Steve Potts
Phil 1:6

TruthQuest

IMPACT

TruthQuest™

IMPACT

STUDENT MINISTRY
THAT WILL TRANSFORM
A GENERATION

EDITED BY STEVEN PATTY
STEVE KEELS / GENERAL EDITOR

BROADMAN
&HOLMAN
PUBLISHERS

NASHVILLE, TENNESSEE

10-digit ISBN: 0805425845
13-digit ISBN: 9780805425840

Published by Broadman & Holman Publishers,
Nashville, Tennessee

Dewey Decimal Classification: 259.23
Subject Headings: CHURCH WORK WITH YOUTH
                  YOUTH MINISTRY
                  YOUTH—RELIGIOUS LIFE

Unless noted otherwise, Scripture quotations are taken from the Holman
Christian Standard Bible®, © 1999, 2000, 2002, 2003 by Holman Bible
Publishers. Scripture quotations also include those marked NASB, the New
American Standard Bible, © the Lockman Foundation, 1960, 1962, 1963,
1968, 1971, 1972, 1973, 1975, 1977; NIV, the Holy Bible, New International
Version, © 1973, 1978, 1984 by International Bible Society; and Phillips, from
J. B. Phillips: The New Testament in Modern English, revised edition, © J. B.
Phillips 1958, 1960, 1972 (Macmillan Publishing Co., Inc.).

1 2 3 4 5 6 7 8 9 10 09 08 07 06 05

Contents

Contributors

Clark Blakeman is a graduate of Multnomah Bible College. He spent three years as a street evangelist focusing on runaways and street youth in the Portland, Oregon, area. He served with a church-planting team in Tigard, Oregon, for three years and ministered for nine years as a youth pastor at Trinity Fellowship in Portland. He is married and has four children.

Judy Glanz is an adjunct faculty member at Multnomah Bible College and Biblical Seminary, director of Northwest Women's Youth Network director, and a conference speaker. She has served in children's, youth, and women's ministries in various churches throughout the Pacific Northwest. She resides in Tualatin, Oregon, with her husband, Randy, and daughter, Julia.

David Jongeward is associate academic dean at Multnomah Bible College where he teaches youth ministry, theology, and psychology. He received his education from Wheaton College and Graduate School and Western Conservative Baptist Seminary and is currently in the doctoral program in leadership at Gonzaga University. He was born and raised in the mission field in Africa. Prior to his position at Multnomah Bible College, he was youth pastor at West Side Baptist Church in Yakima, Washington. He, his wife Debbie, and their four children make their home in Portland, Oregon.

Chris Kainu has worked with youth and young adults for the past eighteen years. He is currently the lead pastor of Summit View Church in Vancouver, Washington, and assisted in planting Summit View ten years ago. Since then his focus is youth ministry. He has a degree from Multnomah Bible College where he is an adjunct faculty member. He resides in Hockinson, Washington, with his wife, Diana, and their three children.

Byron Kehler is founder and executive director of Agape Youth & Family Ministries, a Christian counseling and educational agency in Milwaukie, Oregon. He has worked in the juvenile justice system and youth ministry, spoken at high schools throughout the Northwest, and taught in public education and at Multnomah Bible College for more than ten years. He is a member of and is a board certified expert in trauma recovery by the American Academy of Experts in Traumatic Stress. He and his wife, Vickie, have two children and have shared their home with more than one hundred teenagers during thirty years of marriage. He maintains a counseling practice specializing in adolescents and childhood trauma recovery.

Dave Patty is the founder and director of Josiah Venture, a ministry that trains young leaders for churches in Central and Eastern Europe. In the early '80s he initiated and directed Malachi Ministries to reach young people of military families overseas. He is a graduate of Multnomah Bible College and received an MA in educational ministries from Wheaton College Graduate School. He resides in the Czech Republic with his wife and three children.

Steven Patty chairs the department of Youth and Educational Ministries at Multnomah Bible College. He has a decade of youth ministry experience and is currently leading a church planting team in an urban area of Portland, Oregon.

Gene Poppino is director of student ministries at Grace Community Church, Auburn, Washington, where he has served for seventeen years. A graduate of Multnomah Bible College, he began his youth ministry career in 1974, serving in three ministries before coming to his current position. He is a trainer for Sonlife Ministries and an international trainer with First Wave and has served as an adjunct faculty member at Trinity Lutheran College, Issaquah, Washington. He and his wife Anne have been married for twenty-eight years and have two grown sons.

David Schroeder is general director of Cadence International, an evangelical outreach to the U.S. military and other militaries. Prior to this appointment in 1995, he served for ten years in Cadence's youth ministry division called Malachi Ministries. He is a graduate of Multnomah Bible College and Grace Theological Seminary. He and his wife, Joyce, and their four children, Kerith, Justin, Kyrie, and Jonathan, reside in Englewood, Colorado.

Jeff Vanderstelt is student ministries director of Centrifuge and oversees youth pastors of two churches in the Seattle/Tacoma area. He is also a trainer and associate staff member for Sonlife Ministries. Prior to moving to the Northwest, he worked with youth ministry at a Christian juvenile home, Wedgewood Christian Acres in Grand Rapids, Michigan. He also worked in high school ministry at Christ Community Church in St. Charles, Illinois and Willow Creek Community Church in Barrington, Illinois. He received his education at Trinity College, Calvin College, and Fuller Theological Seminary. He and his wife, Jayne, have a daughter, Haylee Grace.

Preface

ACCORDING TO MATTHEW 28, the goal of youth ministry (and any ministry in general, for that matter) is to make disciples. We know from Jesus' summary of God's commandments (Matt. 22) the core of this effort is developing in young people an abiding love for God and for people. No true disciple will fail to love God and people. And no true youth ministry will fail to make disciples.

The Matthew 28 commission from Christ is unmistakable: *We must make disciples.* Against no other criteria will the success of a youth ministry be judged. Evidence of numbers, creative programming, great relationships, exotic mission trips, the satisfaction of parents, the praise of senior pastors—none of these measure effectiveness. Instead, the extent to which ministry produces true, loyal, and enduring disciples is the mark of its success.*

This disciple-making course is not easy to chart and maintain. We have in mind a picture from the Scriptures of what mature disciples should look like. We know generally that they are to love God and people. But they need to know, do, and feel much more in order to effectively love that way. Much needs to be formed and transformed in them. And usually we are starting with raw material. Like Jesus, we, too, begin with two primary kinds of people: (1) scribes and Pharisees and (2) sinners and tax collectors.

Church kids can tend to be like scribes and Pharisees. They have been around the faith long enough to know it well. They can pray, recite verses, and share testimonies. They can answer tough questions and distinguish between truth and error. They can practice the faith, for they are very familiar with the

---

* Note that we are not talking here about personal success. That is measured by faithfulness in a personal life dedicated to the glory of God. One can be personally successful as a loyal disciple without having a successful ministry.

practices of the church. But like rich kids who inherit wealth without appreciating its cost, these kids have received more than they get. They possess more than they own. And so they are too often cynical, suspicious, bored, impassive, and jaded. Their faith can be filled with activity that has little vitality and life.

Youth ministry exists to somehow get these church kids, these adolescent versions of scribes and Pharisees to be true disciples. That is its purpose. It has no other.

The sinners and tax collectors are unchurched kids. They come in all shapes and sizes, with all manner of questions and all shades of suspicion toward the gospel. Some are ignorant, untouched by any true message of Jesus and often unconcerned with the Christian faith. Others are resistant, hostile toward any advance on their hearts by another—even if that "other" is God. In any case, these sinners and tax collectors think in ways that must be transformed; their minds are darkened. They behave without the purpose of the saving gospel; their lives revolve around illegitimate pursuits. And their passions—the seat of their emotions and commitments of the heart—reflect nothing but their own selves; their desires are misguided and their hearts are truly dead.

Youth ministry exists to somehow get these unchurched kids, these adolescent versions of sinners and tax collectors to be true disciples. That is also its purpose. It has no other.

Do you know this picture of church and unchurched kids? Students from the church filing into the youth room, excited about everything except God, bored with the whole "church" thing, daring you to somehow make them feel something? Or students so secular, pierced and tattooed, living only to secure a college scholarship, thinking only of how to get with girls . . . or boys, wrapped up only in the latest computer games? These kids need to be captured by Christ. They need their lives to be rearranged by Jesus. They need to love deeply both God and people. They need to be made into disciples.

And you have seen this picture too. A sixteen-year-old gets up at six to pray before school. A junior starts a Bible study with his friends during lunch. A middle schooler shares his faith and wins his best friend to Christ. You have seen kids consistently love even horrible parents, resist amazing and persistent sexual temptation, speak eloquently of their faith before hostile teachers, and make commitments of their lives for missionary service. And these kids graduate and go to college and volunteer in Young Life or turn a fraternity into a place of worship. Some give up athletic scholarships to go to Bible college and pursue the ministry.

These are disciples. These adolescents exhibit such a profound love for God and for people that it defines their hearts and transforms their lives. To that end

youth ministry is geared. And all that youth ministry does is for that purpose: to develop churched and unchurched kids into devoted disciples of Jesus.

Everything that we will write about in this book is dedicated to that aim. We will tell about skills, techniques, ways of thinking, ways of being—all kinds of useful things about the ministry. But we tell you this not so that you will get good at running retreats or giving talks or staying balanced. We tell you this so that you will be good at making disciples. That is the point. Look at all you see in this book through that disciple-making lens. What should it profit a youth leader to have a great youth ministry but not make disciples?

1.
A Starting Frame
STEVEN PATTY

WE HAVE ALL STUDIED BOOKS on systematic theology. Most begin with something called a prolegomenon. A prolegomenon introduces the reader to the frame of reference from which the author writes. It is like a philosophical preface, letting everyone know about the assumptions the author makes as he or she goes about doing theology. It lays out the author's core beliefs about approaching theology. Prolegomena are helpful to catch a writer's frame of mind and see *how* he thinks before you read about *what* he thinks. This youth ministry book is not a work in theology (although theology will permeate it), but we will still begin with a prolegomenon.

The contributing authors to this work have diverse backgrounds. You will read from veteran youth pastors, an adolescent therapist, two leaders of international youth ministries, and a couple of youth ministry professors. We share a common understanding of how to approach youth ministry. Even with our diversity we agree on a prolegomenon. This is the frame from which we write about doing youth ministry.

We have a lot to tell you in this book. But let me fill you in on the crucial elements of this mental frame before we jump into a discussion about what to do to have a disciple-making youth ministry.

Youth Ministry Is a Spiritual Activity

I spoke at a high school winter camp a couple of months ago. A few churches had joined together and combined resources. They put on a great camp. They held it in a beautiful, large log chalet just minutes from the ski slopes. The setting was magnificent: deep snow, cozy fireplaces, and unmatched views of the Cascades.

The program was solid too. It had been a long time since I have laughed that hard at skits. The "funny man" was truly funny. Preparing those videos, gathering appropriate costumes, and practicing the timing on those jokes required a lot of energy and creativity. The presenters had music themed to characters and video clips woven into ongoing stories. The hero even fell from the sky, and the mascot went up in flames fabulously on the back deck. It really was impressive.

The worship band was outstanding too. The musicians did a great job. Obviously, they had practiced long and hard to get just the right sound. They were better than most youth bands I've heard. I enjoyed it.

Even the speaker was good. I know I've laid my share of eggs at retreats and conferences before. But this weekend, I was on. The messages rolled out with what I thought were clarity, humor, and some degree of elegance.

The weekend went well. No major problems. No serious injuries. No big discipline issues. Everything was as it should be—except that there was no real evidence of spiritual activity.

I felt uneasy driving away after it was all over. How can a retreat go so well and there be so little evidence of God moving anywhere? How can such a high-quality church program display so little spirituality?

I don't think it was a matter of hard hearts or stiff necks among most of the students. These were good, honest, malleable kids. And it certainly was not because God was uninterested in working in the hearts of these students.

I'm sure I'm overstating things here. That God must have touched the hearts of students in ways indecipherable to me is certain. But still I was deeply concerned with what I saw—or didn't see, to be more accurate. The whole experience made me wonder at the ease with which youth ministry can become something other than a spiritual activity.

Youth ministry is not a business, primarily dependent on presentation, programs, strategy, or market share in order to flourish. It's a spiritual activity. Youth ministry is not social science, primarily dependent on cultural insight, research, or precision in order to flourish. It's a spiritual activity. Youth ministry is not a human activity, primarily dependent on human interests, human relationships, or human nature in order to flourish. It's a spiritual activity.

We should not lose sight of God's work in youth ministry. We, his human ministers, are important but peripheral to the primary nature of ministry. Business lessons, social science insights, and human endeavor are helpful— they give us many tools for ministry. But God initiates. God woos. God calls. God teaches. God comforts. God convicts. And apart from God's ministry we are doing activities for youth, not youth ministry.

Because youth ministry is a spiritual activity, then his Word must be central. The Bible is his revelation to young people and cannot be dismissed. Prayer needs to be central, for we need to ask for his movement and listen closely to his prompting in our hearts toward students. We must use spiritual tools like repentance, belief, faith, and truth. The real work of youth ministry is accomplished spiritually in the hearts of young people and then is evidenced in their behavior. We are utterly dependent on God for this to happen.

The Goal Is to Make Disciples

We will address this issue of making disciples more completely in a later chapter, but here we need to include it in our prolegomenon because it's a core belief we share about youth ministry and it will define all that we say about youth ministry in the upcoming discussions.

The short of it is this: The goal of youth ministry is to make disciples. Take a look at the Gospels accounts and particularly the commission of Matthew 28. The priority of making disciples is unmistakable.

One day in a college Greek class, my good friend attempted to translate *mathetes* as "student" instead of "disciple." The professor, a very portly and serious old man with silver hair and piercing blue eyes, sighed deeply and corrected him. "Young man, a student is one who sits barely listening, keeps looking at the clock, and lives for the time that school is out. A disciple leaves his boats and his nets and risks everything for the sake of the gospel. The word is *disciple!*" Ah, now that's a goal worthy of pursuing!

So many other goals vie for your attention when you initiate youth ministry. You want to have the support of the congregation because you need a mandate and a vote of confidence. You want to have happy parents because it is their own children to whom you are ministering. You want to have the pastor and the church board excited about your efforts because there is little better than a board that publicly and enthusiastically affirms your ministry and your giftedness. But these are unsatisfying goals compared with making disciples.

Even more critically, you may feel the desire to have the support of the young people in your care. It is nice to have students excited about youth group. When they are impressed with all that you do to them and for them, you feel indispensable. When they express love to you, you experience a kind of adoration the likes of which very few others will ever experience. Adulation from students feels great. It pales compared to disciple making, however.

Some youth ministers seek to secure a kind of support from the self, to prove some untested ability to minister. The early days of my ministry were propelled by a need to be proven. I was twenty-one and right out of Bible college, not yet sure if I could do this thing called youth ministry. I knew what a privilege it was to pastor these students, but I was so uncertain about my own abilities. As a result, every meeting, every interaction with students, every word of feedback worked on my self-identity. I wanted to know if I was capable. A lot was on the line—this was my training, my career, my life's dreams. And this, too, was an insufficient goal compared to making disciples.

Our eyes need to lock onto the goal of making disciples. We need to serve as pastors and shepherds, correctors and confidantes, exhorters and encouragers in order to see the young people in our care presented maturely before Christ (Col. 1:28–29).

Jesus the Model for Doing Youth Ministry

We believe Jesus models good ministry practice for us. Even though we live in a different culture and at a different time and place, the values of Christ's ministry are astoundingly powerful. We would do well to emulate these—his priorities, timing, values, strategy, teaching, and ministry ethos.

Some people contend that doing ministry "Jesus' way" is impossible. They argue that he is God and we are not, and as a result he has access to ways of ministry that we don't. But remember our doctrine of Christ's humanity: Jesus was also fully man. He ministered under the authority of the Father and in the power of the Holy Spirit. His resources are the same as our resources. His ministry should not so quickly be disregarded as our model.

Others argue that there is not much to learn from one who lived in such a different place and time. "Should we then," they wonder, "walk around in sandals and teach from the bow of fishing boats? Certainly, our modern ministry must look different than his, shouldn't it?" Whereas some of the elements of Jesus' ministry are bound by the context of his culture, the values of his ministry are unmistakably transferable. His ministry priorities are normative for contemporary youth ministry in the twenty-first century. The lessons from the development of his ministry demonstrate a direction that our ministry trajectories should follow.

We too often take our cues from venues other than Jesus. Think of the modeling power of our own education, for instance. For years we have received lectures—taking notes and writing papers, cramming for tests, passively receiving information to produce it again on exams in order to pass on to the next class. And so we take that model for youth ministry. We accept that young people are primarily students with minds. And we believe that if we teach them, our job is complete. Jesus' ministry encompassed so much more of the person than only the mind.

The model of therapy—a focus on the individual psyche of the student as the primary residence for ministerial intercourse—also pulls hard on us.

Another entertainment model pushes us to think about the adolescent as a spectator, one who watches and is moved by what we provide for him or her and do in front of him or her. The marketing model alerts us to the activity of recruitment and retention, of finding the adolescent "magnets" and wooing them into the social center of the youth ministry.

In any case, all kinds of potential forces pull on us for attention. But Jesus stands alone as God's pure example of ministry. Jesus is our one chance to see with our own eyes God moving among men as one himself and doing ministry. Probably even the majority of Jesus' own disciples were young people themselves. Surely we can lock onto his posture and follow him in ministry.

Intentional, Life-Changing Relationships Vitalize Youth Ministry

There is no substitute for life-on-life. No program can achieve the kind of persuasive influence that human intimacy can. No presentation can match the holistic, multidimensional teaching like that mediated by human relationships. As Howard G. Hendricks is fond of saying, "You can impress people from a distance, but you can only impact them up close." God's method is to impact us up close.

When God initiated his most clearly potent self-revelation, when human history in relation to God reached its apex, its climax, and turning point, God chose to come near to us. He used the vehicle of relationship. He broke into our existence and penetrated our world to walk and talk, eat and breathe, sleep and wake with us. He could have used all methods of communication and divine persuasion. And we see Jesus: God coming near.

Theologians call this the incarnation—God wrapped in human flesh to be with us. And looking at the ministry of Christ, we see his obvious model of incarnational ministry and his expectation for his followers to do the same. Listen to the words of Robert Coleman in *The Master Plan of Evangelism*: "It all started by Jesus calling a few men to follow him. This revealed immediately the direction his evangelistic strategy would take. His concern was not with programs to reach the multitudes, but with men whom the multitudes would follow. Remarkable as it may seem, Jesus started to gather these men before he ever organized an evangelistic campaign or even preached a sermon in public. Men were to be his method of winning the world to God."[1]

Do you see this life engaging life? This is not just cohabitation, people hanging out together with no specific purpose. This is not manufactured friendliness to somehow convince another that you like them enough for them to agree with you. This is not a force of personality to overcome a person's volition and personal dignity. Rather, this is God revealing himself in and through relationship.

Revelation is the key to the incarnational relationship. Somehow, in some way, shape, or form, God must be revealed through one life for another. And so God must be freely active in the one's life, palpably present and bearing the fruit of Spirit relationship. Then the one must be close enough that the other may see Christ, hear Christ, taste Christ, feel Christ in him. This is the essence of youth ministry.

The Base of Youth Ministry Is the Local Church

The church is an irreplaceable means of God's grace, the context in which youth ministry best sits and out of which it expresses mission to the campus and the world. Youth ministry efforts should not be attempted apart from the local church. As alluring as a nimble, free-floating, untethered ministry to youth may seem, the best base of context is the people of God acting as the body of Christ in local expression. We are not trying to undermine the potency of the church universal, the family of God to which all believers belong, and to somehow disparage the efforts of ministries outside of the life and authority of the local church. We are merely affirming that there is peculiar vibrancy and fidelity to a ministry that is within the daily living of the Christian church as expressed in a local congregation.

Campus-based ministries are powerful. An orientation toward the secular place where so much of an adolescent's life happens affords a youth minister special sensitivity to the cultural nuances that make the gospel relevant. There is no substitute for going where the students are. We need to show up on campuses. We need to sit through volleyball games. We need to watch countless drama productions. Why? To understand, enter in, and communicate Christ effectively to kids. We can't sit in church offices or youth rooms and expect kids to come to us. The secular and unchurched will not. We need to go to them. But we need to go from the base of the local church.

Event-oriented ministries can be tremendously impacting too. Every summer I recruit some of our best collegiate ministry students and gather some of our best theology professors. We provide two weeks of a high-intensity spiritual learning experience for high school students in the Northwest. We rent a couple of beach homes on the beautiful Oregon coast and spend two weeks talking about theology, wrestling with life questions, and encouraging one another. The experience changes students' lives. (It changes the professors' lives, for that matter.) *Credo* is so valuable and impacts lives so deeply but has nothing close to the influence of each young person's own home church. The home church ministry is real and potent and enduring.

We'll talk about the church more completely in a later chapter. But here we want to say that in spite of its difficulties and complexities, troubles and frustrations, no organization or effort can replace the local body of believers, the bride of Christ, the family of faith. The extent to which organizations and efforts resource the local church, support the local church, and provide for the local church is the extent that they participate in the clearest present means, apart from the family, of God's grace.

Youth Ministry Is Developmental

Youth ministry can be initiated from a variety of points. A personality-driven ministry, for instance, orients the style of ministry around the personality of the primary leader. A gregarious person will often develop an outgoing group and a reflective one will grow a sensitive group. A gift-driven ministry likewise starts with the particular gifts of the primary youth leader and develops a ministry oriented around those. A minister adept at relating with fringe kids will have a fringe-kid youth group. A minister gifted for in-depth discipleship will gravitate toward serious students of the Word. An opportunity-driven ministry will tend to capitalize on the particular open doors available.

A developmentally driven youth ministry, however, will seek to meet students each at their point of interest and growth and challenge them to the next step of growth. This requires that a youth minister understand where the students are, where they need to be, and how to get them there. It takes seriously the individual's stage of spiritual development and urges him or her forward toward the likeness of Christ.

Youth Ministry Is an Equipping, Multiplying Endeavor

The apostle Paul maintained that God provides the church with a variety of gifts "for the training of the saints in the work of ministry, to build up the body of Christ, until we all reach unity in the faith and in the knowledge of God's Son" (Eph. 4:12–13). The people of God are to be equipped for works of service.

Here is the question: Is youth ministry primarily *to* students or *with* and *among* students? This may sound like a preoccupation with prepositions, but I believe that ministerially the distinction is key. If ministry is *to* students, then young people are the objects, the recipients, and the end points of our ministry. If ministry is *with* and *among* students, then we see as our job to share the ministry with those to whom we minister. In other words, we need to equip young people with the maturity, skills, and resources to minister to one another.

Peer ministry has been championed recently among leaders in the field of youth ministry. Certainly, one could so thoroughly place the ministry within the adolescent context such that no effective impact from adults could be felt. According to our doctrine of the church, to relinquish the place of influence of the older to the younger within a church is to deter health and growth. Spiritual direction from spiritual adults is critical to any young person's growth.

However, this growing emphasis on student-to-student ministry is biblical. Young people should be equipped to do the work of ministry. Young people, as true disciples, should multiply themselves in the lives of their peers. Again, listen to Robert Coleman: "Jesus intended for the disciples to produce his likeness in and through the church being gathered out of the world. Thus his ministry in the Spirit would be duplicated many-fold by his ministry in the lives of his disciples. Through them and others like them it would continue to expand in an ever-enlarging circumference until the multitudes might know in a similar way the opportunity which they had known with the Master. By this strategy the conquest of the world was only a matter of time and their faithfulness to his plan."[2]

Youth ministry is not primarily a show, a program, an event, or an expenditure of energy and talent. It is the making of young disciples who will go and make more young disciples.

Guiding Precepts

I am no airline pilot. Occasionally, squeezed in a passenger seat, flying across the country in the dark of night, I've wondered how the pilots of this metal tube know where to go. How do they keep this flying vehicle on course?

It helped me relax a bit when I once took the headphones and listened in on the conversation between the pilots and the air traffic controllers. I heard the controllers from fixed locations on the ground pass the plane from one "center" to another. These were points of reference and control spaced across the country by which the pilots could be oriented and guided.

These centers provide a fine picture of our prolegomenon. So many competing impulses vie for the attention of youth ministers. Without clear centers to guide us, we will fly around in the dark, unable to steer straight to a disciple-making destination. Keep these in mind as you read. And keep them in front of you as you set out to do ministry.

Notes

1. Robert E. Coleman, *The Master Plan of Evangelism* (Old Tappan, N.J.: Revell, 1969), 27.
2. Ibid., 97.

Part 1

Developing Pastoral Abilities

2.

Casting Vision

DAVE PATTY

RECENTLY I SPENT A DAY bumping along the back roads of South Africa, headed for a game park with Bill Hodgens, director of Campus Crusade for Australia. It was a long hot trip, so we filled our time with interesting conversation.

Curious about the founder of Campus Crusade I asked Hodgens, "What exactly is Bill Bright like? I've heard so much about him but never had the opportunity to meet him personally."

"Mate, he's not what you would expect," Bill replied, his Australian accent lilting as he spoke. "He is a normal man, not a brilliant speaker, no starlike quality to his personality. When he speaks, it generally comes back to one of two topics, the uniqueness of Christ for nonbelievers or how to be filled with the Spirit for believers. Sometimes it sounds as if he doesn't have anything else to say."

He paused thoughtfully and then continued. "But he is a man of great faith, with an absolutely single-minded focus and vision." "What is that?" I asked, sensing I could probably get close without even asking. "The fulfillment of the Great Commission in our generation," Bill replied, without a moment's hesitation.

He went on to describe how the organization had grown from a single college ministry in the early '50s to a team of twenty-seven thousand full-time staff today, serving in all corners of the globe; how the *Jesus* film has become the most widely circulated movie of all time; and how hundreds of thousands of volunteers are trained each year. As I listened it was hard to even get my mind around the extent to which Crusade has marked the cause of Christ in our generation. One thing was clear to me, however.

Such is the power of vision.

"I have a dream," Martin Luther King declared to a crowd of two hundred thousand people gathered before the Lincoln Memorial in Washington, D.C., in August 1963. "I have a dream that one day on the red hills of Georgia the sons of former slaves and the sons of former slave owners will be able to sit down together at a table of brotherhood. I have a dream that one day even the state of Mississippi, a desert state, sweltering with the heat of injustice and oppression, will be transformed into an oasis of freedom and justice. I have a dream that my four children will one day live in a nation where they will not be judged by the color of their skin but by the content of their character."

Five years later Martin Luther King was dead, killed by an assassin's bullet. On his tomb was chiseled these words: "Behold the dreamer. Let us slay him, and we will see what will become of his dream" (Gen. 37:19–20). The dreamer was gone, but the dream lived on. His vision of a future reality was so vivid and compelling that thousands rallied to the cause and the entire course of a nation was turned.

I've seen videos of his life and read copies of his speech. I've studied pictures of the marches, but I still have a hard time comprehending exactly how it all happened. Still, one thing is clear.

Such is the power of a dream.

At Englewood High School, in the southern suburbs of Denver, Colorado, the student body president ranked at the top of the popularity and prestige ladder, somewhere near the drum major in the marching band and the head cheerleader. But somehow Rolf seemed just like one of us as he talked to the packed classroom. I don't remember exactly what he shared—my lowly sophomore mind was full of English literature and math problems. I do know that he spoke from the heart about the change Christ had made in his life since putting his trust in him a year before. His words were earnest, honest, and so full of concern that others in our school would come to know Christ as the only source of life.

"The reason I called you together," he said, "is to ask you to join me in intercession for our school. We can't share Christ in the classroom, but we can pray. We can't make our friends see Jesus, but we can pray that God opens their eyes. I believe God wants to do a powerful work in our school this year and that he wants to begin by calling a number of you to persistent prayer."

My heart started beating faster. If God was preparing something special in our school, I certainly didn't want to miss out.

Rolf had a specific plan. "Seven thirty, every morning before school, in the courtyard where everyone can see us, I will be there to pray. Any of you want to join me?"

The next morning forty of us joined hands for prayer in the courtyard. It must have looked crazy for those who didn't know what was going on. Words of derision rang out from several passing students. Unfazed, the next person in line prayed for them in particular, that God would open their eyes and call them to himself.

Every morning for the entire year, I gathered with Rolf and a group of students to pray for our school. God did incredible things, and we were a part of them.

Such is the power of vision.

Do you lead with vision? If someone were to ask about your dreams for the youth group, could you tell them what you believe to be God's vision for these students? Is your gaze firmly fixed on a future reality, one that you can describe to others in a way that makes them want to go there with you, whatever the cost?

I suspect that many common problems we face in youth ministry actually stem from our inability to lead with vision. Why is the ministry team meeting last on the priority list of your key students? They say they are just busy. Could it be that you have not captured their gaze with a compelling vision?

It's tough to get the money you need from the elder board. The elders say the economy is tight, and there is not enough to go around. Could it be that they are seeing only activities and not outcomes as you talk about the year ahead? Is your vision clear?

Volunteers are not as motivated as they were in the past. In fact, it is hard to find adults willing to help out at all. People just don't have a heart for young people as they used to. Maybe, but the state of the heart is not a static thing. Could you change their priorities if you led with vision?

Some of my models of visionary leaders are world class, like Bill Bright and Martin Luther King. Others are normal folk who spoke vision into my life in powerful ways, like Rolf. Some seem to be born with a special calling from God, while others may have to sweat bullets to find the way. Wherever we start, I'm convinced that every step down the road of growth in leading with vision will be a step toward greater fruitfulness and broader impact.

You can learn to lead others with vision.

What Is Vision?

In his book *Courageous Leadership*, Bill Hybels laid out one of the clearest definitions of *vision* I've seen: "a picture of the future that produces passion." "Vision is the fuel that leaders run on," he continued. "It is the fire that ignites the passion of followers. It's the clear call that sustains focused effort year after year, decade after decade, as people offer consistent and sacrificial service to God."[1]

Too many times we see our ministry as a string of activities. As we look into the future, our minds merely extend that stream of events—youth meetings, retreats, conversations over a Coke, and more activities. The eyes of vision, however, are filled not with activities but outcomes. They see change, movement. They envision a fully formed reality in a future that is different from the present.

But before you point others to that picture, you must have it yourself. What can you do to sharpen your gaze?

Take a Trip to the Future

Someone once told me that poor people should take rich people out to lunch. I took him at his word and arranged an appointment with the most successful businessman in our church. Good leadership leaves footprints, I reasoned, and I wanted to see what I could learn from this man who had founded a string of companies and motivated hundreds of key leaders with his vision.

"Most people don't realize that I am not living in the same time zone as they are," he said. "I live, think, and breathe at least two years down the road. While others are anticipating tomorrow's sale, I am preparing the one two years from now. While others are picturing how their company will look a month in the future, I am envisioning where we will be in five years. When we actually get there, it is already long finished in my mind. The picture for me is generally clear years before it becomes a reality."

"How do you do it?" I asked, wondering if it might be possible to borrow a time capsule from one of his companies. "You go there in your mind," he said. "Fast-forward time and walk around. Feel, observe, sense. Try out various scenarios and then back up and go at them again. Work at it until the future reality is as real to you as the fact that you are sitting in my office today. Then come back to the present and figure out how to get there."

His words have rung in my mind for many years since our meeting—maybe he anticipated that as well. I realized that the furthest point in the future many of us can see is next month's retreat, the one that still doesn't have a brochure designed for it. It requires a conscious choice to travel beyond the current time, to set aside space and energy to dream of how it could be. A choice well made, however, for one who wants to lead with vision.

Wait on the Lord

As believers we possess a huge advantage in developing vision. The God we serve is a God of the future, seeing what will be as clearly as if it were today. The most powerful visions are not conceived but received from the hands of the King who is weaving a tapestry that encompasses all of history. The thread of your life is included there as well.

In a recent study through the book of Acts, I was struck by the fact that the most important breakthroughs were unexpected, often meeting resistance from those who should have been charting the course. Saul, a converted believer? Impossible. Peter eating with Gentiles? Unacceptable. An assignment to write letters from a Roman prison? Certainly it wouldn't seem a good use of apostolic energy.

A habit of waiting on the Lord allowed the early church fathers to navigate these unexpected turns in the road without being derailed, in spite of their initial hesitations. Ananias received a vision from God with clear instructions to restore Saul's sight (Acts 9:10–16). Peter was confronted with God's plan for the Gentiles when he retreated to a rooftop to pray (Acts 10:9–23). Paul and Barnabas were set aside for the work of the ministry as the elders were engaged in worship and prayer (Acts 13:2–3).

A similar pattern emerges in the lives of Old Testament heroes. Before Nehemiah had a chance to present his request to the king, he recorded, "I mourned for a number of days, fasting and praying before the God of heaven" (Neh. 1:4). When Daniel did not know how to proceed after the revelation of a great war, he fasted and prayed for three weeks. Only at the end of that time, on the banks of a river, did an angel appear to him with instructions and words of encouragement (Dan. 10:2–21).

Toward the end of my studies at Wheaton Graduate School, I faced an acute vision vacuum. It was unclear if I should return to the ministry where I had earlier served or branch out in an entirely new direction. Inspired by the examples of Scripture, I grabbed my Bible and notebook and headed for a lakeside cabin in Wisconsin for two days of fasting and prayer.

I set aside the first day for cleansing my soul and getting my spirit in tune with the Lord. I read Scripture for hours, prayed through every request I could think of, and asked the Lord to reveal areas of sin or surrender that needed his purifying touch. It was a sweet time of communion, heightened in intensity by hunger pains.

The second day I dragged a chair partway into the water so I could cool my feet, took out my notebook, and asked the Lord for a vision of the future. What followed in the next hours has marked my life for the twelve years since then. As fast as I could write, the Lord revealed a picture of a ministry to train youth leaders in Eastern Europe. Specific steps came into view, as well as unique characteristics of the work God had in mind. The vision was compelling, motivating, and filled my heart with passion. What is more, it was a vision received, not simply conceived.

When we leave a place of prayer, convinced that the Lord has laid plans on our hearts that are from him, the task of speaking with conviction about those plans comes naturally. It is not so much that we possess a vision but that a vision possesses us.

Again, it seems that one of the greatest challenges comes in the seeking. If you want to hear God's voice and discern his heart for the future, you must create the proper conditions for listening. There must be space, a receptive heart, listening ears, and an expectant spirit. When your vision falters, you must retreat to the rooftop, the riverbank, or the upper room.

Think what energy could be saved if you responded to a vision God prepared. Peter fell asleep in the garden. When the guards came, he could engage only in the activity which seemed most appropriate to him. It was wasted effort, a flailing sword that lopped off an ear, but it was out of sync with God's purposes. Christ had to step in and repair the damage, however well intentioned.

Contrast this with the obedient steps of the Savior, remaining on course with God's design in the face of unrelenting pressure, accomplishing a vision conceived by God before the foundations of the world. We, too, must not leave the garden until we have heeded the command of the master to "watch and pray" (Matt. 26:41 NIV).

Get in Touch with Needs around You

Sometimes vision is not developed in a flash of insight or a revelation from God but in response to an awareness of the needs around us. Nehemiah took the initiative to inquire about the state of the captives in Israel, and the news brought by his brother Hanani drove him to tears (Neh. 1:4). David was comfortably settled in his palace of cedar when he noticed with consternation that the ark of God was still in a tent (2 Sam. 7:2). A sensitivity to needs around them motivated both of these men to dream about a future reality, one that their vision later propelled into place.

Cameron Townsend was passing out Spanish tracts in Mexico when he came upon a Cakchiquel man. "Do you have one in Cakchiquel?" the man asked. "There are none, I'm sorry," replied Townsend. "Well," retorted the man, "if your God is so great, why can't he speak my language."[2] In one decisive moment Townsend understood that God had called him to translate the Bible into the language of this Guatemalan tribe.

He threw himself into the work with vigor, and as the translation began to progress, he became aware of many other tribes that likewise did not have the Scripture in their tongue. In response to this need, Townsend spearheaded the founding of Wycliffe Bible Translators. Rallying around "Uncle Cam's" vision, a growing team has translated the Bible into all or part of fifteen hundred languages, and plans to tackle another two thousand during the next twenty-five years.

An amazing effort—all started by a sensitivity to need.

What are the unique needs in your local high school, your community, your city, or your state? What conversations have moved you to tears? What statements continue to ring in your mind? How could you picture a future reality in your youth group that would make a difference with those needs?

Communicating Vision

Once a leader begins to see the shape of things ahead, he must communicate to others in a way that they begin to also see. Those who lead with vision must work hard at the art of vision casting because the power of a vision is closely tied to its ability to energize and engage others.

As we begin to communicate vision to others, we must answer three crucial questions.

1. *Where* are we going?
2. *Why?*
3. *How* will we get there?

Remember my hero Rolf? Listen to his vision casting with this in mind. (*Where* are we going?) "The reason I called you together," he said, "is to ask you to join me in intercession for our school. (*Why?*) We can't share Christ in the classroom, but we can pray. We can't make our friends see Jesus, but we can pray that God opens their eyes. I believe God wants to do a powerful work in our school this year and that he wants to begin by calling a number of you to persistent prayer." (*How* will we get there?) "Seven thirty, every morning before school, in the courtyard where everyone can see us, I will be there to pray. Any of you want to join me?"

I don't know if he knew we were asking those questions. But like the good leader that he was, he intuitively provided us with the answers. This is crucial to the vision-casting process.

What about Martin Luther King? Here again are excerpts from his famous speech. (*Where* are we going?) "I have a dream that one day on the red hills of Georgia the sons of former slaves and the sons of former slave owners will be able to sit down together at a table of brotherhood. . . . I have a dream that my four children will one day live in a nation where they will not be judged by the color of their skin but by the content of their character. . . ." (*Why?*) "This is our hope. This is the faith with which I return to the South." (*How* will we get there?) "With this faith we will be able to hew out of the mountain of despair a stone of hope. With this faith we will be able to transform the jangling discords of our nation into a beautiful symphony of brotherhood."

Each of these questions is crucial to vision casting. The "where" gives the compelling end, the future reality. The "why" provides the motivation. Without this, there is no reason to engage in the hard work of getting there. One of my mentors often reminds me that until the "why" question is answered, the price is always too high.

The "how" tells me what to do and lets me know my place in fulfilling the vision. Without this step, the listener is only a bystander, cheering you on, but unaware of how he or she can make a difference. A good vision caster makes clear what the next steps are and shows places where different people can put their hands to the plow.

Those who lead with vision also know that the manner in which these questions are answered is extremely important. If the answer is too complicated, dry, or out of tune with reality, the listener leaves untouched or with the perception that you are just pumping sunshine.

A good vision will burrow into the mind and capture the imagination. The dynamic that makes a vision grab and sparkle can be summed up in three words, which form the first three letters of the word *vision*. A compelling vision is *vivid, inspiring,* and *succinct*.

Your Vision Must Be Vivid

"By this time next year I want you all to be more committed." This may be a great vision, but it won't capture my attention. It is not vivid enough. The overused words and bland structure cause it to fade from my mind like vanishing ink. It is gone before I can take a breath to respond.

A good vision caster, on the other hand, uses words that are alive, that sparkle, words that create pictures in the listener's mind and are easily remembered.

"I have a dream," said Martin Luther King, "that one day even the state of Mississippi, a desert state, sweltering with the heat of injustice and oppression, will be transformed into an oasis of freedom and justice."

Wow, do you hear that leap off the page? Every word counts, every line rings with living pictures and rich images. I can just feel the heat of injustice as he speaks, and I long for the oasis of freedom he describes.

I wonder how long he worked on those few lines. Sometimes it takes hours to find just the right image or turn of phrase that will capture the listener with the power of a vision. In winning people over to our vision for the youth of eastern Europe, I describe the "hinge of history" that was created by the "velvet revolution" in the Czech Republic. I tell how we dream of a "movement of God" among the youth of eastern Europe, one that "finds its home in the church and transforms society." I have worked on these phrases and others like them for years, searching for the best way to capture the passion God has placed in my heart for these precious young people.

A story or anecdote can also be powerfully used to make a vision come alive. Cameron Townsend's brief interchange with the obstinate Indian embodies the heart of Wycliffe Bible Translators. I'm sure he told the story thousands of times, and my guess is that many of the people who heard it remember it to this day. It is every bit as good as the best mission statement they could come up with, particularly because it is charged with vivid life.

Your Vision Must Be Inspiring

I devour biographies of great leaders for one simple reason: They inspire me. Not long ago I read the story of Sir Ernest Shackleton's failed attempt to reach the South Pole. After an unusually thick ice field destroyed the expedition's ship before even reaching the shore, Shackleton faced the almost insurmountable task of surviving the long winter and then getting his twenty-seven men back to safety with only a few longboats.[3] The ensuing hardships form an incredible tale of leadership and courage, one that made me grateful for warmth and civilization.

I finished the book inspired but not by the information; I doubt I will have need for his finely honed skills of surviving on an ice floe. But it was Shackleton's determination, commitment, courage, and unflagging commitment to the goal that energized me.

Inspiration has much to do with the emotion that a listener feels when a vision is shared. More than anything else, that emotion is tied to the person and passion of the vision caster. A good vision is shared not just from the mind but from the heart as well. It comes from a place of passion, carries the weight of personal conviction, and is supported with determination and courage.

Mel, a key leader on our team, is filled with a heart for young people and a passion to reach them. Often when he shares his vision, only a few sentences make their way out before he is choked up and has to stop. Not long ago he didn't get far enough for us to even make sense of what he was saying. As he stood in the front of the room with his fist over his mouth, fighting back the emotion so that he could continue, someone called from the audience, "We don't know where you're going, Mel, but we'll all go there with you."

The laughter that followed showed everyone else agreed. Feeling the depth of Mel's passion was enough for the people who knew him. If Mel is going to lead this charge, then sign me up.

The vision caster must embody the vision, and many decide to follow more because of their confidence in the person than because they fully understand the goal. One who leads with vision ties himself to the mast of the ship, personally placing himself on the line as proof that the cause is a worthy one. We all knew that Rolf would be there at 7:30 for prayer even if he was alone. Because of that conviction, he wasn't alone.

When you share your vision, kick in your heart. Don't make anything up, but let yourself feel. Make sure, before you invite anyone else into the boat, that you have tied yourself personally to the mast. People will sense the depth of your resolve, your personal conviction, your determination.

Lead with a vision that inspires.

Your Vision Must Be Succinct

Remember that successful businessman in my church? He was also a generous philanthropist, a man who didn't like to waste time. Once he called the leader of a Christian organization into his office and told him, "You have five minutes to convince me that I should support your work." With that he reached over and hit a timer on the edge of his desk.

What would you say? What if you had just two minutes, or one? Could you paint the picture in only a couple of sentences? Could you embody your passion with a phrase?

If you cannot share your vision succinctly, then you probably cannot share it at all. Though our eyes can take in an entire panorama before us, we can focus only on a small portion of that picture at a time. If your vision doesn't capture that part of my gaze, it will be quickly lost in background noise.

I don't know what the ministry leader shared before the timer ran out. But I do know that he walked out of the office with a check for fifty thousand dollars. At times it pays to be prepared.

The purpose statement of Willow Creek Community Church has become almost legendary because it succinctly captures a vision: "To turn irreligious people into fully devoted followers of Christ."⁴ Brief, to the point, memorable. Because it can be easily passed on to others, this vision has resurfaced in a wide variety of ministry locations all over the world.

Coca-Cola drives its billion-dollar global empire with a vision statement that's even more compact. "A Coke within reach of every person on the planet" is the company dream. So far it seems to be doing quite well.

The vision statement for an entire ministry may take months or even years to develop. That doesn't mean that short-term vision casting has to be this finely tuned. You may have to cast vision with a moment's notice or paint a picture of the future in the light of a particular upcoming problem. The key is to keep it short and power packed, focused and to the point.

Look at Jesus' vision statements. "For even the Son of Man did not come to be served, but to serve, and to give His life—a ransom for many" (Mark 10:45). "Those who are well don't need a doctor, but the sick [do need one]. I don't come to call the righteous, but sinners" (Mark 2:17). "For the Son of Man has come to seek and to save the lost" (Luke 19:10).

As Christ expresses his mission, we see the same thought expressed over and over. It's communicated in a variety of ways, but they all share the common characteristics of brevity, compactness, and focus.

Put a timer on your desk. Give yourself no more than five minutes. Can you convince me to climb in the boat with you? Take out a pen and a piece of paper. Rough out your vision for the future. Can you communicate your passion in a compact sentence? Can you focus my attention on the goal with a single phrase?

One final piece of advice. A good leader reminds people of the vision over and over. Since the mind is porous, vision leaks. Management experts urge leaders to communicate a vision clearly, and then multiply that communication effort fifty times. Only then, they argue, is the average person beginning to see and own the dream.

Bill Bright's relentless return to the Great Commission has burned his vision into every corner of Campus Crusade. Cameron Townsend's single-minded focus kept Wycliffe on track through fifteen hundred languages. These men never seemed to tire of saying the same thing over again, and saying it each time with a passion as if that were the first time.

Vision. Eyes of faith allow you to see the future, and the words of motivation enable you to take others to that goal. It is the difference between half-hearted activity and devoted passion. It is one of the leader's most powerful tools.

Learn to lead others with vision.

Notes

1. Bill Hybels, *Courageous Leadership* (Grand Rapids, Mich.: Zondervan, 2002), 31–32.

2. Janet and Geoff Benge, *Cameron Townsend: Good News in Every Language* (Youth with a Mission Publishing, 2000).

3. Margot Morrell, Stephanie Capparell, and Alexandra Shackleton, *Shackleton's Way: Leadership Lessons from the Great Antarctic Explorer* (New York: Penguin Books, 2002).

4. Hybels, *Courageous Leadership*, 35.

3.
Shepherding

CHRIS KAINU

I WAS STARING right through the kid. But I was sure he couldn't tell. I'm certain my face had an engaged look. Barely noticing his lengthening pause, I faked my involvement in the conversation by saying, "That's cool." I may have even been looking intently in his eyes. I don't remember. But I do remember the cold anger of his response. "No. That's not cool. My mom just left my dad for another man." I was busted and embarrassed.

His confrontation hit my consciousness like a bucket of ice water, waking me up from my pastoral preoccupation with other things. A feeling of shallowness coated me. I quickly apologized for my lack of listening. I probably could have justified my distracted mind by listing my many responsibilities as a youth pastor. But I sensed this was a symptom of a deeper, heart-level problem; perhaps this was even a correction from the Lord. God sent that sophomore prophet to catch me in the act of shallow-hearted shepherding.

That glance in the mirror happened nearly fifteen years ago, but the image I saw was so unsettling that it speaks to me even today: "Don't forget to love them . . . for real."

This chapter is written especially for those of us who like to excel and perform, who major in "doing" and minor in "being," who feel more eager to achieve than to love. We bypass the life-given discipleship of a caring shepherd. If you want to be God's tool in building a life-altering youth ministry, then you can't be caught up in other things: activities, burdens, excitements, and responsibilities that distract your heart and mind from impassioned, genuine, and helpful shepherding.

By contrast, you must stick to the commandments that have no superior: loving God and loving people. You cannot produce healthy disciples of Christ without healthy pastoral care. Leadership is not enough.

God Rejects Shallow Shepherding

The leaders of Israel failed as shepherds. They neglected the true pain of the people. They blew it because they were distracted. Such costly distraction made God furious. "For from the least to the greatest, everyone is gaining profit unjustly. From prophet to priest, everyone deals falsely. They have treated superficially the brokenness of My dear people, claiming: Peace, peace, when there is no peace" (Jer. 8:10b–11).

The truly sad part is that the religious leaders never even noticed their own failure. They were so busy chasing their *self-appointed* priorities they didn't have time to notice the gross neglect of their *God-assigned* priorities. They wanted to get rich with self-importance and that required time and focus. So the people got squeezed out. These religious posers got caught up in other things and lost sight of the aching needs of the ones they were called to shepherd.

What distracts you from God's priority of caring for students? Is it writing the message, preparing for Sunday morning, or an impending event? Is it the quest to appear busy and important? Hanging out with your favorite volunteers? Building your own career, finances, or personal life? Dealing with your own personal fatigue or pain? Perhaps your seemingly noble desire to see everything done with excellence (which is often a wonderful justification for unhealthy perfectionism) keeps you from this priority. Take a moment and write down the distractions from your job as a shepherd.

Becoming a Better Shepherd

Pray for Brokenness

I had heard about Jeff Colker. I had never seen him or met him, but I knew I needed to be more like him. I was just starting an internship in a huge church with a huge youth ministry. Jeff had been a volunteer there for years and I kept hearing his story. He was a "man's man" kind of guy—super competitive, funny, and hard-working. It was the story of his tears, however, that challenged me.

I inherited responsibility for the campus where he had worked for years. He used to drive regularly to the parking lot and pray for hours for the students. He didn't pray pretend hours; he prayed real hours. He would pray for the ones he knew. He would pray for the unknown and the lost. He would pray for the teachers and administrators. And as he prayed for them, he was often brought to tears in concern and care for them.

Stories of heroic missionaries and their tear-saturated prayers have always inspired me, but they lived in a distant place and time. This guy was real. And I had seen the result of God's work through him. The lives of hundreds of students were permanently altered. Though Jeff was obviously talented in youth ministry, it was his brokenness that challenged me. I had to ask myself, "Chris, when was the last time you cried for someone besides yourself?" It was a bothering irony that my whole future was being refined for youth ministry, yet I experienced more emotions about the delivery over my Wednesday night message than over a kid's experience of divorce.

Jesus wept. Not because his friend was in the tomb. Not because the situation was hopeless. Jesus wept because he cared. He cared about his followers' relationships, losses, griefs, joys, disappointments, and victories. But his care didn't stop there. He craved the chance to console his enemies. "Jerusalem, Jerusalem! The city who kills the prophets and stones those who are sent to her. How often I wanted to gather your children together, as a hen gathers her chicks under her wings, yet you were not willing!" (Matt. 23:37). Does this kind of passion and brokenness drive you in your youth ministry? Yes or no, I guarantee the answer is obvious to others.

When was the last time you sat in a school parking lot, on the football field, or at the mall and prayed with intensity for one solid hour, asking for God's intervention in lives of your students? How often do you ask God for a brokenness and extreme compassion for your kids? Having heard about Jeff's commitment to prayer, I drove to that same parking lot and began to pray for my students—and myself. I asked God, "Please break my heart for these students." I'm a bit embarrassed to admit that it took about two years of this consistent request to God before my actions and emotions began to show evidence to a Christlike brokenness. If you normally lack deep-hearted compassion, it will likely take some time to gain it. Don't bypass your pursuit of such character; it's vital to your life and ministry.

Though the rest of this chapter is designed to be highly practical, you must settle this issue of heart condition first. Without a heart of ever-increasing compassion, applying the practical tools will amount to little more than second-rate acting. Evaluate yourself before you go on.

On a scale of one to ten, where do you rank in terms of brokenness for your students? Since Jesus is off the scale, make the apostle Paul a ten. Make the priests and prophets of Israel a one. Then ask yourself two questions: (1) What prayer do I need to pray for my own heart condition? (2) What action do I need to take to increase my compassion and brokenness for students?

Listen

One of the greatest acts of kindness you can extend to another human is to listen to him or her. Yet, for some strange reason, we leaders too often feel the necessity to *say* something. I love the folk proverb, "Those who talk a lot need to." Ironically, the more we mature in leadership, the less we should be saying and the more we should be listening. James said we are to be "quick to listen." Are you a good listener? Eugene Peterson suggested that pastors should focus on fewer priorities to become the truly spiritual leaders we are called to be.[1] He suggested that the three most critical priorities of a pastor are praying, preaching, and listening. For the youth pastor, I believe equipping workers and personally discipling leaders outrank preaching. Yet I see prayer and listening as extremely high priorities for the youth pastor.

Most of us reflexively talk more than we listen. Why? Because listening is hard work. German theologian Dietrich Bonhoeffer aptly described us: "There is a kind of listening with half an ear that presumes already to know what the other person has to say. It is an impatient, inattentive listening, that despises the brother, and is only waiting for a chance to speak and thus get rid of the other person."[2]

Listening requires that we rid ourselves of our own preoccupations in order to receive another, attend to another, concentrate on another.

Are you willing to do the hard work of listening? I want to share with you two homework assignments I gave as a part of a class called Communication to Youth. I challenge you to do them both.

1. *Who listens to you?* This is a study of one individual who currently listens to you at length and in such a way that you are personally encouraged or comforted. Describe the significance of this individual in your life, focusing in detail on how his/her style of listening has ministered to you.

2. *Forty-five minutes of listening:* Engage someone in conversation for forty-five minutes. The person must not be aware that you are doing this as an assignment (until completion of the conversation). You must "win" this person over. The focus of the conversation must be on him or her. Every time the conversation turns to you, you must quickly and skillfully turn it back to the other person. Write a very brief summary of the conversation (what you learned about this person, if you can share it), and list the skills you used to keep the person engaged in conversation.

If you do these two assignments, I guarantee you'll learn more about listening. You'll also gain powerful illustrations for a message on listening.

Certain listening activities, such as *dealing with drainers,* require special consideration. For example, we all dreaded Karla. She was as sweet as could be, but she was absolutely draining. Her upbringing had left her emotionally malnourished and socially handicapped. Most kids (and leaders) walked the other way when they saw her coming. Others made polite excuses about why they had to leave, immediately. The nice Christian kids who did try to listen usually began to drown under the endless stream of her personal problems. They became her personal captives of conversation. She was boring, depleting, and, apparently, clueless to boot.

Some youth workers allow huge chunks of their precious time to be swallowed by the Karlas of their youth group. Others ignore them, hoping that such drainers would learn to avoid such certain rejection. As shepherds, we must find a balance between the two extremes.

The next time a draining student is walking your way, don't panic. Subtly glance at your watch as you quietly pray, *Lord, give me wisdom.* Then, pick an amount of time—five, ten, or fifteen minutes. Give her your undivided, warm, and sincere attention. Listen to what she is saying. Ask her thoughtful, personal questions. Ask her if she wants some advice. If you can give her some in the time allotted, do so. If not, tell her one useful step to take. (For example, ask her to write out three possible solutions to her situation. Or have her write a letter to the person bothering her but not send it. Tell her to bring it to church on Sunday when you'll talk about it and pray for her.) When there is only about two minutes left in your time, start silently praying, *Lord, please graciously get me out of this conversation.* I'm serious. In all my years of youth ministry, those were my number-one and number-two prayers. That may not sound very spiritual, but as a shepherd of so many, you must ask for God's guidance moment by moment. Especially, when so much of your ministry happens in the context of interpersonal conversation.

Know and Grow Individuals

The unity was unraveling around me. Summer camp always puts the pressure on a team of volunteer leaders, but this year the strife was abnormally abundant. I could feel a minor-league mutiny brewing. Staff members were irritable and unusually defiant. They were mature enough to take good care of the students, but I was getting a lot of resistance from nearly all of them. Finally, I asked Steve, a longtime leader, what the problem was. In a moment of penetrating honesty, he let me know that the problem was the youth pastor. I was the problem.

Steve went on to let me know that the staff members felt like employees and that I didn't really care about them. When I asked what I could do differently, he said, "Just once, why don't you hang out with us on your day off." Ouch, that hurt. But I got the message. They felt uncared for. They felt like a means to my end. I had allowed the good goals and real pressures of kingdom work to turn the ministry into a business. I was the chief executive officer. The volunteer leaders were the employees, and the students were the customers.

I had to admit that though I was long on personality, drive, and conviction, I was short on nurturing, care, and compassion. I needed to make some lasting changes in my approach to leadership, but I wasn't sure how.

Good leaders often make poor shepherds, even when they genuinely want to love their students. Can you relate to shepherding failure? Do you ever find yourself running over people as you build the kingdom? Do you neglect the personal lives of your students? Do you forget to actively develop the whole person of your staff members? Don't give up your desire to love more genuinely. There's hope. You *can* learn to love better. But you must be willing to study those who are better at shepherding than you.

Good shepherds often make poor leaders, even when they genuinely want to lead their students to greater spiritual depth and personal development. Do you find yourself extending a lot of nurturing but see little change in the lives of your students? Do you give your leaders a lot of attention, only to find them struggling with the same distractions to character development? Don't give up your desire to encourage more growth in their lives. There's hope. You *can* learn to lead better. But you must be willing to study those who are better at leading than you.

I was so bothered by my care-deficient style of leadership that I began to study the "teddy bears" on my leadership team. I needed to learn from the big-hearted, love-driven volunteers who continually cared about individuals. What was it that they did to make people feel so loved and cared for? I wanted to care more about people.

I had noticed that shepherding friends were very good at paying attention to the small, personal details of a person's life. Furthermore, they naturally took action to respond to those personal details. Sounds basic, but I was consistently overlooking such care.

I also began to study leaders who consistently developed individuals in a very thorough and holistic manner. These leaders weren't just trying to make their students feel good or keep their volunteers from quitting. They were doing an effective job of life-altering discipleship, the kind that results in significant character change and genuine spiritual growth sustained over the long run.

It was apparent the leaders who initiated a deep level of life change in others were continually thinking about specific areas of relational, emotional, and spiritual development. I was doing a decent job of leading the whole ministry but wasn't seeing the lives of individuals dramatically changed from my personal mentoring.

My observations led to the development of a tool I call the Individual Assessment Form. I have used this form many times as a tool to think thoroughly through the lives of individuals and make specific plans toward their

holistic maturity in Christ. It has also been an invaluable prayer guide, resulting in tangible changes in the lives of those under my care. A form like this may seem stiff and impersonal, but for unnatural (or ineffective) shepherds it is a path to more Christ-like pastoring. If you are creative in developing your own form and use it consistently, you will see the lives of many more individuals dramatically altered by God's work through you. (See IAF at the end of the chapter.)

Jesus, the Ultimate Leader-Shepherd

Jesus' main strategy to reach the lost and grow the found was *not* by way of Sunday morning services, Wednesday night youth groups, or weekend retreats. Nor was it by taking his disciples to ministry conferences offered by the best ministry minds of the day. Christ's plan for world impact depended on his personal leadership and shepherding of a few men who would receive the transfer of his life into their own. He knew his followers well. He prayed for them. He encouraged, challenged, and called them to become more like him. And they did. These men went on to change the course of human history.

In youth ministry especially, we must not see preaching, teaching, and training meetings or events as the prime conduit of life change. These are important tools but insufficient for large-scale, long-term growth of adolescent believers. Without the aggressive life development of individuals, such programs are inadequate for multigeneration impact. And as a youth pastor, that development of people starts with you.

Do you believe Jesus is the best leader-shepherd ever to walk the planet? Do you believe his model of ministry is worth a lifetime of study? If you do, then you are among those who regularly scour the Gospels for clues to his leadership-shepherding style. You watch closely for insight into how he tempered Peter or emboldened the woman at the well. You look for principles from the way he balanced his daily schedule and how he dealt with the racism in James and John. And these studies will translate into action you take in lives of your people.

Does personal ministry to individuals mark your leadership? Jesus' ministry did. Do people see you as a consistent source of both comfort and challenge? Do you spend time and prayer preparing for intentional conversations?

Jesus' ability to inspire the redirection of world history flowed centrally from his love and leadership in the lives of a relatively small circle of followers. Clearly his message was bigger than life, and, indeed, that enticed passionate men and women to fulfill their deep cravings for greatness. But he built the bulk of his plan for world impact on the development of individuals. What is the bulk of your plan built on?

How well do you know your students? When was the last time you thought through the details of their lives and attempted to discover how the Lord wants to use you in their entire growth? This evaluation form has been created not only as a practical tool but a prayer guide too. Pray your way through this form as you consider what your students need from the Lord and how you can guide them in their life development. Of course, this is only one example of how a worksheet like this can be designed. Be creative. Expand this concept and adapt it so that it will work for your own ministry. A fictitious student named Kyle is the example.

Individual Assessment Form

(Confidential)

The Basics - *How well do you know them? The little things matter.*

place of birth: Longview

temperament: charismatic, funny, emotional

age/birthday: 17, June 12

passions: girls, Jesus, snowboarding, music

born again: 14 at summer camp

key relationships: Pete's parents; girlfriend Katie

mentors: Coach Miller, Curt

current issues: college decision; struggling with sex

Strength Areas	Growth Areas	Other Distinctives
very fun & amiable	weak commitment	stepfamily issues
smart	short-term focus	highly extroverted
influential	too emotional	
loves Jesus	sexual past	

Individual Assessment Form

(Continued)

Basic summary—*How would you describe him to someone who didn't know him?*

Kyle is a great guy who everyone enjoys. He was a church kid until fourth grade when his parents divorced. His folks get along, but they all drifted away from Christ. He has relied on his personality to get by, so his character is lacking. But since his freshman recommitment to Christ, he has passionately pursued the Lord. He could become an outstanding leader if he's willing to grow in his character.

What attitudes, relationships, or actions need to change or begin?

He must stop being his mom's emotional crutch because his step-dad is such a jerk to his mom. It would be great for him to get more time with Pete's parents as a "second mom and dad." He's got to get his physical relationship with Katie under control or get out of it. He must increase his character, especially in the areas of commitment and servanthood.

What does he need from God? *Grace, reassurance, identity, guidance, comfort, direction, etc.*

Release from the burden of emotionally carrying his mom; assurance that God can take care of her. A prompting in the heart of Pete's parents to commit more of their time to Kyle. A clear directive about his relationship with Katie (and more conviction about his sin). Strength to choose character development over emotion-driven living.

What does he need from me? *Encouragement, advice, confrontation, prayer, hugs, etc.*

To ask a few questions about his role with his mom and some advice on how to draw boundaries. To talk to Pete's parents without Kyle knowing; I should suggest they pray about mentoring him. A long talk about his relationship with Katie and how he can grow it in a healthy way (or get out). A challenge to commit to the servant-leadership team in our youth ministry; get in or get out.

Notes

1. Eugene Peterson, *The Contemplative Pastor: Returning to the Art of Spiritual Direction* (Grand Rapids, Mich.: Eerdmans, 1993), 29–30.

2. John Stott, *The Contemporary Christian: Applying God's Word to Today's World* (Downers Grove, Ill.: InterVarsity, 1992), 109.

4.
Raising Disciples

DAVE PATTY

I HAVE A TALL STACK of books in my library on discipleship, perhaps more than on any other single subject. It started on a family vacation years ago when I read the biography of Dawson Trotman, the founder of The Navigators. His single-minded passion for Christ inspired me, but it was his particular emphasis on discipleship that marked my sixteen-year-old soul. He became my hero, and from that point on I devoured everything I could pick up on the subject and added books to my collection. *The Master Plan of Evangelism* soon followed and then other classics like *Disciples Are Made, Not Born.*

These books deeply marked me, and a passion for disciple making began to drive all of my major decisions in ministry. Soon it became coupled with a conviction that disciple making contains the most powerful model for spreading the kingdom of God. Even today, nothing, other than Christ himself, fires my passions more than true living discipleship.

But I am not sure I understand it.

I must confess that my mind is cluttered with competing images when I hear the word. The term *discipleship* is tacked on thousands of programs, materials, strategies, and ministries, like an evangelical "proof of purchase" seal. I wonder if the label has become an icon in and of itself, so much so that we have forgotten the substance it describes.

Once on a missions trip in Korea, I slipped out to a market to buy a present for my wife. The stalls were stacked with inexpensive clothes, but I had something special in mind. After digging through a pile of shirts, I remarked to the salesman that I was searching for something that had more of a name brand. "What name brand would you like?" he said with a half grin, opening a cigar box. "Adidas, Nike, Channel, Gucci, we have them all." I could see that he did. There in his hands were the designer labels for each of these companies. "Just pick the blouse that you want and tell us the label. We will have it ready in five minutes."

I was amused. And just as he promised, my bag was soon packed with something very top-of-the-line. Somehow, however, the label didn't keep the dye in the blouse from bleeding and the seams from unraveling the first time it was washed. The label stayed fresh, colorful, and inspiring. Still it didn't make up for the lack of substance in the garment.

As I watch what is called discipleship unravel at the seams, I wonder if we are aware that we might not be holding the real thing.

Perhaps it would be good to begin with what discipleship is not. Discipleship is not a twelve-week course. It is not a manual nor a program. It is not a weekly meeting nor a small-group Bible study. It is not an institute and not a prayer journal.

Discipleship may use some of these tools, but to confuse the garment with the life underneath would be like saying that my son is the clothes he wears. I can't reach into his closet and say I am holding my son only because I am touching his shirt. His life is much more than the jeans he puts on in the morning. And the presence of his jeans does not necessarily mean he is there.

Discipleship is also not just for professionals, for people who have time, or for those who possess a particular gift. It is not an option, an elective, nor just a recommendation. I am convinced that a Christian who is not making disciples is not an obedient Christian. Even though discipleship seems to be quite difficult, it's not nearly as complicated as most people think.

Being Discipled

Rich's question caught me off guard because it was so unexpected. "Could you join us for dinner this week?" I knew the pastor of an eight-hundred-member church had other things to do with his time. Besides, I was a no-name Wheaton College student. I tried to give him an easy way out.

"No, I'm serious," he insisted. "How about Friday at five?" I nodded in agreement and then realized I had no idea what my schedule was for the week. *If there is something on Friday I can cancel it,* I thought. *Dinner at Rich's house? What is this all about?*

I wondered what he had planned. But when I showed up for dinner, it seemed nothing was planned, other than a meal with his family and a time of prayer around the table. Then we retired into the family room. Again, nothing in particular was prepared. Rich asked me questions about school, then shared the gist of the sermon he was preparing for Sunday. "What do you think?" he asked. Two hours later I looked down at my watch. *Where had the evening gone?* I thought. *And how did the conversation end up on spiritual issues that I desperately needed to hear?*

The next week Rich pressed me for a lunch together. I showed up with my Bible and notebook this time, but again it seemed that no lesson had been prepared. During an awkward pause I asked about a passage I hadn't understood in my quiet time. Soon our Bibles were open, and it was so interesting that my french fries got cold on the plate. When we bowed our heads to pray, the passion in his voice caught me off guard. This man really seemed to love his Savior. I walked away with a strange hunger to study the Bible. His excitement for the Word of God was somehow contagious.

At church he pressed a book into my hands. "You'll love this," he said. "Let me know when you're done and we can talk about it." I had hundreds of pages of required reading due that week for school, but the book Rich gave me was finished in four days. On my way to meet for coffee, I suddenly realized something. *I am being discipled,* I thought to myself.

And I was.

It had been a long few weeks, but somehow the guys had gotten under my skin. I poured my heart out in prayer for them on my knees, glancing back at a smudged list of requests we gathered during our small-group meetings. *Brian is headed into a tough final today,* I thought. *I wonder if he is keeping his eyes on the Lord.* Almost absentmindedly I picked up the phone to give him a call. I couldn't wait until next Tuesday to find out what happened.

A voice rang bright on the other end of the line. Brian told me how God had given peace in a subject over which he normally sweated bullets, but that wasn't the reason for his joy. "You know, Tom, the guy on my list of friends I want to see come to know Jesus," he said excitedly. "Well, he asked me how I felt about the test, and I got to share with him that all of you guys are praying for me. He snickered at me at first, but somehow the conversation kept going and I told him how Christ has changed my life."

Brian's words were tripping over one another in haste to get out of his mouth. "Tom asked some questions I couldn't answer. Could we talk about them next week at Bible study?"

I promised him we could, and as we talked I felt a wave of love wash over my heart for this precious high school student. "Something is changing," I said to myself as I hung up the phone. "This started just as a guys Bible study, but about three weeks ago it began to be different. Something is happening in their hearts, and mine as well. I think maybe this is discipleship."

And it was.

My wife Connie can write text messages on her mobile phone faster than any person I know. I tell her it is born genius. She tells me it's practice. Last night it was multitasking. With one hand she sorted laundry while the other hand pressed that tiny keypad. "Who are you writing?" I asked. "Marketa" came back the answer, without a pause in either the laundry sorting or the typing. I should have known.

Marketa trusted Christ in our youth group seven years ago but struggled to keep her head above water in the atheistic family in which she had been raised. She needed more intensive care, so we invited her to move in with us for a year after graduating from high school. It was an adventure for all of us but represented a deep labor of love for my wife. They talked about things of the Lord around the dinner dishes and over late evening cups of tea. Marketa saw our family at its finest and watched us try to sort out things at our worst. In the process, God transformed her life and wove the character of Christ deep into her thirsty soul. Today she is walking with the Lord at her university and dating a fine Christian man.

"How often do you text Marketa?" I asked. "I don't know," Connie replied, "I don't keep track." I could hear her scrolling down the message box. "Four times so far today. But you wouldn't believe what God is doing in her heart." I told her that the details would have to wait. "I have to write a chapter on discipleship," I said. The key chatter stopped.

My wife looked up at me. "Dave, do you think a lot of people feel pressure when they hear that word?"

"What do you mean?" I asked.

"It just seems to me that people think *discipleship* is some special formula, some program, some kind of neat package. If someone takes you through the right steps you can say you have 'been discipled' and if you do it to others, you can say you are 'discipling them.' I just think it has a lot more to do with following Jesus, and pulling some people close to you so they can follow Jesus too."

I thought back to an event earlier that week when I walked into the room to find Connie on the phone with an open Bible in her hand, reading Scripture to Marketa. Or a few days later when she stepped out of the health club to pray with her over the phone about a situation at home.

"You know, Connie," I said, "I think what has happened between you and Marketa, that really is discipleship."

"Maybe so," she said, reaching down to finish up her message.

And it is.

I still don't understand it. But I have experienced it and I long for more of it. I wonder what could happen if true disciple making characterized each of our ministries. What could be the cumulative transforming effect if young people in each of your youth groups were truly shaped into the image of Christ through discipleship relationships? What if disciple making began to take on a life all its own, bigger than any program or structure or calendar of events? How could history be different if young people left your ministry and continued to make disciples for the rest of their lives?

Here are some principles to keep in mind as you try to comprehend the real thing.

Begin with a Passion for Christ

Oswald Chambers says it well: "There is only one relationship that matters, and that is your personal relationship to a personal Redeemer and Lord. Let everything else go, but maintain that at all costs, and God will fulfill His purpose through your life. One individual life may be of priceless value to God's purposes, and yours may be that life."[1]

Every effective disciple maker I know is passionate about Jesus Christ. This passion is contagious, giving substance, meaning, and purpose to the activities of discipleship. Rich taught me a great deal. But more than anything he modeled the Christian life before me. I wanted to experience the kind of walk with Christ I saw displayed in his life, and for years afterward I mined every memory of our times together for clues as to how I could know Jesus as he did. He pointed my gaze to Christ because that was where his gaze was directed.

Sometimes I cringe when I hear the phrase "my disciple." This is a term we find in the New Testament only coming from the lips of Jesus. Paul talked about "my son" Timothy or "my brother" Epaphroditus. A group of young believers was called "my children" and coworkers named "my fellow servants." But the authors of the New Testament never addressed a fellow believer as "my disciple" or "my follower."

The disciples we make never belong to us. We are to make disciples of Christ, not of Dave or Bob or Laurie. In 1 Corinthians, Paul responds with horror when he hears that some are calling themselves followers of Paul or Apollos. "Is Christ divided?" He wrote with evident frustration. "Was it Paul who was crucified for you? Or were you baptized in Paul's name?" (1:13). He knew the Great Commission commands us to make disciples of Christ, not of ourselves. If their attention is to be on Jesus, our attention must be there as well.

Once during my high school years, a seminary student started a "discipleship group" with myself and some of my friends. We dutifully met at 6:30 a.m. once a week because discipleship is all about commitment. We held one another accountable and discussed a lesson because discipleship is about growth and obedience. At the same time, the entire experience seemed dull and burdensome. I could see no particular fruit being born in my life, and I sensed the same from the other participants.

After several months, our leader confided that he had lost his passion for Jesus in the press of his theological education. Quiet times had slipped to the wayside, his communion with the Savior practically nonexistent. With no fire in his soul, there was nothing but dry wood in ours. A passion for Christ is contagious; unfortunately, the lack of it is contagious as well. Our meetings had all the structure of discipleship but none of the life. Jesus was absent.

I came across the following poem in college, from an unknown author, which deeply marked my life.

Not only in the words you speak,
to you so dear, to me so dim.
But when you came to me you brought a sense of him
And from your eyes he beckons me
And from your lips his voice is spread
Till I lose sight of you and see the Christ instead.
Is it a beatific smile, a holy light upon your brow?
No, I saw his presence when you laughed just now.

Discipleship begins with a passion for Christ.

Invite Others to "Be with" You

In Mark 3:14, Christ appointed twelve, "named them apostles—to *be with Him*, to send them out to preach" (emphasis added). We see here Christ's initiative in challenging men and calling them to who they would become. We see his vision, that they would touch others and preach the good news of the kingdom. But before this vision could be realized, we see him calling them to "be with him."

As we follow the disciples from this point on, their training appears chaotic. Christ's teaching and preparation is intensive, but it often seems to be haphazard, designed to shape and mold whatever raw materials life had thrown at them in a given day. What remains consistent, however, is the characteristic of Christ's presence in their lives and their presence in his. They were with him and he with them.

A colleague of mine likes to remind me that Christ's discipleship activities—his teaching, leading, and shaping—were all set in the frame of life rather than in the frame of a program. This seems like a subtle difference, but the reality is very profound. The container can indeed have a significant impact on the content.

We might wonder, "How can I create the frame of life to place around my discipleship?" It doesn't need to be created, it already exists. In fact, created life is always a bit plastic and inert, bearing none of the pulsing richness of the real thing. You already have a frame of life. You live in the midst of it. Now you need to invite others to be with you in it.

For my wife this means talking with a young believer about spiritual things when she is standing at the sink doing the dinner dishes or text messaging a word of encouragement while she is folding laundry. For me, it means taking Tom with me when I go to speak at a retreat, studying the book of Philippians in my quiet time with Michael, or sharing openly about my struggles at our Sunday night small group.

This is why discipleship is so hard to describe to someone who has not experienced it. It can take so many forms, yet the common characteristic of sharing life remains the same.

Though not stated in his challenge, the fact that Jesus called these men to be with him meant he was also with them. We find him in their homes, having dinner with their friends and even healing their relatives. In entering their environments, he brought the transforming impact of his presence and teaching, often marking their worlds in radical and enduring ways.

As you think about the activity of discipling a young person, begin by moving to be with them. Step into whatever frame of life they currently find themselves. Join them and then begin to use the raw materials of life to shape and lead them.

Many Paths but the Same Destination

"Where do I lead them?" we might ask. This is a common roadblock in discipleship, the sense that we don't know exactly what to do. It causes us to latch on to a list from the experts or try to mimic someone who already displays disciple-making fruit.

Rich didn't seem prepared for our meetings. But on the other hand he was. Somehow he always seemed to know where to take me, responding with an almost intuitive sense of what was ahead. How did he know where to lead me and on what basis did he choose the next step?

I live at the foot of a four-thousand-foot mountain, the highest in our region. It is a favorite destination for hikers, and on weekends the roads are often clogged with cars, discharging groups of nature lovers for a day on the trail. Because the valley provides many places to start the hike, there are scores of paths up the mountain. Each has its unique views and challenges, but all converge at the top, where there is a breathtaking view of the surrounding countryside.

Not long ago my son and I decided to take a jaunt up the peak. Because I had already explored most of the paths on our side of the mountain, we decided to pioneer a new route directly up the face. It was more difficult than most and involved hundreds of decisions. Should we go to the left of this rock or to the right, around the patch of bushes or through them? However, at each point it was only necessary to see two things: the terrain directly in front of us and the top of the peak in the distance. Because the destination was always in view and our immediate surroundings as well, each decision had a clear context, and the steps forward flowed naturally one right after another.

Because every person begins in a different place, no discipleship path will look exactly the same. What gives the disciple maker a context for choosing the route forward, however, is a clear view of the goal in the distance, coupled with a keen sense of the immediate surroundings.

Paul described this goal in Colossians 1:28–29: "We proclaim him, admonishing and teaching everyone with all wisdom, so that we may present everyone *perfect in Christ*. To this end I labor, struggling with all his energy, which so powerfully works in me" (emphasis added, NIV). Our goal for every disciple is that the student reaches maturity in Christ, that the student's life begins to look like Christ's. This vision gives our work focus, allowing us to throw everything into the labor with the power of his energy.

An artist was once asked how he learned to carve a piece of stone into a beautiful statue. "You see a square pillar of stone," he said. "But I see a beautiful woman inside of it. As I gaze at the stone I look at her, and then simply chip off what doesn't belong to her form."

Our task is similar. The picture of Christ should always be before us. What doesn't belong to his form needs to be chipped away. Other descriptions of maturity in the Bible can focus our eyes even more clearly on this image. The fruit of the Spirit is a helpful starting place, as are examples of men and women of God in Scripture. These pictures can clarify our view of where we are going and give us a context for knowing the next step.

Our work has an additional dynamic because what is being formed is living. Part of what we need to provide is the proper conditions for growth—the daily intake of the Word of God, the exercise of obedience, and the regular cleansing of repentance. We have access to the shaping power of a community of believers, the nurture of prayer, and the warmth of God's grace and love. All of these can form believers into the image of Christ.

Discipleship Flows from Who God Made You

The Word of God is clear that there are a number of different spiritual gifts, but it is equally clear that everyone should be involved in the work of disciple making. This means that your disciple-making energy will flow through your unique gifting and out of the natural context of who you are. In that, it will have your unique signature and form.

When the disciples were given the task of feeding the five thousand, their attention immediately went to what they did not have. They said to him, "Should we go and buy 200 denarii worth of bread and give them something to eat?" (Mark 6:37). It was a useless discussion, full of frustration and doubt. Though it was easy to picture how this sum of money would meet the needs of the people, their assessment was an exercise in futility. They couldn't give Christ something they didn't have.

On the other hand, when they engaged what they did possess in meeting the needs of the people, through Christ it multiplied and stomachs were filled. It is easy in disciple making for our gaze to drift to what we do not have or to what we wish were true. We don't have enough time, energy, resources, or talent. It's easy to picture how everything could be different, if the missing elements we needed were somehow available.

This is an exercise in futility. You can't give someone what you don't have. But you can step out in faith and invest what you do possess, asking the Lord to break it, bless it, and multiply it.

My wife doesn't have the gift of teaching. She disciples through the gifts of encouragement and prayer. I, on the other hand, don't have the gift of administration. But I can disciple by leading and teaching. I know a woman who disciples through the gift of hospitality and another who visits women and helps them organize their homes. She has the gift of service, and God most powerfully uses her to shape others when the two of them are elbow-deep in the back closet, bringing the world back into order.

God will also use our unique talents and experiences. Todd has discipled many with a basketball in one hand and a Bible in the other. It is a natural combination for a Moody Bible School graduate who was also an all-American athlete. Victor disciples around a pool table in his front room, Cari through her uncanny knack for conversation and mastery of the fine art of hanging around.

The key is an engagement of all we are in the disciple-making process. Whatever God has built into you, bring it to bear in expectation that God will use it. Learn your unique style and become comfortable with it. Trust that the resources he gave you are an expression of his wisdom. He wants you to say with Paul, "We cared so much for you that we were pleased to share with you not only the gospel of God but also our own lives, because you had become dear to us" (1 Thess. 2:8).

Discipleship Is Not Complete until the Student Becomes a Teacher

My favorite work by Dawson Trotman is a slim pamphlet titled *Born to Reproduce*. It's a power-packed piece with only one main thought—nothing is fully mature until it begins to reproduce. This must be kept in ·mind even when a believer is still a spiritual infant, Trotman argued. One day they, too, will need to impart Christ's life to others. Every step forward from birth needs to prepare them to reproduce.[2]

The power of this thought is even understood in the business world. In the training process at McDonald's restaurants, workers are not just instructed in how to flip a hamburger but simultaneously taught how to *teach* someone to flip a hamburger. Those who learn with a view to pass on their skills to others have a much higher mastery over the material covered.

Jesus sent his disciples out to serve without him. He warned them they would need at some point to carry the message on their own. The path would be a dead end if Christ just recruited students. A disciple was prepared from the beginning to make other disciples, who in turn made other disciples, who made still more disciples. And so the gospel reached you and me.

I'm still convinced there is no better model for spreading the kingdom of God.

Notes

1. Oswald Chambers, *My Utmost for His Highest* (Grand Rapids, Mich.: Discovery House Publishers, 1992), November 30.

2. Dawson Trotman and Dave Trotman, *Born to Reproduce* (Colorado Springs, Colo.: NavPress, 1975).

5.
Leading into Worship

CLARK BLAKEMAN

PICTURE YOURSELF ARRIVING at a youth meeting about twenty minutes late. The still and quiet room is filled with students. You see about half of them on their knees. Many press their faces to the floor. Others simply bow their heads. Some are seated, looking at open Bibles or praying silently. You see a few standing, faces uplifted and smiling, arms raised as if offering themselves to God.

On the stage, you see a band—a group of teens. They, too, take various postures, silently connected with God. Someone begins to sing, but it is not one of the leaders up front. As others join in, the song crescendos in energy, volume, and passion even though no instruments are playing. A seated worshipper then reads loudly from the Psalms. When she's finished, someone else speaks out praise to God for his power and gracious interest in humanity.

In time a quiet, clear note sounds as a bow is pulled across violin strings. Soon a sustained dampened keyboard adds depth. A soft cymbal counts out a beat. Other instruments join in—a guitar, a bass—and then students begin to sing again. The song magnifies Jesus as the ruling King of the universe. The worship builds in volume and proclamation, then transitions to another song. This is a song of celebration. Kids begin clapping. Some shout, some dance, some sway and nod; others stand still in reverence. All are engaged. After another song the leader of the band guides the group through the reading of an old creed and then encourages everyone to partner-up. He instructs them to pray for one another to be changed by the truth they have just proclaimed and the truth they are about to hear.

Does this describe your group's worship times? Or does this seem surreal to you? This kind of God-ward, truth-filled, sincere, and relevant worship is not beyond the possibility for any youth ministry. It could be the norm. It takes attention to the process of disciple development just like everything else in our ministry.

First, delineate your worship values, undergird, energize, and frame all efforts to lead into worship. Here are my worship values. You may use them, change them, add to them, or if necessary even take away from them as you develop your own. I ask only that you evaluate and study the Scriptures as you develop guiding values for worship.

As you develop your own worship ministry, think about what the Scriptures reveal concerning the values you want to embrace and communicate to your team. Study, ask questions of students, leaders, professors, and other youth pastors. Biblical values are where you begin leading into worship. Your values will influence everything you do in the worship ministry of your youth group.

God-ward

Leading people to God-oriented expressions must be a goal for worship leaders. Communication that has God as the subject or is spoken directly to him is God-ward. Worship is not really about you or me, how we feel, or what we commit to Christ. True worship reflects on a God who is wonderful, holy, exalted, and gracious. I've seen so-called worship services focus primarily on another individual or my own characteristics. The main subject was self. This is communication going horizontally and directed man-ward. Consider, for instance, a line from the popular song "In the Secret": "Pressing onward, pushing every hindrance aside out of my way / 'cause I want to know you more."[1]

This is a good sentiment coming from a person hungering for our Lord. He is pleased with our desire to know him. But what have we exalted about him? How has he been magnified in our own minds and hearts? Who is the subject? I am the subject. This song amplifies our own commitment to Jesus, which is good. However, the result is somewhat off the target of praise: the focus is more man-ward than God-ward. This kind of song can appropriately express our hearts. But I would be careful to choose a majority of worship elements that purposefully magnify or exalt the Lord, his attributes, and his work.

Worship encompasses much more than songs. When selecting any elements of a worship service, whether it's responsive reading, the use of an image or illustration, an instrumental interlude, or a scripted prayer, we should take care that they focus on God.

Truth-filled

In Luke 24, on the road to Emmaus, Jesus confronted the disciples' lack of understanding about his identity. They were distraught because they didn't know where their Messiah's body had gone. They had missed the truth, even the revealed truth of God's Word. Their misunderstanding led to wrong attitudes and poor behavior. However, when Jesus used the Old Testament Scriptures to teach about himself as they walked along and later as they shared a meal, they became overjoyed. Their eyes were opened to the truth of the Resurrection. Their response of joy, belief, and action culminated when they returned to the other disciples to tell them of their greater understanding. These fruit often spring from truth-filled worship. When we become encouraged by the truth about Jesus, we feel joy. When we are reminded of truth, we are moved to God-honoring action.

A change in belief and action occurred again as the story continues in Luke 24. When the two disciples returned to tell their story (proclaiming the truth about God—this is God-ward worship), some still doubted. But the Lord himself showed up to confirm their words. He revealed the truth. And the truth brought joy into their hearts. The last verses of this story say that, "After worshiping Him, they returned to Jerusalem with great joy. And they were continually in the temple complex blessing God" (Luke 24:52–53).

Worship must flow from the truth. Truth flows from the Scriptures. Therefore, songs or any other element of a worship service must be grounded in the Scriptures. This can be difficult with the current flood of worship CDs, songbooks, bands, and conferences. We must evaluate our selections on biblical integrity. Ask, "Does this song (or worship element of any kind) accurately represent truth? Is it supported biblically?"

Let's look at an almost perfect song. "Above All," sung by Michael W. Smith, is a good, reflective song of proclamation. It chronicles the life of Christ poetically and beautifully through the verses and then the chorus concludes, "You took the fall, and thought of me / Above all."[2]

A bunker buster is buried deep in this song, in the last phrase of the last line. Everything is so God-ward and truth-filled until right at the end when suddenly the message explodes, becoming man-ward and untrue. What was on Christ's mind above all? The scene in the garden of Gethsemane reveals that doing the will of his Father was what was foremost on the mind of Christ. "Yet not my will, but yours be done" was his concluding request as he anticipated the misery of the cross. I'm not minimizing his love for me, which is so powerful nothing in all of creation can separate me from it

(Rom. 8:35–39). But Jesus certainly did not think of *me* above every other person of the human race. Be careful to value worship that is filled with good, biblical truth.

Planned

There was a wonderful worship service in Jerusalem just after Nehemiah rebuilt the walls (Neh. 12:27–47). He organized an incredible celebration and recruited musicians, singers, and priests from surrounding villages. The ministers underwent a purification ritual before the celebration. He researched the Psalms and followed the instructions prescribed by King David. He choreographed a parade. Then, on the appointed day he had musicians, singers, priests, and the people stationed in specific locations throughout the city. Two different choirs led music, one that ascended the stairs to the top of the walls on one side of the city and another choir on the opposite side. They marched to their locations. They sang to one another from their positions. Then they continued to the temple. Scriptures were read and all the people participated so enthusiastically that "Jerusalem's rejoicing was heard far away" (12:43).

This great celebration could be accomplished only through careful planning. Nehemiah was a strategic planner. Leading people, even youth, in worship also requires strategic and diligent planning.

I occasionally pick up a negative attitude toward planning from some youth leaders. There is a thought that the Spirit may be restricted by overly planned services. I do believe we can become so committed to (or dependent on) what we've planned that we cannot sense what the Lord may be doing during the service. However, better planning can free the leader from the tunnel vision of concentrating on what's next, allowing for greater sensitivity to God and those he's leading. Good planning actually results in greater freedom and responsiveness to the moments when the Spirit moves in unexpected ways.

Relevant

Worship expressions that fail to interest the people gathered for worship may be legitimate forms of worship; they may even be God-ward, truth-filled, and reflect good planning. Nevertheless, worship expressions that don't connect with kids are often ill-fated. The problem could lie with uninterested or immature youth. It could be that they need instruction or correction. However, maybe the musical form or lyrical genre just doesn't relate. Remember the camp songs? They don't fly with the current generation. A good worship leader is sensitive to what connects with those she's leading. She understands the culture of those she's leading. Being relevant requires study of and sensitivity to the culture.

Youth pop culture explodes into every realm of society. We pastors need to recognize the potential to reach churched and unchurched youth alike through worship. God-honoring worship and contemporary youth culture can meet in three key ways:

1. Passionate Sincerity

Both God and the current youth culture highly value sincerity. Both God and youth value passion. In the youth vernacular, anything that seems contrived or passionless is bogus. When students feel required to say things they don't mean or feel, they feel manipulated and hypocritical. They can't stand that. Neither can God. Numerous passages reflect the Lord's attitude toward empty words and rituals. Here are a few to consider: Psalm 51:17; Isaiah 29:13–14; 58:2–14; Zephaniah 3:9–12. A particularly poignant passage is found in Amos 5 in which God says he despises insincere religious activities. He says he won't listen to the noise of hypocritical songs.

We must be sensitive to God and young people by cultivating a sincere expression of worship to God. Most important to the development of sincerity is a sincere leader. Jesus sees our hearts. He is more interested in our hearts than the words we say, songs we sing, or musical skills we possess. Students can also read us. They are very perceptive about sincerity. Be a sincere worshipper. Develop this sincerity by worshipping in private. Make worship a lifestyle.

Lead students into sincerity too. Help them make worship from the heart by encouraging them to participate in some specific and personal ways. Give them a good example and then call them to it.

2. Experiential Participation

The postmodern youth loves freedom. He wants the freedom to add his own individuality to whatever he's doing. He is, after all, a unique, indefinable, nonstereotyped individual. When it comes to worship, if those up front manage every aspect of the service, kids tend to feel fenced in, controlled, and moved along like cattle. To escape, some kids disengage from the experience. Disengagement in worship breeds insincerity. Most students who disconnect still try to be respectful and so they go through the motions. Others will simply find other things to keep themselves entertained. They may carry on conversation, sit and doodle, write notes, or gawk at the most attractive or interesting among their peers.

For a young person, experience gives meaning and provides value. Experience is a picture of a contemporary teen. The good news is that God desires us to experience him. He implores us to "taste and see that the LORD is good" (Ps. 34:8). He offers us peace, joy, and love. These are experiential concepts. When students are called to participate in the worship experience, they begin to recognize God's goodness more fully.

It is not only the worship team that I encourage to pay attention to experiential needs. I encourage all those present at the meeting to lead us in worship expressions that spontaneously flow from their own hearts. Establish an expectation by giving opportunities for praise after instruction, by the public reading of Bible passages, starting songs a cappella, writing letters to God, or simply sitting quietly in his presence together. These opportunities will greatly enhance the worship experience for everyone.

3. Variety

The current generation also values variety. Teens hate boredom, and repetition bores them nearly to death. "I've already done that." "We always play the same games." "I hate this CD." (Usually, these were the same games and songs that they just recently loved.) "I'm not going to that show tonight; I already saw it." It's a good thing the Bible is full of variety in expressions of worship. Reading through the Psalms you can find examples of worship that include singing, standing, shouting, dancing, laying down, meditating, playing instrumental music, reading Scripture, responsive congregational reading, writing songs or prayers, marching, and quoting memorized Scripture. I don't believe we have an exhaustive list of possible ways to worship God.

One glance at creation and it's clear God loves variety. As God's image bearers, we have some freedom to be creative in our worship of him. This creativity expressed in variety encourages freshness. It keeps students thinking and participating. They are less likely to devolve into vain repetition.

Mixing things up is one way to add variety. Using liturgical prayers and spontaneous moments of personal prayer within the same meeting is great for youth. The liturgy instructs while they participate, and the spontaneous moments provide opportunities to practice. Elements of declaration such as the Nicene Creed or portions of the Westminster Shorter Catechism read in unison can give a more historical, formal sense to a service. In the same service a video of the Crucifixion could be shown with Delirious's song "Jesus Blood" lending a contemporary and passionate moment.

Atmospheric conditions can be changed for a variety of purposes. Lots of candles, lowered lights, and slow bass-heavy music create an ominous mood great for personal meditation. That might be what you want for Good Friday or other contemplative services. Bright lights, chairs arranged in a U formation, and lively music encourage community and joy. This would be for a celebration such as Easter. No chairs and nothing plugged in can represent a homey atmosphere. Intimacy and vulnerability within the group can motivate some to connect more with God because of the perceived safety of the setting. Straight rows of chairs all facing forward bring a formal and reverent feel.

Related photos or video behind the song lyrics projected on the screen can connect with visually oriented people. Varied musical styles help connect a broader range of people. Moments of instruction within the worship service elevate the mind. Instrumental segments allow people to put their own thoughts and prayers into the song. There are many ways to bring variety to our worship services. Your students will learn to love it, and variety will help keep them engaged in worship.

Developing a Discipling Worship Ministry

Now that you know your need to clarify your values in worship, the more practical steps for developing a discipling worship ministry can be considered. Because God has set things up to work from the top down, we begin with the leader.

Prepare the Leader

If you are the leader, your first job in developing a discipling worship ministry is to *be* a worshipper. You and I must first worship our Lord. Before we can lead others to worship him, we must truly worship. Matt Redman introduced the term "lead worshipper" in his recent book *The Unquenchable Worshipper*.[3] I find this term immensely helpful. The one who would aspire to lead others in worship should be a participant in worship. He is not simply a signpost ("go that way to worship"); he is also the escort ("come, follow me as I worship"). Being a worshipper has implications both during a given worship service and on any day in a leader's life. A lead worshipper is one who worships his Lord when no one is there to be led. This lifestyle of private worship lays the foundation for authenticity when people are present. *Consistent private practice results in authentic public leadership.*

Second, gaining Christlike character must be a priority. We don't know if Jesus could play any instrument. We know he sang a hymn, but we don't know if he could carry a tune. I wonder if he was nothing better than average with music. At least, none of the Gospel writers highlight his musical ability. And yet he led into worship. I find this thought comforting, partly because I struggle with gaining ability in music.

One thing I know: "man sees what is visible, but the LORD sees the heart" (1 Sam. 16:7). We should emphasize developing our character more than our musical prowess. If we are spending more time with our guitar than our Lord, we reveal that our service is more about our own exaltation than it is about God's praise. I don't mean we should disparage practice or fail to push ourselves. David said, "play skillfully" (Ps. 33:3). It is just more important to have a heart fully given to the Lord and character that reflects him to the world than it is to have great musicianship.

Plan the Service

Planning will increase your group's ability to glorify God through worship. Glorifying God develops a sense of connecting with him that satisfies the deep desire everyone has to be close to our Lord. The NOIPE process for planning, explained in chapter 18, is useful in planning worship services and developing worship teams. As with any program, the leader must determine the needs of his group, choose objectives, gather ideas, develop plans, and evaluate the event's success.

As you prepare a worship service or develop a worship team, plan early. Communicate frequently. Organize worship elements thematically. Coordinate with the speaker if there is one.

As you work to determine your theme, prayer is your greatest tool. In prayer ask the Lord what the needs are in the group. How do students need to connect with him? What do they need to learn about him? What is the teaching topic, and how does that topic lend itself to worship?

Then as you begin to grasp a theme, prayerful evaluation will help you identify some objectives. What should the students know, believe, feel, or do after or during this service? Take these questions to the Lord. As you discover the answers, you also find your objectives.

Ideas are next. Use creativity in developing different elements for worship. Imagine the whole service. Put yourself in the kids' seats. Think of their responses, their preferences, their distractions, and their capabilities. Select Scriptures. Decide how to use the Scriptures. Would graphics help? What songs support the theme and objectives? Could the songs build sequentially toward an ultimate truth? What transitions can you use? Would environmental changes enhance the experience? How can you get the students personally active?

As you come up with a list of ideas, develop a plan. What ideas do you use? Which do you save for another time? Don't succumb to the temptation to use lots of your ideas in a single service. The cheesy KISS principle still applies today. Keep it super simple. Super is not an adjective of simple; it is a stand-alone concept meaning choose only the best.

People need time to practice their parts. So all this planning must be done early enough so those involved can prepare. A schedule is very helpful for planning weeks or months in advance for the elements that require greater practice or work. Multiple musicians, computer programs, video scenes, and dramatic presentations all require planning.

Evaluation is the final step. It should be done both after the plan is set and after the event occurs. Again, question liberally. Did you meet the needs you saw? Did you accomplish your objectives? Did the elements seem to flow? Were the students relating?

Build the Team

Developing a team of people (including students) to lead worship provides a rich context for raising up disciples. You can develop the hearts of young people powerfully as you teach them how to lead worship. Keep these five elements in mind:

1. Find a Place for Anyone Who's Interested

When you invite students to join the worship ministry, you will get interested students from all different backgrounds, styles, maturity levels, and skill levels. Each one is a set of mixed motives, fears, and hopes. Down to the minutia of their ear hairs, God loves and values them all. So must you. This can be very difficult.

One thing that has helped me with loving and valuing each student is to assume that most Christians who want to truly serve the body of Christ have at least some prodding from the Holy Spirit. True service is not natural to humanity. I make it my aim to find them all a place. During the process, we discover what it means to serve, what options are available, and what are the students' skill levels.

Think of worship ministry more broadly than music and song. As mentioned earlier, there are many ways one can express worship. Therefore, there are many ways to lead worship. If a student is not a good guitar player, maybe she's a computer genius. She could make lyric slides with a creative flare unmatched by anyone else. If a student can't sing, maybe he can read dramatically. If a student has no rhythm, maybe he can set up sound equipment. If a student is too shy for up-front ministry, maybe she can find Scriptures extolling the character of God and copy them onto three-by-five cards for others to read.

What about the goof-off musician types? Of course, maturity plays a big role in readiness to lead worship, but don't lose sight of the fact that youth are young. I have seen squirrelly, fringe kids come alive to responsibility and move to the center of the youth group because they discovered they could be used by God. They felt useful and challenged, as if they could make a difference. For guys especially, the need for significant contribution (or impact) is so great they often don't care whether it's positive or negative impact. They just need to make a dent in something. If they are given an opportunity as important as being a part of the worship team, many rise to the occasion with surprising sobriety.

What about underskilled musicians and vocalists? Don't give up on them too early. Protect them for a time by burying them in the midst of a solid group of musicians. Allow them to play without being heard. This produces confidence, and practicing with better musicians or vocalists usually improves their skills. In time, they will be ready for fewer crutches.

The role of a shepherd disciple maker is to lead people to their places of service. Build your team with this in mind.

2.   **Call for Servant-Leadership**

Model for your team biblical leadership, just as Jesus did for his team. He turned the understanding of leadership upside down. The biblical leader is the servant of all. He is the one who washes feet. "Washing feet" in our worship means putting away the instruments, coiling the cords, moving the speakers, making photocopies, arriving early to set up, calling to make sure everyone can make it to practice. Hold up the sacred ministry of service for those on the worship team. They need to know from the beginning that they cannot participate for the glory of the position. If they lead, they also wash feet.

3.   **Teach Your Values in Worship**

Communicate your values to team members. Give them a handout. Refer to your values during planning sessions. Have the values become common parts of your worship team vocabulary. Remember all the times that Jesus talked about the nature of ministry with his ministry team. Likewise, we need to instruct students so they imbibe scriptural values.

4.   **Prepare Them for Responsibility**

Students need to understand that greater service is a privilege. Up-front ministry is in many ways a greater service. Like teaching, any kind of up-front leadership (even those who silently play their instrument) comes with a greater responsibility. It is a reward for faithfulness in small things. But for many youth, the drive for attention sometimes competes with the desire to serve God and others. Rock stars are very cool. Youth group bands can provide an opportunity to showcase a kid's cool. Carefully guard against such motivation.

I frequently think of leading into worship as a sacred service to God and others by imagining my job is to pass through Solomon's temple and reveal the Lord whose presence is behind the veil in the Holy of Holies. My job is to step up to the curtain before the gathered people, take hold of the bottom hem, and begin to pull back, allowing the brilliance of the glory of the Lord of Hosts to flood the temple. As the people are pierced with his beauty, they are inspired to praise, exalt, and magnify the great I Am. They can't help but worship him.

To help students see the sacredness of leading worship, I share this picture of pulling back the veil. I call them to see the intensity of the Old Testament imagery. Priests wore ropes around their legs when in the Holy of Holies, in case they did something wrong and were struck dead by the Holy One.

Additionally, teach through example, instructing both formally and informally and providing or restricting opportunities for them. Students must see their leader live a worshipper's life. They must know their leader worships in private. They must observe how your values influence your approach to worship. They must see that you are more interested in your own character and theirs than you are in musical perfection. Make sure you deliberately pass on the principles that prepare the leader.

5. Apply the Discipleship Principle

This principle is a progressive teaching and then transferring of skills and responsibilities to another. At first, give many small opportunities with specific instructions. Require them to write out their prayer or call to worship the first few times they lead during a worship service. Help them by editing if necessary. Assign readings. Encourage them to practice so they are free of nervousness and can read with emotive emphasis. Challenge them to develop a musical transition or instrumental segment.

Set up regular practices for the worship team. This gives you lots of opportunities to demonstrate servant-leadership, teach your values, involve students in planning, and assign elements of the upcoming worship times.

Leading into Worship

Again, I try to remember the veil picture because it's the job of the lead worshipper. He must be purified, ready to perform the sacred duty, and understand the biblical values of worship and know how to connect with the people.

Helping others learn how to pull back on the veil, becoming leaders into worship is the job of the disciple maker. The leader who builds a disciple-making worship ministry transfers his values and shepherds his disciples.

God-ward, truth-filled, planned worship services that contain elements relevant to young people is a real and constant possibility. You can lead a team to minister in sincerity and passion, experiential personal participation, and variety. Through preparing yourself as the leader, planning your services strategically, and building and guiding a team, you will see your whole group enter into meaningful God-honoring worship on a regular basis. That is a worship ministry that makes disciples.

Notes

1. Andy Park, "In the Secret," © 1995 Mercy/Vineyard Publishing.

2. Michael W. Smith, "Above All," *Worship*, © 2001 (label: Maranatha, Integrity, Vineyard).

3. Matt Redman, *The Unquenchable Worshipper* (Ventura, Calif.: Regal Books, 2001).

6.
Evangelizing

I SERVED AS YOUTH PASTOR at two Willow Creek Association churches— Christ Community Church in St. Charles and Willow Creek Community Church in South Barrington, Illinois. In each place God expanded my heart for the lost and solidified my commitment to the starting point of disciple making found in the Matthew 28:18–20 commission. Jesus asked his disciples to participate with God in reaching those who are lost.

Those pastoral experiences marked my life. I will forever have embedded in my memory the words of one of my senior pastors, Bill Hybels, as he regularly taught on Luke 15: "Lost people matter to God." In this passage Jesus pointedly responded to religious people who couldn't understand why he befriended "sinners." He told three stories about three lost items that were each so dear to the one who had lost them that an all-out search was made to find them. The shepherd left the ninety-nine sheep to find one lost sheep. The woman cleaned out her house to find a lost coin. The father threw a huge celebration for the son who was lost but now was found.

In each case, the lost consumed each person's thoughts and activities so much that they reoriented their whole lives around the pursuit of finding. Jesus made it clear: those lost matter greatly to God. They matter so much that he is on an all-out search for them and will do whatever it takes to bring them home. Jesus didn't just tell this story to help the religious leaders of his day understand the Father's heart. We have his words today so we will not lose focus on what matters most to the Father. Apart from his own glory, what matters most to God is people. And lost people matter so much to God that he has called his church to partner with him in finding those who are lost.

In youth ministry we find one of the greatest of harvest fields. We work with students who are in the formative stages, discovering what they believe and making life-long decisions based on those beliefs. We work with students who have to spend the majority of their day, five days a week, together in school where they are legally free to talk about their faith with one another. And they spend the majority of their extracurricular time with their peers as well. They may not have another time in their lives when they have this kind of freedom and time to hear and respond to the gospel as well as be messengers of it to their friends.

If Jesus were to look over a junior high or high school campus today, as he did the Samaritan field of souls in John 4:35, he would say again, "look at the fields, for they are ready for harvest." And he would again, as he did with the young disciples he called to follow him, turn those teenage souls into harvesters for the kingdom. So, let's look at how we can follow his example in raising the evangelistic temperature in our youth ministries and impart the Father's passion for lost people, enough to rearrange how we do youth ministry.

Doing or Being?

Often in ministry we say, "We do evangelism." But I have always had that uneasy feeling in my gut that we're missing Jesus' true call. I look back to my first youth ministry. Once at a summer evangelism-training event in Seattle, for a week our students did evangelism. Then we went home and not much changed.

Later, I stepped into a very public ministry in Saint Charles, Illinois. It had gained attention, first, because of its quick growth and, second, because of a very public moral failure of my predecessor. The measuring stick for evangelism in this place had been attached to the number of students attending the large event that was called seeker-targeted night. For awhile, I also found myself thinking, *We're doing evangelism because we have students showing up to our evangelistic gathering.* Again, I knew in my spirit that this was not the whole call of Jesus.

At Willow Creek, outreach events also took priority. One creative outreach, called Mosaic, was a thoughtful, well-crafted, student-led program targeting teens with broken lives. Students would share how God had taken the broken pieces of their lives and through Christ and his work on the cross was building in them a beautiful mosaic. Students shared through personal story, song, dance, creative art, and drama. Many students brought their friends. I remember leaving at the end of the night, encouraged by how well the event went but still feeling uneasy because something was missing.

The Missing Element

All of these programs certainly raise the evangelistic temperature of a group. However, doing evangelism is different than being evangelistic. It's possible to prepare evangelistic events, host evangelistic retreats, even take evangelistic trips or a getaway for training and still exhibit a lack of lifestyle evangelism. In each ministry I realized over and over again that I needed to see the evangelistic priority of our ministry reflected every day in the hearts and lives of our students. This is different than just calling them to participate in an evangelistic event. It is so easy for us youth ministers to create groups that do evangelism and yet remain evangelistically ineffective in the way they live.

The missing element is found in the second word of Jesus' commission in Matthew 28:19: "Therefore, go" (NIV). In its original language, this word is a participle, an -*ing* word. Like the other participles in this passage (baptizing, teaching), *going* denotes an ongoing, active, enduring process. In other words, Jesus was calling his followers to a way of life, to a pervasive kind of living. He was calling them to an evangelism lifestyle. If that is so, then wherever we are, whatever we do, and whichever position we find ourselves in, we should be making disciples. And making disciples starts with introducing those in our circle of influence to the love and life-giving power of Jesus Christ. It translates into building relationships, loving people, and sharing what is most important to us in everyday living.

I'm not suggesting that our evangelistic events were misconceived. I'm saying that we missed getting students to live evangelistically—with their whole lives. We needed to shift our focus from seeing evangelism as events or activities to seeing it encompassing lives. Even our language needs to change from "I do evangelism" to "I am evangelistic." In each ministry, as we made this shift and began to implement the principles found in this chapter, we saw our students move from those who did evangelistic events to those who had evangelistic lifestyles.

Real-Life Shifts

In Seattle, Luke Williams made the decision prior to his senior year to leave the Christian school he had been attending for years to transfer to a public school near his home. He transferred in order to widen his relational realm with students who didn't know God personally. At his Christian school, Luke was class president, a star athlete, valedictorian-to-be, head of the chapel committee, and an all-around, well-liked student. Yet Luke realized that doing evangelistic events or activities accomplished nothing when he had no friends who needed to meet Jesus. He looked around and concluded there were no non-Christians who would consider Luke their friend. And he changed his life to make that a reality. That year Luke made the shift from doing evangelism to living an evangelistic life.

Greg Flannigan caught the vision for seeing his peer group impacted by his friendship and his personal walk with God. He began openly living his God-changed life at school and in his extracurricular activities. As a result, Nick Rendleman, one of his friends, began seeking God. Later, Nick prayed alone in his bedroom to surrender to God. Then he came to our student ministry gathering. Now, for those of us who measure our evangelistic effectiveness by the number of responses in a program, this response never showed on the radar. However, Nick's conversion was the result of Greg's open life of faith, not just participating in a program. As a result of this evangelistic influence, more than twenty students were led to make decisions to follow Christ in Greg's and Nick's peer group that year. Most of those students came to Christ as a result of seeing Nick's life change and then hearing directly from Nick about his relationship with Jesus Christ. Greg was living a lifestyle of evangelism, which led to Nick living it as well.

A Relational Process

In order to shift our understanding, we need to acknowledge that making disciples is a relational process, not a mechanical program. But our tendency is to throw programs at people instead of relationships because programs are neater, controllable, and more visible. Relationships tend to be slow in developing, messy, confusing, unpredictable, and behind the scenes. However, people do not come to faith in Jesus Christ because they attended a program. Most people have been loved by the people of God and have seen faith lived out in a community of loving followers of Christ. A program may have been a tool in the process, but it never replaces relationships.

One day I asked one of my students how her relationship was going with someone she was trying to share Christ with. She said, "Oh, I'm not really talking to him anymore." I was surprised and asked why. She responded, "Well, he's made it pretty clear that he isn't going to buy into what we believe." She went on to explain how difficult it had been trying to share her faith with him and how she was not ready to continue talking to him because his reaction was so adverse.

My response needed to be measured. I wanted to carefully shepherd her and not trample her feelings. She was obviously hurt by the cynicism of her friend. So we spent some time walking through that together. However, I also wanted to teach her through this circumstance that our goal is not just to convert people. Our goal is to love in the name of Jesus and in the context of a relationship. That's the reason we should share the gospel in the first place—because we love our peers. But we must never give up on a relationship. We need to keep on loving even if our friends are only willing to receive God's love through us instead of through him directly. That means when they reject the message, we as the messenger must refuse to reject them.

When an expert in religious law asked Jesus, "Teacher, which commandment in the law is the greatest?" He said to him, "Love the Lord your God with all your heart, with all your soul, and with all your mind. This is the greatest and most important commandment. The second is like it: Love your neighbor as yourself. All the Law and the Prophets depend on these two commandments" (Matt. 22:36–40).

Jesus made it clear that our highest calling is love—to love God and love others. Jesus didn't speak empty words. He lived this calling. He loved the prostitute caught in sin, the greedy tax collector, the promiscuous Samaritan woman rejected not only by the Jews but even by her own people, a betraying disciple, a denying disciple, and the angry mob who shouted at him on the cross. Listen to him: "Father, forgive them for they don't know what they are doing." Jesus loved those who accepted his message and those who rejected it. He even wept over Jerusalem because of his love for them, even though they were hardhearted. His calling to all of us who follow him is to love others tenaciously.

That means that we don't build relationships with people far from God just to see them come to faith in Jesus Christ. We don't make people our projects, which, as Brian McLaren describes in his book *A New Kind of Christian*, prostitutes relationships with people for the purpose of evangelism.[1] Instead, we build loving relationships with them because we are called to love. If they never respond in surrender to Jesus Christ, we continue to love them, because the goal is building loving relationships.

The Starting Point: The Messenger

Rarely do we find a gospel presentation that results in life transformation through students who are not personally experiencing life transformation. This is especially the case today when truth needs to be seen and experienced in real life before it will be heard. Nor do we find students eager to share the message of Jesus' transforming power and love if they have no experience from which to share. That's why it's so important that our evangelism strategy starts with the personal transformation of the messenger—our students.

If Christians who don't experience spiritual transformation are challenged to tell their friends about the good news of Jesus Christ, their messages will lack power and authenticity. To encourage them to do this is a grave disservice to the message of Christ and to the students we are leading. I'm not surprised at how often this happens. When youth ministers become driven by their egos and *need* programs that attract large numbers of students, the spiritual health of the students entrusted to them too often suffers. If our students are growing in their love for God and one another, however, it will be out of the overflow of their hearts that their mouths speak, not just because we told them to do so.

Listen to Paul's words: "knowing your election, brothers loved by God. For our gospel did not come to you in word only, but also in power, in the Holy Spirit, and with much assurance. You know what kind of men we were among you for your benefit" (1 Thess. 1:4–5) and "we cared so much for you that we were pleased to share with you not only the gospel of God but also our own lives, because you had become dear to us" (1 Thess. 2:8).

The Process: Three Stories

You may train your students in how to share the gospel, how to answer challenging questions, and how to defend what they believe. But those skills alone will not produce a lifestyle evangelist. Most junior high and high school students are ill-equipped to build loving relationships. Just stop and watch your students interact with one another. They stumble all over themselves because of their insecurity, awkwardness, and self-focus. Many of our students have never seen this modeled by their parents and so their deficiency runs deep. However, if we're going to move our ministries away from doing evangelism to being a ministry of students who are evangelistic we need to equip them with the skills necessary for building loving relationships.

Every person has a story. Life is a collection of stories building on one another. We cannot exist without the stories that preceded us. And we cannot interact apart from the stories that shape one another. Building loving relationships requires that we hear and participate in one another's stories.

Story One—Their Story

If we carefully listen and observe our students interact with one another, we quickly discover that much of their focus is on themselves. But we know that relationships are built when we move from centering on self to centering on others. We must equip students with the ability to be more concerned about others than themselves. This means they need to hear and know the other person's story before they share their own. We must first seek to know before we are known.

Ask questions. This goes a long way. Most people are just waiting for someone to take an interest in them. All people want to be known by someone else. Students are no exception. We need to train students to be seekers of others' stories. We must teach them how to ask questions of another's life.

Our tendency is to tell someone else what God has done in our lives. We give people information about ourselves before they are even interested in it. Or we give them answers to our own questions, not the ones they are really asking. Is it any wonder we find our attempts at sharing the gospel so ineffective? We may be talking to people who have an entirely different set of questions or life experiences, but we treat them like ourselves because we don't know their stories.

Training students to seek out the story of God in the lives of their peers is the first step. I don't mean ask a bunch of "God" questions. Instead, help them ask questions that invite their peers to share their own stories while paying attention to God's activity in the midst of that story. If students listen closely to one of their friends, they will find a whole set of real questions and real issues that can lead to really significant spiritual conversations.

Serve. We are rarely freely given the right to enter into someone's story. We earn that right. And the way we earn it is through serving. Jesus told his disciples that he came not to be served but to serve and give up his life as a ransom for many. He entered others' lives by serving their needs first.

Most needs of people fall into three categories: significance, security, and belonging. We need to train students to recognize their peers' needs and serve them by meeting those needs in appropriate ways. If a student is seeking significance, he needs to be accepted and loved for who he is, not what he does. This means we teach students to look past behavior to the heart of a person and actively care for him regardless of what he might do. At some point he will need to hear that God loves and accepts him for himself and not for what he has or hasn't done.

If a student is seeking security, she will be served through consistency in our time with her. She probably doesn't care as much about what someone does for her. She's more concerned about whether someone is willing to consistently spend time with her. Eventually, she may come to see that God is faithful and she can be secure with him.

Many students need a sense of belonging. Students have an incredible opportunity to serve these kids by including them in our community. We need to train our students to be inclusive and not exclusive in their groups. They need to see the community of faith as a place to invite others to and not a place to exclude them from.

Students will see their peers merely as projects if they distance themselves from entering into their story. Jesus didn't stay at a safe distance from those he served. He entered into their stories. Students need to be encouraged to become a part of their peers' stories. We can help them think about this in a variety of ways:

- Picking up a shared hobby
- Attending performances and events
- Getting their friends to teach them a sport or skill
- Finding out where they spend time and joining them

As students listen to the stories of their peers, serve them according to their needs, and enter into their worlds, they will better understand how God has already been at work preparing their peers for an encounter with him. They will have a clearer picture of their peers' spiritual hunger.

Story Two—Our Story

I have found that my personal story of God's work in my life has the greatest impact when it interconnects with another person's story and experience. When I share how God has continued to shape and refine my life through difficult and painful circumstances, another person in pain gets a spark of hope that God might do that for him also. When I share my story of how God moved me from trying to please people to courageous and principled decision making, a person enslaved by the expectations of others will wonder if God can do the same for him or her.

God works intentionally to connect us to people who need to hear our story. When we listen to and enter another person's story, we begin to discover that God intends for our story to intersect with another's story and lead to him.

One of our responsibilities is to train our students to be able to share their story with their peers. We may need to start by teaching our students how to tell a story. This can be done using Paul's example in Acts 26. He shared his story with King Agrippa in three parts:

1. His life before Christ (BC)
2. How he met Christ (MC)
3. His life after Christ (AC)

Familiarize your students with this outline. You can train them in the skills of a storyteller together as a group before they work on telling their stories individually. After they experience this together, ask them to work on their personal story of how Jesus has affected their life. They can use Paul's model as a guideline (BC, MC, AC). Then have them come together and share their stories with one another.

Another way to convey the value of storytelling is to ask students to share their stories regularly in your gatherings. These can be stories of how they met Christ or stories of how he is actively involved in their lives. The great thing about our stories is that they're always developing so we always have more to share. For years I tried to connect a student story with the weekly ministry. This kept the value of storytelling in front of our students and illustrated the power of stories to communicate truth.

As you teach students to tell their stories, help them identify their key learning experiences. For some students this will be a broken relationship, a divorce, a significant failure, a rejection, giving in to peer pressure, having it "all together," or not wanting to give up something. Each of these may serve as a connection point with the story of the person they are reaching out to. As you identify their key learning experiences together, have them stop and identify the areas of need within the peers they hope to reach. They may need some help at first, but they will find it exciting to see how the story of God in their lives can intersect with a friend's story.

Story Three—His Story

When we've taken the time to listen, serve, and enter into someone else's story and to connect God's activity in our lives with the need in another's life by sharing our own story, we're ready to start sharing his story—the gospel.

We must prepare our students by teaching them clearly what the gospel message is and how to share it with someone else. Romans 6:23 is a great one-verse picture of the gospel message: "For the wages of sin is death, but the gift of God is eternal life in Christ Jesus our Lord." There are several key parts to this verse. First, because God is a righteous and just God, there is a consequence for sin. That consequence is death, physical as well as spiritual death, which is eternal separation from God. If our sin is not dealt with, we cannot be in relationship with God because he is perfect and holy. However, God is also loving, therefore he wants us to have a gift. He made us to be in relationship with him and to experience life abundant and eternal. His gift was sending Jesus Christ his Son to die on the cross to pay for our sins and forgive us. This makes it possible for us to receive forgiveness and to be made righteous and holy like Jesus Christ so we can be in a relationship with God. However, in order to receive this gift we must believe and receive. We must believe that Jesus is our Forgiver and then receive him into our lives as our Leader (our Lord).

Another way is by writing "DO" on one-half of a piece of paper or napkin and "DONE" on the other half. Then explain that religion is spelled "D-O" because it's about all the things we need to do to impress God and measure up to his standard of perfection. But Christianity is spelled "D-O-N-E" because it's about what God has done for us through Jesus Christ to forgive us of our sins and give us his righteousness in exchange for our sins (2 Cor. 5:21).

There are many different ways to share the gospel. Train your students in one or two ways. Then have them practice with one another so they gain confidence in sharing.

We must also prepare our students in how to call their friends to respond to the gospel message. Jesus made it clear that we were to *repent* and *believe* (Mark 1:15; Luke 13:3, 5; John 1:12; 3:15–18). This involves turning away from sin and self-governance and looking to Jesus as the forgiver, redeemer, and leader of our lives.

When I'm training students in this part, I often take them through an experience of personal repentance so they're reminded of what it feels like to repent. I ask them to take some time and identify any activity, thought, or word that is incongruent to the character and priorities of Jesus Christ. I encourage them to ask the Holy Spirit to identify both sins of commission (ones we commit) and sins of omission (things God has told us to do, but we have not obeyed). I encourage them to write everything the Holy Spirit brings to mind. After this I invite them to repent of those sins.

Once we have experienced this together, I ask them to share how it felt. Often I hear descriptions like, "I felt ashamed or embarrassed," "I am sad to admit that I am still struggling with this," "I feel so relieved to get that off my chest," "I feel clean and renewed." After we share, I remind students that we are inviting our friends to something they have never done before. They don't know what it's like to repent and then experience God's forgiveness and refreshing. We need to enter into each situation with extreme care and sensitivity as we invite them to take this step of faith.

Finally, we must teach students to listen closely to the Spirit's promptings and leadings and be sensitive to each person's journey. At some point it's most appropriate for us to only ask questions and seek to better understand their story while we serve them and enter into their life story. At other times, they need to hear our story and see how God's activity in our lives may intersect with their need for his activity in their lives. And, as God opens the door for the gospel, we may have the opportunity to share his good news with our friends. Whatever the case or situation, we must do all these things from a position of prayerful dependence because ultimately it's God who changes a heart, not our personal story or clever presentation.

A Visible Example

The evangelistic temperature of a group stems from the life of the leaders. Jesus said in Luke 6:40, "A disciple is not above his teacher, but everyone who is fully trained will be like his teacher." When I'm coaching or consulting a ministry leader about a particular issue, problem, or inadequacy in his or her ministry, I pay close attention to the life before me. I ask probing questions to reveal what the leader believes and does. When a leader tells me his group of students is not reaching out to their peers, I start by checking whether the leader is reaching his peers. I ask if there are any non-Christian peers in his life who would call him a friend. Most often what I discover with youth leaders is a commitment to the evangelism priority of the Great Commission with students but not with their own peers. We may be compelled to share the gospel with teens and encourage teens to share the gospel with their peers, but we ourselves fail to do what we're challenging kids to do.

The tendency of most of us is to minister down. We choose the group of people who are not a threat to us—an age or population that will not destroy us if they reject us. Often that equates to ministering to the age below us. When we get out of college we do youth ministry, then when we get older we do college ministry. So why should we be surprised when our teens have no problem doing evangelism through vacation Bible school or children's ministry but refrain from reaching their own peer group? They're just doing what they've seen us do. Why should they take the risk of having their peer group, those whose opinions matter most to them, reject them?

If kids see their leaders taking that risk, they might follow. If they heard us talk about the neighbor we are befriending, they might realize they have people in their circle of influence God has called them to befriend as well. When they see us interacting with other adults in the community who don't go to our church or share our beliefs, maybe they'll come to realize that evangelism doesn't just happen in a church building or at a church event. But how will they know if they never see it? I have often heard it said, "We teach what we know. We reproduce who we are." If we want our students to live evangelistic lifestyles, we must start by living evangelistically ourselves.

So before you continue reading the next chapter, stop and pray for those whom God has put in the circle of influence in your life who don't yet know him personally. Think about how you can take time to get to know their stories. Do it today or this week. Be a listener and servant yourself to those who are lost around you. Enter into their stories and pray that God intersects your story with theirs and opens a door for you to share his story.

Notes

1. Brian D. McLaren, *A New Kind of Christian: A Tale of Two Friends on a Spiritual Journey* (San Francisco: Jossey-Bass, 2001).

7.

Spiritual Tools

DAVE PATTY

FROM AS EARLY AS I CAN REMEMBER, I loved to build. At the age of five I discovered a hammer and nails and immediately proceeded to scrounge scraps of wood from a building project next door. A small house was in mind when I started, but the best I could manage was a flimsy half wall that would hold together only when it lay flat on the ground. I threw my whole heart into it, however, and would sometimes pound the wood without a nail just to hear the hammer strokes echo off the nearby fence.

I attempted next to master the saw but managed only to create a huge pile of sawdust and destroy a few chairs in the process. Christmas arrived, and Santa blessed my life with a set of screwdrivers and a pair of pliers. A telephone and toaster were deconstructed into a fascinating pile of parts, never again to be returned to their original state.

Tools were some of my most prized possessions. They were almost magical, making it possible for my pudgy hands to accomplish unbelievable feats of skill. But they had limitations as well. It took a great deal of energy to push that saw back and forth, and my lack of coordination made the cut anything but straight. That hammer sent nails into the wood, but it also produced plenty of blisters and sore muscles.

I began dreaming of the day when I could use power tools. I knew from watching grownups that power tools were of a different world altogether. The circular saw my dad used could rip through a thick beam in just seconds, producing a ruler-straight cut. When he sank screws into the wood, a drill did the heavy lifting. He just held the pieces in place. Power tools did more than just extend his energy to the task at hand, however. They were an independent source of power, carefully designed to fulfill a special task.

Oh, the possibilities, I thought longingly. *If I were just old enough to use power tools.*

Let me share with you a fear of mine. Youth ministry professionals have more resources at their fingertips than at anytime in history. We have books of carefully designed games, stacks of ready-made talks, and facilities that would make the leaders of another generation green with envy. We can rent houseboats, take ski trips, storm amusement parks, and then relive it all when we get home on a video filling a wall and blasting us with surround sound. We can go to Christian concerts, give away our custom-designed T-shirts, and surf the latest trends.

But in all the excitement we may never grow up to use power tools.

Could it be that we miss powerful resources? Could your frustration and weariness come in part from a ministry leaning solely on your manual work and limited energy? Don't forget that a designer hammer with a fish logo is still only a hammer, and a pair of pliers in a color-coordinated case with a ticket to the pliers' convention is still just a pair of pliers. Power tools are of a different nature altogether.

What did ministers do during the last two thousand years when all of these current resources were unavailable? I believe they leaned heavily on a simple set of tools that possess built-in spiritual power. Though the list could be longer, I will focus on five of particular significance.

Repentance

John the Baptist had a hefty assignment for a reclusive prophet with a wardrobe problem. "Prepare the way for the Lord; make His paths straight! Every valley will be filled, and every mountain and hill will be made low; the crooked will become straight, the rough ways smooth" (Luke 3:4–5).

Remember that this was before the advent of Caterpillar tractors and huge, earth-moving machines. We don't even know if John had a shovel. His to-do list seems like an impossible assignment. What did God expect him to use as raw material—a couple of locusts swarms and a stack of wild honey?

In his shoes I would find it difficult to sleep at night. So many people depended on his success. John's road is to open the "way for the Lord," to prepare the path for a salvation that "all mankind" would see. This was serious business. This was a daunting task.

Somehow, however, John remained calm. He reached into his camel-skin coat, pulled out a major power tool, and began to preach "a baptism of repentance for the forgiveness of sins" (Luke 3:3). Scripture records that "[people from] Jerusalem, all Judea, and all the vicinity of the Jordan were flocking to him, and they were baptized by him in the Jordan River as they confessed their sins" (Matt. 3:5–6). Something amazing began to happen.

Do we understand the power repentance possesses to prepare the way for the Lord? Do we realize that repentance could turn a winding dirt road into a highway for his blessing? Do we know that the kingdom of heaven starts to arrive in a convoy when repentance has cleared the way?

Martin was a mess. After years of wandering far from God, his life was in shambles and he knew it. "I want to come back to God," he said with tears in his eyes. "But I don't know how. I have so much garbage in my life, so many bad habits, so much debris from all my sin. I'm afraid I won't be able to make it back. It's just too far."

At this point, what should I do? I could start dissecting his bad habits one by one, pointing out the errors and compiling lists of right behavior for him. I could hold him accountable and give him feedback, but we would be exhausted long before the work was done. He needed the power of God, a visit from the Savior. He needed the kingdom of heaven to roll into his life. And I know, from the witness of John the Baptist, that repentance makes the path straight.

"Martin, your situation is hopeless," I said. "You think it is bad, but the reality is even worse than you realize." I could have called him a "brood of vipers," but I thought he was getting the point. "That is the bad news. The good news is that this realization is the first step to repentance and that repentance can clear the way for the power of God. Let's start by filling in those valleys, and see what he decides to do."

We began to meet weekly with only one purpose in mind—to lead him through steps of repentance. I would ask him what the Holy Spirit had convicted him of that week and what needed to come into the light. Generally, recent issues surfaced first. Then a whole slew of old garbage came connected to it—ugly sin that was difficult for both of us to see. We would bring it out into the light and then take it to the Savior in prayer. Martin named his sin without making excuses, expressed his sorrow to God, and then asked for forgiveness and cleansing. I then laid my hands on him and prayed for healing and renewal in the area we had just covered.

It was hard work! But what a joy to see the kingdom of God released. As soon as an area was cleansed, the fruits of the Spirit became immediately evident. A spiritual sensitivity began to emerge along with a passion to follow hard after God and please him in that area. It was not logical or explainable. But it was very biblical.

Repentance prepares the way for the Lord.

Recently Peter knocked on the door of the room where I was writing. Peter was fulfilling his civil service in the center we run to train young leaders in the Czech Republic, so we frequently saw each other during the course of a day. "I just had a great time in prayer," he said excitedly, "and I wanted to tell you about it." Listening to him speak, I shook my head in amazement.

I remembered my impression of him over the previous months—sullenly shuffling from one task to the next, locked in a permanent bad mood, difficult to get along with. We knew, however, that his behavior was the reflection of his spiritual condition. Then God brought him to his knees, and he spent the evening weeping before the Lord.

The young man who emerged from his room the next day bore no resemblance to the Peter we knew. Now every time we turn around we see huge steps forward in areas that once seemed hopeless. It's like the power of God has descended on his life. I find myself filled with joy and amazement. But I guess I shouldn't be surprised.

Repentance prepares the way for the Lord.

Are you leading young people to repentance? Are you going there yourself?

Not long ago I noted an area of my life in which I was missing God's presence and power. Knowing that a dear friend was coming to visit, I called and asked if he could spend the evening with me in repentance and prayer. (I take seriously the instruction of James 5:16a which says, "Confess your sins to *one another* and pray for *one another*, so that you may be healed.")

He agreed, and we worked through the area together. It wasn't fun to name the sins that God brought to light, but the release that repentance provided was deep and sweet. The best part was the kingdom of heaven started showing up once the mountain was removed.

Faith

The disciples had a tough time with faith. They assumed their proximity to the Master was sufficient and kept forgetting to pull out the power tool he urged them to use. A storm raged and they broke their backs at the oars. One of them broke away to wake Jesus to give him their expert assessment of the situation. "We're going to die!" he said.

He asked them, "Where is your faith?" (Luke 8:24–25).

Another time Peter could have expected a commendation. After all, he was the first to notice that the strange aberration coming across the water was actually their teacher. He was the first to recommend a course of action and the only one to jump out of the boat and try out this water-walking mode of transport. It seems surprising, then, that in place of praise he received a mild rebuke from Jesus.

"You of *little faith*, why did you doubt?" (Matt. 14:31, emphasis added).

Still another time someone had to take care of the food. And that some-one forgot. What made it worse was that Jesus already seemed to have noticed. How could they expect to rule in a future kingdom if they couldn't even keep track of lunch? This was embarrassing, but maybe it could be quickly fixed. "Thomas, you head off to the city as soon as we hit land. Philip, see if you can get a theological conversation going with the Master to distract him. Let's see how we can fix this."

"Aware of this Jesus said, 'You of *little faith!* Why are you discussing among yourselves that you do not have bread? Don't you understand yet? Don't you remember the five loaves for the 5,000 . . . ?'" (Matt. 16:8–9, emphasis added).

This seemed to be a common occurrence. In fact, the disciples were rebuked more for their lack of faith than for any other single thing! The role of faith was so central that Jesus even connected it to his miraculous power, "Let it be done for you according to your faith!" (Matt. 9:29). In his hometown of Nazareth, a lack of faith shut down the work. "And he did not do many mir-acles there because of their lack of faith" (Matt. 13:58 NIV).

Scriptural faith is not based on naive optimism or hopeful wishing but on the person and promises of Christ. This is a firm foundation. Biblical faith is not passive mental agreement or warm sentiment. It is boldly active. Faith is confidently living on the basis of what cannot be seen because we are res-olutely convinced that it's true.

Are you leading your students to faith?

They will attempt to direct your eyes back to the seen. When I challenged Susan to forgive her alcoholic father, she responded defensively, "How will that change the situation? He is still an alcoholic. And how can I forgive when I don't feel it in my heart?" When God began to convict Jerry that he needed to break up with his non-Christian girlfriend, he was paralyzed by fear. "What will my friends say?" he worried. "And how do I know I will find a Christian girl? At least she likes me. What if God has no one else for me?"

At this point we have a choice—to point our students to the seen or to the unseen. We can explain the situation to them logically. We can give them a stack of reasons and good advice. These ploys are insufficient, however. In the final analysis, true solutions come back to faith in the character and promises of God. Without faith it is impossible to please him (Heb. 11:6).

What most people don't understand is that faith is one of the few things we actually can control. I can't control my circumstances, my friends, my par-ents, my health, my image, or my future. But I can choose at any moment, in any circumstance, under any pressure, to believe.

This secret of the Christian life is often misunderstood. I frequently hear students pray, asking God to help them believe and give them faith. They then passively wait for him to respond. Sometimes I have to interrupt them and remind them that God has already answered their prayer and is waiting for them to respond! Faith is one of the few tasks actually entrusted to us. When the disciples asked Christ to increase their faith, he told them that faith as small as a mustard seed was sufficient (Luke 17:5–6). They already had faith enough; what they needed to do was use it.

Amazing things happen when students begin to believe. When Susan chose in faith to forgive, even when everything in her screamed that it was impossible, God stepped in and performed a miraculous work of redemption. Her father is still an alcoholic, but Susan is free of the curse of his sin. When Jerry stepped out in faith to be obedient in the face of immense fear, God provided in miraculous ways for the needs of his soul. He doesn't even know how to explain it today, but he is rich and whole.

The waters do not part, however, until the step of faith places us out into the raging torrent, resolutely confident of what we cannot see. We must not let students convince us that this is out of their control. They are able to believe. And they are fully responsible for their lack of faith. Christ would not rebuke a follower for something beyond that person's control. But his words to those of little faith were firm and direct: "Why did you doubt?"

Don't just call your students to join you on the winter retreat; call them to faith. Don't just challenge them to show up on Sunday morning; challenge them to believe. When you see the absence of the power of God, look for the evidence of little faith and let them know this can change. Remind them of the words of Jesus: "Didn't I tell you that if you believed you would see the glory of God?" (John 11:40).

Prayer

I shouldn't have even been in school that day. A head cold made me feel I was drowning. I just couldn't afford to miss another day of class. Armed with a pocket full of pills and a box of tissues, I trudged through the biting cold to the Billy Graham Center, wondering how in the world I was going to concentrate. A fellow graduate student, Karen, caught sight of me as I was making my way through the front door.

"Hi, Dave," she said cheerily, "how are you today?"

I stopped and looked at her through glassy eyes. "Do you really want to know?" I asked glumly.

"Sure, that's why I asked," she said.

"To be honest, rotten. I have a horrible cold and my head hurts," I complained. "I should be in bed rather than standing here and I stayed up half the night catching up on my reading. It's going to be a long day."

"Wow, you do look bad," she said with compassion. Then she brightened. "Hey, has anyone prayed for you yet?"

I was a little surprised. "No, not that I know of."

"May I then?" she asked.

"I suppose so. You mean right here?" I replied.

"Why not? You need prayer right away," she said and, without a moment's hesitation, started in. We were standing in the lobby with students swirling all around us and heading for the next hour's instruction. But for Karen, we had just been transported into the throne room. She prayed for my strength, my spirit, and my body. She prayed for a sense of the Lord's presence and for my perspective. Then, as quickly as it began, the prayer was finished.

"Have a blessed day, Dave," she said as she disappeared into the crowd.

I did—in spite of my cold. And I walked off to class grateful for a friend who knew how to pray—grateful that she didn't give me only a sympathetic ear and a pat on the back but remembered that prayer connects us to a powerful God.

The tool of prayer is well known to us, but precisely because of its familiarity we sometimes forget to use it. We overlook it because it seems so common, forgetting that it connects us with a very uncommon God. We proceed in our own strength, missing out on the benefits and blessing prayer brings.

When the disciples sheepishly approached Jesus to ask why they had not been successful in casting out a particularly obstinate demon, Jesus reminded them they had forgotten something: "This kind can come out by nothing but prayer" (Mark 9:29). I wonder how many difficult situations in our youth groups would be overcome only through persistent prayer.

Next time a student comes to you with a problem, don't let him leave before you've prayed for him. When you see a young person buckling under the weight of the day, put your hand on her shoulder in the lobby and pray. Do you feel you're staring evil in the eye? Face down the forces of darkness with fasting and prayer.

Don't forget the quick prayer—for blessing, encouragement, or strength. Write a prayer to a student in e-mail, or take requests to the Father when you're talking together on the phone. Remember, this is one of your primary responsibilities. When the apostles stripped down their job description to the nonnegotiable elements, there were only two things left: the ministry of the Word of God and prayer (Acts 6:4).

The Holy Spirit

D. L. Moody traced the turning point in his ministry to when he began to personally understand the work of the Holy Spirit. It started with an old man who confronted him after one of his services with a stern reprimand. "Young man, when you speak again, honor the Holy Ghost." Shortly thereafter he noticed two women praying for him in one of his evangelistic services. "Why are you praying for me? Why don't you pray for the people?" "You need power," they answered without hesitation.

Moody ignored them for a time, but the Lord would not let him loose. "There came a great hunger in my soul. I knew not what it was. I began to cry as never before. The hunger increased. I really felt that I did not want to live any longer if I could not have this power for service. I kept on crying all the time that God would fill me with His Spirit."[1]

God honored his request, and Moody began to experience the work of the Holy Spirit in a way that forever marked his life and ministry. Soon after, he left a thriving ministry for a study trip to England, where he spoke in several churches. His gospel presentation had unusual power, and in the course of several months, he was preaching to thousands. The rest is history.

Later he said, "The doctrine of the Holy Ghost has been too much overlooked, as though it were not practical, and the result is a lack of power in testimony and work. If we would work, not as one that beatest the air, but to some definite purpose, we must have this power from on high. Without this power our work will be drudgery. With it, it becomes a joyful task, a refreshing service."[2]

Jim Cymbala, pastor of the Brooklyn Tabernacle, experienced a similar breakthrough early in his ministry. "One day I told the Lord that I would rather die than merely tread water throughout my career in the ministry . . . always preaching about the power of the Word and the Spirit but never seeing it. I abhorred the thought of just having more church services. I hungered for God to break through in our lives and ministry."[3]

The work of the Holy Spirit was so essential for ministry that the disciples were carefully instructed "not to leave Jerusalem, but to wait for the Father's promise. 'This,' [He said, 'is what] you heard from Me'" (Acts 1:4). Earlier Christ had shared that it was actually for their good that he was leaving: "If I don't go away the Counselor will not come to you. If I go, I will send Him to you" (John 16:7).

What does this mean for us practically? We could fill another book with answers to this question, but perhaps two sentences sum up the most important thoughts.

1. Submit to the work of the Holy Spirit in your life and seek to be filled by him.
2. Count on the work of the Holy Spirit in the lives of others and help them respond to him.

Do you remember my talk with Martin? When he began to share, the Lord reminded me that I was not alone and that I was just an assistant to the great

Counselor. That was comforting because I didn't know what to do next. I experience that often—the sense that I am being asked to lead or speak in a way that will move a person forward, and I don't have the faintest idea what to say.

"Martin," I said, "I don't know what to tell you. But I do know that the Holy Spirit is in this room with us, that he dwells in both you and in me. His responsibility is to guide us into all truth. So let's ask him to lead both of us and to bring to your mind the things he wants us to deal with."

He agreed and we prayed for the Holy Spirit's leading. Immediately God brought to his mind the first area of sin he wanted us to deal with. Starting there, we asked the Lord to uncover it fully because his responsibility is to convict of sin (John 16:8). As God brought each area to light, Martin confessed it and then prayed for cleansing. Once that was done we asked Christ, through the Holy Spirit, to lead us to the next step. We did this with confidence, knowing that it's the Spirit's job to take what is from Christ and "make it known" to us (John 16:15 NIV).

When I prayed for Martin, I prayed with one ear open, expecting that the Spirit would lead me as I prayed. I do this because we have a command to "with every prayer and request, pray at all times in the Spirit" (Eph. 6:18). When we met the next week, I assumed the Spirit had been working in his life when I was not with him and asked him how the Spirit was working. I know that the more I get in touch with the Spirit's agenda, the more effective my work will be. I also watched for the areas in which he was experiencing life and peace and the areas in which he was experiencing death because I know that "the mind-set of the flesh is death but the mind-set of the Spirit is life and peace" (Rom. 8:6). These signs were indicators pointing to what was under the Spirit's control and what was still not.

What incredible resources are available to us through the Holy Spirit! His indwelling has hundreds of practical implications for ministry! Unfortunately, we often leave our theology of the Spirit in a dusty textbook high on our shelves or confined to only one particular dimension of his work.

Christ did not leave you alone, and he never expected you to minister with only your human resources. "But you will receive *power* when the Holy Spirit comes on you; and you will be my witnesses in Jerusalem, and in all Judea and Samaria, and to the ends of the earth" (Acts 1:8, emphasis added).

The Word of God

When I was a kid, a friend of mine had a knack for imitating famous people. He could copy the president's voice with perfect intonation and ape the famous comedians of the day so well we would end up rolling on the floor, incapacitated by laughter. But my favorite was his rendition of Billy Graham.

"The Bible says . . ." he would begin, and then continue with all the force of the famous evangelist, filling a stadium with his voice. For emphasis he clenched the Bible in his right hand, holding it high in the air as Billy did when he spoke, pacing back and forth across the front of the room. I was so inspired I could even picture the upcoming invitation!

Later I saw Billy Graham in person. As I watched him speak I noted that my friend had lifted his accent perfectly, even to the often repeated phrase "The Bible says . . ." But as I studied the real thing, I noticed one crucial difference. My friend held up his Bible as you would naturally expect—closed. It is hard to hold a Bible high above your head any other way. But when Graham held his Bible in the air, it was always open.

My friend had the words right and had the right book in his hand. Unfortunately, the book remained closed. Very near to the source of truth he looked but yet so far away.

I assume you believe in the power of the Bible, that you study the Bible, and that you teach about the Bible. How easy it is, however, to hold it closed in our hands. When you talk to kids after youth group, does your Bible come open? As you teach, are theirs open as well? Does it come open when you plan, when you are stuck, when someone asks you a question? Do you begin by saying, "Well, I think . . ." or "God's Word says that . . ." This is a small difference that has huge implications.

The words of God are inspired—yours are not. The words of God are living and active—yours are not. Make sure you don't just lug this power tool around in your briefcase, but that you pull it out every chance you get, knowing that God promises to personally move when his words are proclaimed.

I'm not suggesting that you throw away your shelf of resources. Keep digging through those books (and this one) for good ideas. Don't cancel your creative youth group trip. Ask other ministries for some of their better programming ideas. Work up a great brochure and an impressive T-shirt design. Just remember that all these are mere hand tools.

You're old enough to use the ones that come with built-in power.

Notes

1. Raymond V. Edman, *They Found the Secret* (Grand Rapids, Mich.: Zondervan, 1984), 101–102.

2. Lyle Dorsett, *A Passion for Souls: The Life of D. L. Moody* (Chicago: Moody, 1997), 393.

3. Jim Cymbala, *Fresh Wind, Fresh Fire* (Grand Rapids, Mich.: Zondervan, 1997), 23.

8.
Youth Ministry and Church

STEVEN PATTY

EARLY IN THE DEVELOPMENT of Malachi Ministries—an organization to reach the youth of North American military personnel overseas—we had to make a decision. Officially, we were a youth extension of a missionary agency. We raised support, recruited sending churches, and developed prayer bases from the States. Like other missionaries, we climbed aboard airplanes in front of waving friends and family to join the adventure of overseas ministry. We were set up to be a kind of youth ministry special forces, dropping in from the sky to capture the hearts of adolescents—young people from our culture living in a different culture—with the gospel of Jesus.

But what would we do about the church? For the most part, our strategies were powerfully structured and elegantly refined. We were mobile, responsive, and effective—a light, quick-moving, confident force of youth workers. At the time, we thought we knew what we were doing. And looking back now, I think we really did. We had assembled an amazingly impressive group of gifted youth ministers. So what would we do about the church?

Strategically, embedding our talented teams in the military base or post chapel system (the military equivalent of the local church) made little sense. Sitting through long hours of parish council meetings, even submitting to the recommendation of parish council meetings, seemed unwise and even a bit torturous. Willingly putting our ministry under the authority of a chaplain with whom we may or may not theologically agree and into a system of policies and procedures, red tape and long lines, politics and power pressures felt like ministerial suicide. Why should we willingly engage in such frustration?

For awhile we stared at the fork in the road. The decision seemed monumental for a fledgling organization. And indeed it was.

We could partner with the church but retain our distinction and separateness and enjoy relative freedom and autonomy. Or we could be the church—actually *be* the church, for better or worse.

If we were just to partner, we would merely need to keep the church and its leadership happy with our activity. As long as we didn't cause any problems, we would be free to do as we pleased. (Believe me, the prospect of having freedom sounded so nice to a group of gifted, energetic, strong-willed young youth ministers.) But if we were to *be* the church, then the chaplain, the parish council, and even the base commander of this ministry context would have to become like family to us. We would need not only to impact but let ourselves be impacted, not only to influence but let ourselves be influenced, not only to enter into but let ourselves be entered as well. Such is the implication of having a strong theology of the church.

And so, to borrow from Robert Frost, we took the road less traveled. We decided to *be* church, not just partner with church. No, it was not glory upon glory. Every day was not sweeter than the day before. There were times when we sat opposed and frustrated, stymied and undermined. Yet we still refused to do an "end run" around the church. We decided not to bypass the church system. We were committed, even though at times it felt as if some enormous guy was sitting on top of us as we tried to run with the ministry. This expressed our commitment to a theology of church.

When push comes to shove, you always have to start with revelation and then go to practice, instead of the other way around. And so we decided to start with a doctrine of the church and go from there.

There's a lot of pressure not to connect or embed or immerse or *become* the church—even for church-based youth pastors. It's no wonder that many youth ministries act as if they were an entity unto themselves—satellites to the church, revolving around the mass of adults but not integrated into the authority, life, witness, practices, tensions, and even the more mundane "daily-ness" of the church.   ·

In such cases of disconnected partnership, the youth ministry has its own mission, its own leadership, and its own practices. It touches the church at key points of worship or in meetings with leadership. But in truth, it is truly only a partnership—a pleasant handshake, but not a full-orbed *being* together. These youth ministers tend to develop a tunnel vision that sees people strictly from the time they enter middle school to the time they graduate from high school. The before and the after are foggy hazes in the view of a youth pastor, for those other years do not contribute to the immediate quest of developing a robust youth ministry.

A youth ministry is an expression of the whole, intergenerational church, however, and should be seen in the context of the people of God. *Being* church is not the only implication of a robust theology of church. Consider the following implications of deep belief in church.

If Scriptures Were Central

The Bible stands right at the heart of the church. Protestant reformers held to the notion of *sola Scriptura*—Scripture alone. In the view of these sixteenth-century church leaders, the strength of the church came from the firm instruction of the Bible: "Faith comes from what is heard, and what is heard comes through the message about Christ" (Rom. 10:17).

Through the reading of the Word, the church is nourished, challenged, corrected, and grown. Through the reading of the Word, the church understands its identity and purpose. Through the reading of the Word, the church hears from God himself. Other than hearing the audible voice of God or walking through the first century in the presence of his son, Jesus, the clearest form of God's self-revelation is the Holy Scriptures.

You never find a good church apart from the Bible. Well, there may be a meeting or two every once in awhile, like a potluck dinner or a prayer meeting or a softball tournament that is "church" and where the reading of Scriptures is absent. Not often, however, can a church gather as a church without hearing from the Word. The Scriptures are absolutely central to worship for the people of God.

A youth ministry, if it is to be informed by a theology of church, must also place the Scriptures conspicuously at its heart. Making Scriptures central does not mean talking *about* the Bible, using a verse or two here and there as an illustration within a talk, or even popping in and out of various places in Scripture to make a point. Neither is it going through worksheets or prepared devotionals (although those certainly have a place within the effort to make young disciples). Young people really need to hear from God, in his own words and in his own way. I know of no way of doing this other than getting students in the Word, reading large sections, opening their hearts to the heart of God. Young people need to read their Bibles.

How can you get young people to read their Bibles? Bribe them? That works fine for the short term. Have them compete for prizes? Again, that will help for the duration of a contest. Scold them? Shame is probably not the best approach for a longer view of healthy spiritual development, although it, too, works on the more sensitive hearts in the group.

How can you manage to take uninterested young people, bored with the Bible, and inspire habits of Bible reading?

Let me tell you about Bill, one of my mentors in youth ministry who takes the Bible seriously. Students consistently emerge from his youth ministry with a fairly mature understanding of God and an abiding thirst for his Word.

If you were to drop in on one of Bill's summer camps, you would immediately notice two things. First, you would see all kinds of rafting equipment being prepared for the next day on a wild river in Idaho. Second, you would notice there is no camp speaker. Why? Because camps provide a tremendous opportunity for young people to engage the Bible in a personal and relational way. At camp, students take thirty minutes in the morning to read a chapter out of their Bibles. Immediately following, they meet another half hour or so in small groups, sharing what they've learned. That evening, following the day's activities, the larger group will participate in open and guided dialogue about an important concept from the day's reading.

This accomplishes two very important tasks. First, modeling takes place as students read and study in a safe environment where they have support and can be corrected of misunderstandings if needed. Second, ownership is strengthened as students discover the power of the Bible for themselves and walk away from camp with a growing excitement to learn more.

It is not just Bill's camps that highlight the Bible. His discipleship programs are all oriented around the Bible as well. His prime model is the Bible Read-Through.[1] Youth are placed in groups of three or four with an adult leader. The kids and the adult commit to reading a set amount in the Bible each day. (Students—even middle schoolers—cover amazing amounts of the Scriptures in time.) The group then meets together once a week to talk about what they're reading and to support one another with accountability. At the end of the meeting, they share prayer requests. Even though the meetings last about an hour, they are powerful tools to connect the students to the Scriptures within the context of a group of believers, the church. The Scriptures begin to come alive as students hear the voice of God through his Word.

Another tool that Bill uses is a weekly "rap session." This is an open forum for students to discuss how the Bible relates to the issues of life. In the session, a student raises an issue from his or her life (for example, how to deal with a grouchy mom or what kind of movies to watch). The group then begins to discuss. For the facilitator, the objective is to push the group to discover what the Bible has to say about the issue. In this environment, the kids who are doing Read-Through's begin to shine because they're most likely to have answers found in the Word. It's amazing to watch middle school and high school students paging through their underlined Bibles, reading passages and wrestling together about their application. The implicit learning is powerful: students develop a deep appreciation for the usefulness of the Bible.

Do you see how central the Bible is to this ministry? This is good church. Like Bill, any youth leader can call students to personally engage in the Word of God instead of treat it like a mysterious, indecipherable, only-for-the-experts text. Every true believer should have an appetite for hearing from God.[2] Some young people, like anorexics regarding food, have gone so long without eating they no longer have a desire for God's Word. For them, God's Word will need to be an acquired taste. It may take encouragement, patience, and careful prodding for this type of students to begin to enjoy God's Word.

Students will also read the Bible differently because they are each designed uniquely. Some will find reading easy; others will need to listen to the Scriptures on a CD or read it together with others in a group. In any case, using reading prominently in the youth program is absolutely essential (as in discussion groups and rap sessions). The Word cannot be a tack-on to an already full program. Students need to exercise what they're reading and learning within youth group because exercise always stimulates hunger. You will find that students who ingest the Word and then exercise within the context of the youth ministry will develop a growing hunger that will sustain them long after they leave your ministry.[3]

If Kids Were Priests

Another implication of a deep belief in church is the way that young people should function and relate to one another. The Protestant Reformation introduced the powerful concept of the priesthood of believers. The effort of these reformers undermined the traditional separation between clergy and laity. Traditionally, the clergy were the sole purveyors of spiritual authority and the exclusive ministers of the gospel. The radical notion that all believers are priests upended the hierarchical apparatus of church and dismantled the bifurcation between those who did ministry and those who received ministry. All believers were to be priests, not just the professional clergy.

Church is not meant to be a program, sermon, performance, or Lord's Supper *to* the people. Sure, the expression of church includes programs, sermons, and Lord's suppers. But church is to be the people of God seeking God, reading his Word together, expressing their various spiritual gifts within the context of the community of faith. All those who confess Jesus as Lord and

Savior have been given a part to play and a contribution to make. All believers are priests—even young people. Seeing kids as priests has significant implications for youth ministry.

Youth ministry should be shared with youth. If kids were priests, we would seek to identify the unique contribution God has gifted them to make, provide a context for them to offer that contribution, and then equip and empower them to do so in a way that honors the Lord. The most vibrant youth ministries I've seen have students in all areas of ministry—in prayer, teaching, planning, organization, serving, counseling, showing mercy, confronting, and bearing the vision for the ministry. I'm not talking about a student-led ministry. We wouldn't want to jettison the critical role of mature adults or disparage the influence of those who have walked with God for years. But there is something soundly "church" about believers, even young believers, involved in meaningful ministry.

During college I read a book by Frank Tillapaugh called *The Church Unleashed.* His primary argument was for pastors to equip and empower individuals within the congregation to do the work of ministry.[4] When my thinking shifted from thinking that *I* was the one to do ministry to seeing that I was also to discover the gifting of my believing students and help them discover God's place for them in ministry, the ministry rolled out so much nicer. All kinds of ministry beyond my gifting or energy began to happen. The spiritual energy it created with the youth group surprised me.

Sharing ministry with young people is a little scary. I'm sure church leaders on the other side of the Reformation—the side being challenged—found all kinds of reasons why the priesthood of believers was a bad idea. They, like us, probably struggled with pride, control, concern over quality control, questions about doctrine, and all sorts of other potential ills. But maybe they, like us, thought that the giving away of ministry meant that you had to give up influence, training, authority, and the right to correct, exhort, and challenge. It doesn't mean that. Giving away ministry takes more care and requires more of you than not giving it away. Giving away ministry is more like giving *to* others instead of giving *up.* Sure, it's a little scary. But done well, sharing ministry with your kids is being good church.

If Churches Were the Body of Christ

If churches were the body of Christ, then youth groups would value the contribution of others within the church. They would not sequester themselves in isolation, believing they have no need for the rest of the church.

Understandably, the integration of a youth ministry within the broader activity of the church poses significant difficulty. More than at any develop-

mental period in a person's life (besides the "terrible" two's struggle for autonomy), adolescence is a time of differentiation.[5] Of all the tasks of adolescence,
discovering a sense of self is perhaps the most developmentally significant.
Young people need to develop an identity that's separate from and independent of a family origin or even a church origin. Most young people experience
a powerful and pervasive force toward independence. Consequently, youth
ministries tend to posture themselves independent of the church family. They
reflect the developmental task of adolescence.

To a certain extent, youth groups that mirror the propensity for adolescent separateness promote healthy growth in the lives of kids. Youth directors
challenge students to believe for themselves and not only because their parents do. Small-group leaders encourage students to develop their own code of
morality and their own standards of behavior, based on their own understanding of the Scriptures and not based on the tradition of others. Speakers
work diligently to put the faith into the words of young people instead of the
potentially meaningless phrases of older generations. This encouragement to
make the faith one's own is a key piece of any youth ministry.

However, zealousness to make the faith relevant to kids can push a youth
ministry into isolation. Within the church, isolation is bad theology.
According to the Scriptures, the body of Christ needs every part, no matter
how ignoble it may seem (1 Cor. 12; Rom. 12). That means that young people
need the preschoolers. Young people need the elderly. Young people need their
parents. Ironically, those from whom youth separate, they need.

And the church needs young people. It needs young people not just to
look at or hear from on the occasional "youth Sunday" or to provide for in a
building or a budget. The church needs young people to make it a church.

I watched a sense of church develop in front of me in Lake Forest, Illinois.
I was serving as youth pastor, intent on making the youth ministry as relevant
as possible to the next generation, when I noticed a kind of "church" developing within our church. A group of five or six families started spending a great
deal of time together. It wasn't just parents with parents and children with
children. These were whole families coming together. The parents came to
recitals of the youth. The youth came to the birthday parties of the parents.
They would take off after church to go spend the afternoon on the lake, boat-
ing, talking, eating, reading, laughing, and *being*.

I began to notice the adolescents in this group treat the other parents like
aunts and uncles. They often sat together in church. They expressed affection
liberally. At times they showed up at the houses of their friends just to talk
with their parents. These young people grew up through middle school and
high school with not just one youth pastor and his staff but with a whole web

of adult relationships that formed their spiritual lives. This was much more powerful and formative than any program I initiated.

A youth pastor friend of mine takes the church seriously. He connects the boys in his group with the men in the church. He invites various men to come and train the boys once a month in life tasks. They change oil together, use a shop together, play music, or play ball together. And the women in the church he gets to mentor the girls. The youth ministry sponsors parent-student activities like banquets, outings, or retreats. Granted, not every adult should mentor young people. Not every adult's life is worth emulating. Some can be downright dangerous. But many adults can and should.

At some point, adolescents in a youth group should also notice those younger within the church. I know this is tough. Most adolescents are so happy to no longer be children that they find relating to children excruciating. Still, in order to be the church, they need to look after and invest in those who are younger. Maybe a big brother/big sister program would be worth considering. Maybe an occasional activity that joins with the children's ministry, in which adolescents lead, teach, and love, would help. Maybe just some low-key encouragement to open their eyes and see others in church would do it. However it's done, the teenage years offer a great time to start good habits of intergeneration church within the hearts of those in your care.

Moreover, we youth leaders need to be a part of the intergenerational church. We tend to be a bold-hearted, independent lot. We like to be out in front, breaking trail, overturning traditions with the ministerial avant-garde. But we, too, need to be under the authority of the church. We need to receive instruction, not brace against it. We need to be mentored, not left alone. We need the church to be present, define, and strengthen us in the ministry God has entrusted to us. This commitment to church is personally costly but highly rewarding in time.

If Sensitivity to the Spiritual Grew

The church is a very human entity, made up of human beings with human needs, expressions, pain, emotions, and relationships. But the church is also very spiritual, made up of elements unseen but still very real and very powerful. In Ephesians 6:12–13 Paul reminded us, "For our battle is not against flesh and blood, but against the rulers, against the authorities, against the world powers of this darkness, against the spiritual forces of evil in the heavens. This is why you must take up the full armor of God, so that you may be able to resist in the evil day, and having prepared everything, to take your stand."

It's relatively easy for us to attend to the human element of church. We feel approval and disapproval. We can't help but notice when people show up excited or when they don't show up at all. We see disunity and interpersonal friction or love and charity. But the spiritual dimension can be missed if we're not paying attention.

I'm not one to believe in a complete bifurcation between the natural and the spiritual. You can tell a lot about what's going on in the spiritual realm by observing the expression of the spiritual in the natural and human nexus of relationships within the church and within the youth group. Still, I fear that sensitivity to the spiritual is too often abandoned and replaced with a naturalistic understanding of ministry.

In a naturalistic expression, we youth leaders explain the resistance of students as disinterest, and so we try to make youth group more interesting. We understand their confusion related to the truth to be a function of lack of clarity, and so we work harder on our messages. We blame their lack of spiritual maturity on a lack of motivation, and so we preach with more passion. However, there could be a whole host of *spiritual* difficulties that hinder the students' response to the Spirit of God.

A ministry I was leading puzzled me. No matter how hard we tried, we could not get it rolling. We were all experienced, educated, and talented. There was no natural reason for such frustration and so little return for our effort. We finally found ourselves totally dependent on God. We had no more techniques. We were lost for a next step. We felt totally expended in our natural selves. Out of this experience there began to emerge for all of us on the leadership team a deep sense that unless God showed up, we were lost. This is the theology of the church.

To be informed by church is to attend to the spiritual. We youth leaders should truly be ministers who depend on God. We need to be men and women who fast and pray. We need to have our minds transformed by the Word of God. We need to walk in step with the Spirit. We need to seek the grace of God for the infirmities of our own lives as well as for the lives of our students. We need to hear from him regarding the priorities of his agenda for these young people. We need his blessing for his ministry. We need to see his love for his ministry.

In short, we need God. And we need God desperately. We cannot be church without God. All of the priorities in this chapter could be applied to youth ministry to no avail without God in our midst. But with the presence of God, youth ministry becomes church.

Notes

1. For a more complete explanation, see R. N. Frost, *Discover the Power of the Bible* (Eugene, Ore.: Harvest House, 2000).

2. A. W. Tozer, *The Pursuit of God,* preface (Wheaton, Ill.: Tyndale, 1970).

3. Robert Trenckmann, paper presented as partial fulfillment of requirements for "Spiritual Formation of Youth" (Portland, Ore.: Multnomah Bible College, April 2003).

4. Frank R. Tillapaugh, *The Church Unleashed* (Ventura, Calif.: Regal, 1982).

5. Chapman Clark, "The Changing Face of Adolescence: A Theological View of Human Development," in *Starting Right,* eds. Kenda Creasy Dean, Chap Clark, and Dave Rahn (Grand Rapids, Mich.: Zondervan, 2001).

Part 2

Cultivating Skill in Relating to Adolescents

9.
Understanding Adolescence

BYRON KEHLER

ADOLESCENCE. Would you want to relive it?

As I entered high school, I remember being told by an elderly man that the teen years were the most challenging years of life. Most would agree. Take the word *teenager*. Close your eyes. What images come to mind?

When I ask groups of parents to respond, I hear answers like "trouble, rebellious, self-centered, loud, energetic, moody." When I meet struggling parents, many act as though their child has caught a bad disease that will last at least seven years. As I glance over my bookshelf on this developmental stage, I'm struck by the titles that reinforce such a view. They betray a cultural prejudice.

- *We Never Had Any Trouble Before* (the years after twelve)
- *Almost 13* (Watch out!)
- *Reaching Your Teenager* (They are hard to reach.)
- *Teenagers: The Continuing Challenge* (Sequel to a bad scary movie)
- *How to Live with Your Teenager* (Evidently not an easy task)
- *How to Live (Almost) Happily with a Teenager* (Almost?)
- *Facing the Turbulent Teens*
- *The Nine Most Troublesome Teenage Problems*
- *Surviving the Teen Years*
- *How to Survive Your Teenager*
- *How to Survive Your Child's Rebellious Teens*
- *How to Deal with Your Acting-up Teenager* (Expectation that they will act up)

- *Teenage Rebellion* (It's inevitable.)
- *Teen Is a Four-Letter Word* (Similar to profanity)
- *How to Survive Your Adolescent's Adolescence* (This book is one and a half inches thick.)
- *Normal Adolescence* (This book is only a quarter-inch thick.)

Notice any themes or biases? Much of the writing on adolescence emphasizes survival rather than enjoyment or appreciation. Someone suggested that Mother Nature is providential. She gives us twelve years to develop a love for our children before turning them into teenagers.

How do these perceptions influence our attitudes about expectations of and behavior toward young people? How we perceive people influences how we treat them and interact with them. What perceptions do we hold toward the adolescents we minister to? Do we reflect a cultural bias, or do we let young people define themselves?

Not only does a culture sway our thinking of others, but it also influences our view of ourselves. As teenagers continue to hear these stereotypes, what impact do they have on teen self-image, attitudes, and behavior? When we expect irresponsibility from a group of people, do we somehow encourage it and promote it? Have we indeed made *teen* a four-letter word by how we use it? What attitudes and expectations do you and your staff hold toward those you serve?

I believe we can bring greater compassion and sensitivity to our work with teenagers the better we understand them. Many of us tend to have short memories for experiences that were uncomfortable or troubling. Once we've escaped our own teenage years, we're only too happy to concentrate on someone else's adolescence. As you read, think of how your own adolescence has influenced your approach to the young people you serve, for good or ill.

A number of dynamics influence teens today. Cultural expectations, stereotypes, peer pressure, physical changes, intellectual growth, and spiritual development all contribute to the challenge of adolescence. Trying to explain the intricacies of adolescence in a few pages is a little like describing how to build your own computer on a postcard. We will look at only a few examples in each area, with some suggested implications for ministry to young people.

Cultural Confusion

As a frequent speaker at retreats, conferences, and rallies, I commonly find myself in a confused nightmare, not knowing where I'm supposed to be, running late and not being able to find my place. I can remember many years ago, on my way to speak somewhere, packing my small children with my wife into a car. I'm usually a calm man, seldom raising my voice. As the hour approached for me to speak, I frantically looked for the church. I was lost. I knew I needed to be somewhere important, and others were depending on me. I was in a hurry and had no idea where I was going. My children played in the backseat like on any other trip. This night, however, was different.

Their comments about breathing each other's air or crossing each other's imaginary territorial lines typically would cause me little concern. As the hour grew later, my patience dwindled and I reacted in less than a tender way. What made this trip different? I didn't know where I was, didn't know when I would get there, and was in a great hurry. I wonder if teenagers don't often feel that same way? Their confusing status in our society is a common source of conflict, particularly in their homes.

In some situations we expect them to behave like adults, and in other situations we remind them they're only children. With no clear rite of passage in our culture, is it any wonder they feel frustrated? Lewis Hershey described the problem this way: "An adolescent becomes an adult three years before his parents think he does, and about two years after he thinks he does."[1] Most of us are generally not at our best when we're confused about what's expected of us. Imagine a job in which your responsibilities are undetermined, but the security of your position rests on your satisfying the desires of your employer. One would expect confusion like that to create anxiety, tension, misunderstanding, and even anger at times. The cost of being "inbetweenagers" can easily express itself in rebellion and resentment.

Family Dynamics

You have never met alone with a young person, and you never will. When a teenager enters your office, behind them follow their parents, siblings, and extended family. What do I mean? We're composites of the people with whom we share life. They shape our perspectives, self-understanding, and relationships. Amid all the emphasis you hear about the power of the media and the influence of film and music, nothing compares to the impact of our families. Long into adulthood we carry the lessons we learn within our families. Understand that each young person who sits across from you embodies a story, only part of which you're privy to. Family conditions, birth order, instability, financial status, parenting approach, divorce, dysfunction, or family harmony all leave their mark on the developing adolescent. When you hear teens speak, learn to listen to the choir of those that sit with them. Trained ears can help you understand the influences in their lives so you may minister more effectively to their needs.

Peers

Were you a nerd? Did you know who was? How important was social acceptance to you during adolescence? Do you remember the insecurity you felt? Due to their insecurities, adolescents are particularly susceptible to the influence of others. Acceptance and the desire for conformity often go hand in hand. Young people generally experience the highest levels of conformity around the ages of twelve to thirteen and sixteen to seventeen. The strongest areas of peer influence tend to involve leisure activities, clothing, hairstyles, music, and language. Studies suggest that adolescents who fit in the middle-status category are most likely to conform to others in the hopes of improving their group acceptance and popularity.

What criteria do teens use to establish overall popularity? In boys, it seems to be measured most by athleticism and with girls, personality and attractiveness. In your programming, how do you challenge or accommodate these perspectives? Is your program subtly biased toward those most acceptable? Often we have limited our understanding of not being conformed to the world to not doing the type of things that the world does. We teach that we should restrict the movies we see or the music we listen to but miss the more subtle applications regarding how we measure importance, value, and worth. Those lessons must also be taught.

Physical Development—Growing at Warp Speed

"Puberty, next to birth itself, is the most drastic change we experience in life, but unlike birth, we are acutely aware of the exciting transitions through which we pass."[2] What differentiates this time of growth from all the rest of the life cycle is the rate and magnitude of bodily changes. Young people can feel they are waking up to someone new every day. For girls the growth spurt begins typically around age nine, and for boys two years later at age eleven. It lasts approximately four years and reaches its peak about halfway through that time. Girls gain weight in the form of fat particularly through the hips; boys gain more muscle primarily across the shoulders.

While these changes provide greater strength and endurance, they also provide the challenge of unfamiliarity to the teen. During the junior high and high school years, our home took a battering. A friend of my son's who was always at our home would regularly bump his head into the door jams and hanging lamps or run his feet into the walls. When we grow rapidly it is easy to feel awkward, clumsy, and self-conscious. How sensitive is your ministry to these struggles? Do you talk about them? Does your ministry favor the more developed, more mature? Height and weight aren't the only physical issues to contend with. During the growth spurt of puberty, the adolescent heart nearly doubles in size. Is it any wonder they find it difficult to sit still?

Who's That in the Mirror?

Timing is everything. I don't know if that's always true, but when it comes to our physical development, it certainly seems that way. How many of you would say that you bloomed at just the right time? Not too soon or not too late but just right. Most college students I survey complain that they were either too early or too late. How does this timing affect us?

In one of my first youth ministry positions, I supplemented my meager part-time salary with driving a school bus. At twenty-one years old, I was one of the youngest drivers in our fleet and as a late bloomer looked even younger. One afternoon I was driving on a field trip for an unfamiliar school. I waited for the teacher to appear with her first-graders and pile onto the bus. As I stood by the open door of the bus, a teacher with students in tow approached and asked, "Young man, have you seen the nice bus driver?" Inside, I winced as I indicated that I, in fact, was the driver. Surprised and a little embarrassed, I think, she ushered the children onto the bus, taking the seat directly behind me.

After the bus was started and we were on our way, her curiosity got the better of her. Trying to be slightly more sensitive, but still somewhat uncomfortable, she asked, "How long have you been driving a bus?" Unable now to resist some of my frustration, I remarked, "Oh, this is my very first trip." With that, she slipped back into her seat and nervously studied the traffic through her side window.

The timing of our physical maturation has enormous psychological affects on us. Young people are preoccupied with their bodies and watch and wait for them to change. Research suggests that boys who develop early tend to view themselves more positively, enjoy greater acceptance and popularity by their peers, and are perceived by adults as more responsible. Follow-up studies among boys found, however, that late maturing boys developed a stronger sense of identity and achievement later in life.

For girls who mature earlier, the effects were not as positive. Although they were more satisfied with their bodies and more popular with boys, they also were more vulnerable. They often drew attention from older boys who placed them in situations requiring greater maturity than their actual years afforded. These girls had more problems in school and were more independent. Gaining a more mature and independent self-perception, they requested later curfews and earlier dating and engaged more frequently in early sexual activity. They were more likely to smoke, drink, be depressed, have eating disorders, and spend time with older friends than their less physically developed counterparts.[3]

How do you see the young people in your youth group? Do your activities favor particular young people, depending on their development or size? As you delegate leadership, how influenced are you by appearance? Do you find yourself measuring maturity, responsibility, and potential by physical appearance or presentation?

The Engine Is Racing and I'm Stuck in Park

In addition to growth, during adolescence the body is literally flooded with hormones. These trigger the sexual changes but also effect mood and attitude. One teenager described it as living through five years of premenstrual syndrome.

Puberty itself is changing. One of the common mistakes young people make is they tend to assume that the world has always been as they found it. Didn't people always have cell phones? As youth leaders, we offer valuable perspective on how things were and how they are becoming. We extend the eyes of youth not only upward but also backward and forward.

At what age would you recommend that young people marry? I asked that question to a congregation where I was youth minister during a sermon on Youth Sunday. The responses varied, but most shouted out around twenty-five to thirty years old. And then without much thought, I spontaneously began a survey on the adults. "How many of you married before age thirty?" Almost universally the hands went up. Had I been older and wiser, I would have simply moved on, but now I was intrigued. I continued, "How many of you married before the age of twenty-five?" A vast majority of hands again were lifted. "And before twenty-one?" Many hands still appeared. "And before eighteen?" Still hands were raised. Who did they belong to? Elderly folks cuddled next to each other, toothless and grinning. Most of the adults were encouraging the young people to wait to marry until they were older, when clearly they had not.

Today there seems to be a growing pressure to delay marriage until college is over, careers are established, and financial security achieved. Is this fair and practical? When did young people used to marry? Until recently in Western culture, it was common for people to marry while still in their early to middle teens. I know that is silly and impractical, but we are all here, which seems to suggest that it worked somewhat. We are now marrying approximately ten years later than during most previous cultures, including biblical times.

This information wouldn't be so significant were it not for some other interesting developments. When young people were marrying at ages fifteen to seventeen, when was puberty occurring? Well, according to empirical historical data, the age of menarche (onset of menstruation) in girls around the mid-1800s occurred around age seventeen. Compare that to when girls experience menarche today in the United States at approximately age eleven. The age of puberty has dropped four months every decade for the last century in our country. Among Caucasian girls today, one in seven starts to develop breasts or pubic hair by age eight. The children we minister to are experiencing sexual hormones earlier than ever before in history. Why? Researchers are still investigating, but suspicions include an increase in exposure to light, hormones in meat used to accelerate growth, better nutrition, and the sexual saturation of our society.

We have a challenging set of circumstances. First, we experience sexual hormones earlier and earlier, and second, we're encouraged to marry later and later. First-time marriage occurs around age twenty-five. Whereas throughout most of history young people have married as teens and become sexual later or around the same time, today they feel sexual as they enter adolescence and must cope with those feelings for more than a decade before marriage. If young people experienced sexual maturity at seventeen or older and many had married by then, a number of problems facing teens today were already resolved.

How are we doing? All indicators suggest not very well, both outside as well as inside the church. To suggest to teens that they run another lap, just say no, or take another cold shower may no longer suffice. Teens today must understand how sexuality is changing and that they're fighting a battle that few before have had to fight. We must be honest with them about the type of conviction it will require for them to make godly choices in the midst of physical and cultural changes. We must better equip them not only on the importance of waiting but help them develop strategies on how. And as leaders and parents we must examine our beliefs about what is most important to us—later marriage accompanied by financial and social success or earlier marriage, purity, and faithfulness.

It is certainly not that clear-cut, but the struggles and pressures are real. Paul said if we burn we should marry, and we have young people smoldering around every corner. The solutions are not easily discovered, but the questions and issues must be openly examined.

Cognitive Development

Cognitive development relates to how we think. Although this area is less visible to observers than physical development, the changes here are pervasive and powerful. Paul reminded us, in 1 Corinthians 13, that children and adults think differently. Jean Piaget suggested that adolescents typically move from concrete operational thought to formal operational thought.

Formal operational thought consists of many elements that separate the adolescent from the child. I often describe it to parents in computer terms. Your child has received new software. It represents an upgrade that brings with it a revolution in thinking. They are now able to think in new ways, process material from a whole new perspective, run new applications, connect ideas in ways they were unable to previously. Whereas these new abilities are exciting for young people, they also contribute to the challenge of adolescence. Because they are new, they are frequently expressed in experimental and awkward ways. When we understand this, recognize it, and expect it, we are less offended and confused as parents or youth leaders.

Who Would Have Thought?

One advantage of formal operational thought involves a shift from a very restricted perspective of life to a much more varied perspective. As concrete thinkers, children see their world in two categories. There is safety and predictability in keeping people, events, and circumstances in one or the other category. Some have described this as black-and-white thinking—things are either good or bad. This immature form of perspective forces people and experiences into the only available categories.

Consider popular children's television shows. They often separate the world into two competing categories: cowboys and Indians, Cobra and G.I. Joe, Transformers and Decepticons. Each generation has had its particular set of rivals. This is how children understand their world.

Growing up in a counselor's home has its disadvantages. One afternoon my first-grader was watching one of his favorite television shows when a new character entered the plot. I could tell he was trying to identify which side this new character was on. After evaluating on his own for awhile, he finally asked, "Dad, what side are they on?" Deciding to conduct my own cognitive experiment, I replied, "Well, Son, they aren't on a side. They're neutral." I could tell my answer only increased his frustration as he tried to make sense of the situation. His next question illustrated how children perceive their world. "All right, Dad, if they were going to be on a side, whose side would they be on?"

This type of thinking is illustrated in how the Pharisees viewed life and faith. Resting on the Sabbath was reduced to how many steps you could take without violation of the commandment. This either/or type of thought didn't allow much room for grace, compassion, or growth. This two-dimensional thought creates problems in other areas as well. Children feel responsible for whatever they experience, assuming that they must have caused it. Children view their parents through this two-dimensional grid, drawing the conclusion that parents know everything and can do everything.

Of course, we can reinforce this mistaken thinking by suggesting we do actually have eyes in the back of our heads, can read their minds, and can perform other parental exaggerations. Hoping to avoid this trap and deflect any potential anger from my children by misleading them, I frequently assured them when they were still young that I didn't know everything. I can still remember the dinner conversation when my son had reached about thirteen years old. "You don't know everything, Dad." "I know, Son, you're right, I don't." "No, Dad, I'm serious, you don't know everything." Although I had hoped to dodge the formal operational bullet, it had arrived. He was adamant, irritated, and, I think, disappointed. The realization had finally settled in: Parents were just people. He had been betrayed by his development, held hostage by his childhood, and now he was free. Young people eventually discover that parents are not all-knowing, perfect, all-powerful beings, and they are left with a confusion of feelings: relief, disappointment, criticism, and irritation.

Making such a discovery can be sobering. One evening as I returned home from work my wife and four-year-old daughter met me at the front door. Tightly clutched in my daughter's hands was a plastic baggie with countless pieces of glass. Her voice mixed with sadness and relief, she sputtered, "Daddy, I knocked a cup off the counter and it broke on the floor. But Mommy helped me sweep it up, and we saved all the pieces so you could put it back together." My wife stood just behind her with a mischievous smile. I bent down and with a gentle and compassionate voice explained, "I'm sorry, sweetheart, but there are way too many pieces for Daddy to put the cup back together." She reflected for a moment, as though confused, then responded. "Now, Daddy, don't be lazy."

In her young concrete thinking, it was impossible that I couldn't fix the cup. The only explanation she could find in her child's mind was my unwillingness to take the time or care. As they move from concrete to formal thought during adolescence, they now are able to consider a variety of possibilities and solutions. Their world changes from a black-and-white perspective to a rainbow of color and possibility. While once everything was orderly and clear, now they must consider a wide variety of perspectives, positions, and arguments. It is a movement from either/or thinking to yes-and thinking. Such a transition can be frightening and overwhelming. And all the choices made may not be the wisest. It was so scary the Pharisees were unwilling to go there. Encourage parents not to take it personally. Appreciation for us returns if we navigate the waters of their adolescent discovery well.

With this greater ability to think and reason comes the greater ability to argue and debate. Arguing allows adolescents to hone and sharpen their reasoning skills. I've asked young people if they ever found themselves in an argument with their parents in which they realized what they were arguing about didn't even matter to them. They just smile. I took that as a yes. We believed our daughter was destined to be an attorney at age fifteen because of her incessant debate. I'm happy to report it was only a season that she moved through, and she is now a schoolteacher as well as a good debater.

Arguing is an important part of the developmental stage, even though admittedly it isn't much fun for the rest of us. When as a parent or leader we can detach personally from the debate, we can bring more sensitivity and grace to the young person's need to exercise this growing and necessary adult skill.

Reconceptualizing Past Events

The new software of formal operations also allows young people to run old information through new grids of understanding. Significant events, experiences, confusions, disappointments, and hurts that are too complicated or painful to process as a child are put in storage until necessary upgrades in the software become available. The more stressful the environment while growing up, the less safe it is to feel and talk openly and the more is placed in storage. When formal operational thought becomes available, the backup disks are inserted and the information is now revisited. Painful memories can be resurrected, reinterpreted, and hopefully resolved.

I can remember another meal during adolescence in which my son looked at me and out of nowhere said, "I wanted a blue bike, I asked for a blue bike, and I wanted a blue bike." He was referring to a long past birthday when he had received the wrong color bike, I now learned. That information had sat dormant for years before erupting during a quiet moment at the table. Parents are often surprised when all of a sudden their teens bring up issues from the past. They may want to find their biological parents if adopted, they may want another explanation for their parents' divorce, or they may be confused or upset about a move that took them from their friends.

Whatever the issue, adolescence is often the time when it's reexamined and processed on a deeper level. Disallowing these inquiries or viewing them as intrusions or disrespectful can impair the opportunity to resolve the issues on a healthier and deeper level. Giving permission and encouragement to young people and their parents to talk about these serious life issues can reduce the risk of later tensions in the relationship.

Someone Else Here?

I hear parents frequently complain about how selfish, self-centered, or self-absorbed their teenagers are. David Elkind, building on Piaget's earlier work, has suggested an explanation for this egocentrism.[4] It plays out in three primary ways.

First, the significant focus on self: I can remember my fifteen-year-old daughter (who, by the way, is now a responsible and kind young lady) throwing a slumber party for some of her friends from school. That night at the dinner table, hours before the party was to begin, she made a request of us, her parents. She described her plans for the evening, then added, "Would you guys just stay in your bedroom for the evening, so that we could have the run of the house?" "But of course," I replied. "I don't mind you hiding me out in my room, so you can pretend that you pay the bills, clean the house, and provide all this for your parents."

Teenagers see the world through a lens that they unfortunately stand squarely in front of. They are often self-absorbed by default of development. If we can remember that they may be locked into such perspective by their season in life, then we are less likely to be offended by the fact that they can't see anyone else in the room but themselves. At least that is what I tried to remind myself—to keep from canceling the party and grounding her to her room until she was eighteen. The good news is that such a phase is somewhat short-lived, and afterward they begin to notice others.

One of the other disadvantages of this new awareness in thinking is that now you can think about others thinking about you. And teenagers do. David Elkind has described it as a young person's imaginary audience.[5] Teens take their own audience with them wherever they travel. This is the result of an underdifferentiated perspective, which fails to distinguish between what they think and what others may be thinking about them. Most of us have this. Teenagers just elevate it to an art form. In short, we worry about what others think of us. They have a preoccupation with their peers' thoughts and responses.

One evening I was taking the kids to a movie at our small neighborhood theater. Josh was sixteen and Tiffany was fourteen, fully immersed in her imaginary audience. As we parked the car and prepared to exit, Tiffany let out a blood-curdling scream from the backseat. "My barrette!" she cried out. "My barrette!" "What's wrong, Tiffany?" I inquired somewhat alarmed. "I lost one of my barrettes." My daughter, a little type A, taking after one of her parents who will remain unidentified, had lost one of her hair barrettes.

Josh impatiently reminded us that the movie began in ten minutes. Negotiations began. "Tiffany, we will look for your barrette the moment we return to the car after the movie." Horrified, she refused to move. "I am not going into the movie theater with only one of my barrettes." Josh pleaded, pointing out the obvious as only brothers can do. "Tiffany, it's dark in movie theaters. No one will know." "Not in the lobby, Josh." "Then I'll go in first to make sure the fashion police aren't stationed at the door." We bribed, threatened, pleaded, but to no avail. The dash from car to darkened theater couldn't be risked with only one barrette.

We returned home defeated by the imaginary audience, which evidently ended up enjoying the movie we never saw. I'm sure you can remember your own horror stories of fears that others saw you as you scrutinized yourself. A pimple is not a pimple but a disaster. Glasses, crooked teeth, or too small or too large features all place great stress and insecurity on teens who imagine that others are as preoccupied with them as they are with themselves. Understand that teens are trapped and held hostage by an audience that studies each aspect of their appearance, intellect, sophistication, personality, and presentation. It's not easy getting up in the morning and facing that music.

The companion perspective to the imaginary audience is what Elkind calls the personal fable.[6] If people are paying so much attention to me, then I must really be something special. This overdifferentiated perspective suggests an exaggerated uniqueness. Adolescents believe they're different from others. You hear this in teenagers' comments like, "Nobody understands me," or "It won't happen to me." It fuels behaviors like their willingness to pass on curves and not wear seat belts, placing themselves in high-risk situations, or taking chances that later as adults make us shutter. It helps us understand the failure of condoms as birth control among young people because pregnancy wouldn't happen to them. It explains why they can be genuinely surprised by the consequences of their own choices. It helps us answer the question "What were you thinking?" even if they don't seem to know.

I'm "Me," not "We"

One of the primary tasks of adolescence is the development of a personal identity. This individuation requires time, privacy, and reflection. More times than I can count I knocked on my daughter's door during those teen years to find her lying on her bed staring at the ceiling. "What are you thinking about, sweetie?" It was always the same answer: "Nothing." How could "nothing" take up so much time? I wondered. It never took me that much time to consider. The principle of individuation was in play. Part of the process involves withholding information and desiring privacy. Privacy helps young people develop a sense of their own identity, a sense of self. If this is mine, then I am mine also. Such a sense of personal space can greatly improve their ability later during dating to establish healthy boundaries. Young people also withhold information to give themselves a sense of personal power. They believe that what parents don't know they won't or can't control.

Unfortunately, with most parents this works just opposite. The less we know the more we worry. The more we worry the more we try to control. Individuation is an important step in young people establishing their own identities. If we deny the opportunity, they will seek out and discover ways of their own. Young people want and need to get out of the shadow of their parents to see what they look like.

When my son entered college and began to narrow his career interests, he commented that he thought he might like to do what Pat did. Pat is another counselor at the counseling agency where I work. He didn't say, "I want to do what you do." Instead he would follow his own footsteps and do what someone else does that I do. It's healthy for our children to grow away from us and establish their own lives. That is part of the principle in leaving and cleaving.

Young people during the teen years draw away, wanting to exert influence over their own lives. They want to be "me," not "we." You can watch it happen dropping your kids off at school. I can remember dropping my daughter off for school in sixth grade. As we pulled up right in front of the door, she leaned across the seat and presented me with her cheek and the words "Kiss me good-bye"—right there in front of students, teachers, and the world. Each morning she would insist on a kiss before exiting the car to begin the day. In seventh grade something happened. We would pull up to the same spot in the drive-around, but now she would simply wink and whisper, "I love you," before dashing out the door. In eighth grade it was, "Dad, can you drop me off at the street? I'll walk the rest of the way." In ninth grade it progressed to, "Dad, you can drop me off right here. I'll walk the last block or so." In eleventh it was, "Dad, can I drop you off at work and take the car today?"

Independence empowers and builds confidence. If we don't allow children the opportunity to exert influence over their lives, they'll search for sneaky ways to find it. And generally it goes underground only to come up in dangerous or self-destructive expressions. As a professor at a conservative Bible college, I can usually identify the incoming freshmen raised in homes where few choices were afforded them and little independence. Once the yoke of parental supervision has been lifted, they don't know what to do with the independence and freedom they discover at college. Much of what adolescents experience falls outside their control. They feel adult, but others still primarily make their decisions.

Control is an important element for an individual's sense of identity, security, and self-confidence. When we feel out of control or powerless, we feel vulnerable and often react with defensiveness. Desiring independence is a healthy developmental task, not disrespect.

The Way Things Ought to Be

Since teens can now view the world through a rainbow of possibilities, they can also choose rose-colored glasses to view it. One characteristic of teen thinking is to measure the actual against the ideal. They often demonstrate limited tolerance for hypocrisy, other than their own. It's easy for them to be critical of others, particularly when they also possess insecurity and a self-exaggerated perspective. Naturally those most subject to criticism are those safest and closest to them. This often includes parents. Parents should remember that it's a compliment to their safety when kids target them for polishing their critical analysis.

Spiritual Development

At no other time in life are people as malleable as during adolescence. As they try to define themselves, they also explore the meaning and significance of life. As spiritual leaders, we're presented with a rare opportunity to introduce them to significant truth. To be invited into such a journey of discovery by a young person is a sacred honor and trust. If faith is to truly be theirs, then they must have permission, safety, and support to explore its full meaning.[7] Just as it is wearisome for parents to have a four-year-old continually ask why, why, why, so it's irksome to have adolescents continually challenge authority. Yet probing questions are proportionate to intelligence—the more inquisitive tend to be the brighter. Just as raising questions is a sign of intelligence and therefore a right befitting the child's dignity as an intelligent human being, so, too, is it for the adolescent.

Having achieved the ability to think ideally, to think about ideas and ideals and not only about concrete facts, the adolescent is merely testing this God-given ability, striving to make sense of the world, the church, and all of society's expectations by relentlessly asking why. For adults who are insecure, or who have not developed their own critical faculty, the challenges come as a threat to their authority. And in the "power play," the adolescent may condescend by pretending to submit to the authority. Or he or she may leave the church or family, finding either unbearably unreasonable. Or, saddest of all, the searing vision of youth may be squelched.

Yet it is in the crucible of their questions that all of us can be purged of the dross that keeps us from responding wholeheartedly to the Lord who is

Life. One of the greatest gifts we extend is an environment of inquiry, a place to discover the most important meanings, a place where young people like Peter, Thomas, and Paul can be exposed to Christ and as a result be transformed. Here they drink in a faith that has time to grow, mature, and become truly their own.

Notes

1. Lewis B. Hershey, quoted in Joan Wester Anderson, *Teen Is a Four-Letter Word* (White Hall, Va.: Betterway Pub., 1983), 87.

2. Joan Lipsitz, *Growing Up Forgotten: A Review of Research and Programs Concerning Early Adolescence* (Lexington, Mass.: Lexington Books, 1977).

3. John Santrock, *Adolescence* (Boston: McGraw-Hill, 2001).

4. David Elkind, *All Grown Up and No Place to Go: Teenagers in Crisis* (Reading, Mass.: Addison-Wesley, 1984).

5. Ibid., 40–43.

6. Ibid., 44–45.

7. Suzanne M. DeBenedittis, *Teaching Faith and Morals* (Minneapolis, Minn.: Winston Press, 1981).

10.
Reading Youth Culture

STEVEN PATTY

IF ANYTHING CAN BE SAID about youth ministers over the past few decades, it is that they're experts at being "in touch" with young people. They know how to track culture.

Two forces have given rise to the rather contemporary notion of a distinct youth ministry within the greater ministry of the church.[1] The first is the acknowledgment of a developmental period (both biological as well as cultural) that we term *adolescence*. This adolescent period exhibits contexts, challenges, and perspectives unique enough to warrant specialized ministerial attention from the church. In other words, because the adolescent experience is so unique, it makes sense for the church to develop specialists and specialties for this developmental subgroup.

The second is the emerging force of the culture of the next generation. This new culture is constantly changing. It is always new, for waves of style, conversation, and sensitivities usually begin to build among early adolescents or among the fringes of adolescents and often crest at the onset of early adulthood before washing an influence throughout the larger cultural landscape. And this new culture frames the experience of young people, often in contrast to the experience of adults. This is why adolescents often think of adults as seriously out of touch with the current fashion of language, style, and . . . well, it seems like everything to them. Remember when you thought your parents were just far out of "it"?

Youth ministers, however, are supposed to be the exception. They're supposed to be able to bridge the worlds of the adult and the teenager. They're supposed to be bilingual—fluent in adult talk as well as youth slang. They're supposed to be conversant in the subtle swirls of adolescent posturing and yet be impervious to any personal pressure except that of an internally sponsored adult conviction. In short, youth ministers are supposed to be able to walk with ease in the world of young people and yet retain their maturity and "adultness."

But for some of us, this doesn't come naturally. And so we try really hard to say the right word at the right time, dress in the right way when we spend time with kids, or reference the right artist at the appropriate times. But this doesn't always work out very well.

You've seen, I'm sure, adults clumsily trying too hard. There are few sights as painful as watching an adult attempting to be a kid—especially without the skills to pull it off. It's even a little disturbing sometimes to see an adult act like a kid even when they can pull it off.

So what of cultural relevance? Are we, or are we not supposed to adjust ourselves to the frame of adolescents? Is a knowledge and sensitivity to the developmental place of adolescents enough, or are we supposed to attain fluency in the cultural features that so profoundly impact and even, at times, define the adolescent experience?

Separation and Embeddedness

When I left the front lines of church youth ministry to teach youth ministry at a Bible college, I knew I needed to stay in touch. I determined that I would not be one of those professors of ministry who had no idea about the current state of young people in the world. I would be one to know the newest and the most relevant and not to lose the common touch with kids.

When I was in church ministry, I discovered I'd been blessed with good ears to pick up the latest from my students. (I was relatively young, too, which I'm sure helped a great deal.) But now I had no adolescents in my care. So I decided, upon recommendation, to subscribe to *Rolling Stone* magazine and read it from cover to cover every week. Surely this ultra-in-tune communiqué of contemporary youth culture would help me.

I really didn't want stacks of *Rolling Stone* magazines lying around my house, so I had them sent to my college, addressed to me but in care of the Church Ministries Department.

A problem first surfaced when I realized my significant lack of interest in most of the articles. I didn't really care all that much about the latest band. (In fact, my own musical tastes were going through a slow but significant adjustment. And that felt a little weird for a career "youth guy.") And I didn't really find the articles about the nonmusic celebrities very captivating either.

And then one morning I walked into work to find a note from a secretary telling me that she had adjusted my mail. Evidently, an issue showed up with a naked woman on the front cover—addressed to me at the Church Ministries

Department at Multnomah Bible College. It had been routed through the mail department, carried across campus, and was sitting in my open mail slot next to all the other faculty mail in the faculty lounge.

This was beginning to look like not such a good idea after all.

To what extent does one have to immerse oneself in the culture in order to speak relevantly to the young people in the culture? Is it necessary, in other words, to read *Rolling Stone* and watch hours of MTV? Is catching every movie popular among adolescents a must? Does a youth leader need to tune the car stereo to "Jammin'," "Z-something," "KISS," "Rockin'," or some particularly obnoxious alternative station in an effort to stay informed?

The power of staying informed should not be underestimated. To be able to skillfully participate in the adolescent world and talk their talk, see what they see, and know what they know gives any youth leader a head start in sharing Christ. All through Scripture we have examples of ministers adapting the unchanging truth to the particular unique audience they faced.[2] Awareness gets you so far.

However, awareness is different from immersion. Exposure is different from inculcation. Being conscious of is different from being fixated upon.

To understand the forces that work on the souls of young people in your care is advisable. Sometimes this requires a youth minister to check out a particular artist, movie, or club that's affecting the way young people think or feel. But it's unadvisable to put yourself in the path of the influence, to get so enmeshed with the culture that you compromise your pastoral ability to separate and analyze.

You and those around you who read the culture of youth will be influenced differently. It is important to develop self-awareness to be able to read how your own heart responds along the continuum of awareness versus inculcation. In other words, some elements of youth culture will affect you differently and will be more benign than others. Make sure to watch for your own weakness.

Maintaining this balance is tricky. Notice Jesus' example.

How Jesus Kept Relevant

Dining with Sinners and Tax Collectors

Dining with sinners and tax collectors put him in touch with those who needed to hear and who would otherwise never know. Dining with sinners and tax collectors not only gave him opportunity to share his message, but it made his message relevant. Look at some of the examples from the gospel of Mark:

Then Jesus went out again beside the sea. The whole crowd was coming to Him, and He taught them. Then, moving on, He saw Levi the son of Alphaeus sitting at the tax office, and He said to him, "Follow Me!" So he got up and followed Him. While He was reclining at the table in Levi's house, many tax collectors and sinners were also guests with Jesus and His disciples, because there were many who were following Him. (2:13–15)

Then He went home, and the crowd gathered again so that they were not even able to eat. (3:20)

He got up and departed from there to the region of Tyre and Sidon. He entered a house and did not want anyone to know it, but He could not escape notice. Instead, immediately after hearing about Him, a woman whose little daughter had an unclean spirit came and fell at His feet. Now the woman was Greek, a Syrophoenician by birth, and she kept asking Him to drive the demon out of her daughter. (7:24–26)

Do you see Jesus spending time with people? He went among them, not sitting behind a desk organizing programs and designing games. He didn't read up on culture, sit in lectures, or subscribe to the *Jerusalem Culture Watch*. Sure, that might have been helpful, but nothing close to the sensibilities generated by logging good time with real live people in the places where they live.

Communing with the Father

Withdrawing to connect with the Father kept Jesus' orientation and identity intact. For many of us, too much immersion within a culture starts to change us. We lose our distinction. We forfeit our identity. I love to listen to classic rock on Saturdays. It's a good day to just crank the music up and enjoy. But I've noticed that should I listen all day long, my heart is in a different spot by nightfall. I'm less joyful, less loving, less patient, less kind. The culture of rock 'n' roll has worked its way into my soul. Only by withdrawing to commune with the Father will my distinction return.

Godly distinction is crucial to effective cultural engagement. Without substance, weight, and content to one's identity, the youth worker will be overtaken by culture instead of able to engage with it. I can't engage if there is no distinction between the self and culture. Difference needs to be nurtured and protected. Developmental psychologists have noticed that people can't see clearly what they are embedded in.[3] Notice the priority in Christ's example to get away and withdraw in the Gospel of Mark:

Very early in the morning, while it was still dark, He got up, went out, and made His way to a deserted place. And He was praying there. (1:35)

After He said good-bye to them, He went away to the mountain to pray. (6:46)

Then they came to a place named Gethsemane, and He told His disciples, "Sit here while I pray." (14:32)

Engaging and Withdrawing

Is it possible to get close *and* stay apart at the same time? Yes, and this is not the activity of a schizophrenic. You don't need to have two minds, two personalities, or two lives. If you tried, you would compromise the integrity of your person. Rather, think of positioning yourself in the model of the incarnate Christ, who displaced none of his divine nature to clothe his message and even himself within the human context (Phil. 2:6–11). Nurture your connection to and dependence on God so that your identity oozes with a holy separateness. Simultaneously, engage in the life and culture of the students to whom you minister. You will then be set to bring the presence of the divine into the experience of the human, just as did Christ.

I think of Rick, a youth pastor friend who bears the responsibility of one of the largest ministries in town. The first few hours of every day in the office is spent with the door closed as he reads the Scriptures and prays. He fills himself with God's presence. Then he mobilizes a contemporarily gifted staff to attend to and connect with the experience of the kids in his care. As a result, his ministry is unmistakably characterized by godliness and yet is profoundly relevant.

Practically speaking, how does the second part of this activity happen? How can you as a youth leader sensitize yourself to the context of your kids? Simply, develop the skills of reading your students and reading their culture.

Reading Adolescents—How to Listen to Students

The pursuit of understanding begins with attention to people. Every student is unique. Every youth group is unique. Every middle and high school, every town, every region in the country, and every country in the world is unique. There is no substitute for spending time with your own unique students. In other words, reading *Rolling Stone* every week may teach you a few things about kids, but nothing compares to going and being with the kids in your care.

The art of appreciation can't be underestimated in this endeavor. Mere proximity doesn't guarantee the development of understanding if proximity isn't accompanied by receptiveness. Youth ministers, filled with their own agendas, their own stories, their own pain and insecurities, their own needs to prove themselves in the ministry, relate autobiographically with students. The relationships become groups of individuals doing Christian activities in the same place, instead of true human interchange, receiving and giving.

I once caught the best middle school youth pastor I know standing at the foot of a staircase at a middle school youth rally, watching the kids surge down past him and into the meeting hall. Leaning up next to him, I asked, "Greg, what in the world are you doing?" "I'm just enjoying these kids," he responded. "Look at them, all this excitement and energy. Look at how they talk to one another. See those girls over there—how they relate. Isn't that interesting?" It's no wonder he was able to connect to middle school kids like none other. He actually had developed appreciation for them, even with all of their strange idiosyncrasies.

Don't underestimate the need for appreciation. Elliot Eisner, a brilliant educator at Stanford University, wrote similarly about the task of educational criticism: "Effective criticism, within the arts or in education, is not an act independent of the powers of perception. The ability to see, to perceive what is subtle, complex, and important, is its first necessary condition. The act of knowledgeable perception is, in the arts, referred to as connoisseurship. To be a connoisseur is to know how to look, to see, and to appreciate. Connoisseurship, generally defined, is the art of appreciation."[4]

The best youth ministers are connoisseurs of kids. They see. They pay attention. They watch for the subtle, the complex, and the important. And they truly appreciate the young creations of God in front of them. This takes practice and work. But it is well worth it.

A particularly helpful skill in understanding young people is to pay attention to how you feel when you're around them. For years, psychologists have been training therapists to watch how they feel pulled and pressured by their clients during counseling sessions. Pressures, agendas, insecurities, pain, the problems of individual stories—these often unfold in real time and leave relational clues on your own heart as you interact. When you pay attention to what is going on in your own spirit as you relate to students, you find a rich source of data to understand them. And the more godly and mature you are, the more reliable will be that data stream.

Reading Popular Culture—How to Listen to Cultural Signals

Reading culture well takes good eyes and ears. You need to be able to see and hear not only the microculture of your own students but also the broader cultural milieu in which your students live. Think of a dramatic presentation—a play or a musical. You see specific actors, each with their own personalities and characters in social interaction with one another. But you also see the backdrop of their activity, the setting in which their personal drama is placed, the stage on which their stories unfold. This backdrop—the stage, context, setting, history, milieu—modifies everything about their individual experiences. This macroculture influences the ways that the particular stories of your students unfold.

The cultural backdrop of adolescents is often quite unlike that of adults because of a growing generation gap. As a result, the texts that frame their personal stories are not always immediately accessible to us. We grew up on a different stage, with a different backdrop. The stories of my childhood—Watergate, *Star Wars*, *Saturday Night Live*, the Cold War, Steve Martin, *Saturday Night Fever*, KISS—are different than the ones that impact the broad consciousness of adolescents today. I did not grow up with stories of AIDS, the destruction of the Amazon rain forests, Internet chat, and Harry Potter. I'm familiar with them, but they don't frame my way of understanding as they do for young people today.

The defining and formative events of their age are not only stories. They are legends. They are bigger than merely commonly recognized data—things that every kid knows about. They color the way students think, feel, act, hear Scripture, develop their self-identity, and serve the Lord. At a recent conference in South Africa, a youth leader described that one in four adolescents suffer from HIV infection. For this generation of South African youth, everything is seen through this grid. In less dramatic but no less influential ways is the potency of the Internet, the "alternative" scene, and the issues of globalization on the shared consciousness of young people. These are scenes in which students play out their lives. Legends always mark a culture.

A youth minister who seeks relevancy needs to track down the legends of youth culture today. How do you do that? Watch and listen. Observe and probe. Paying attention to the "what" of their cultural experience will keep you from assuming that your interaction falls against the backdrop of your own cultural context. Also, ask a lot of "why" questions. "Why is uncut, acoustical music so popular?" "Why is reality-based television so captivating?" "Why is retro-dress so attractive?" I recognize that by the time you read this, these questions may make no sense. Every few months and certainly every few years, significant shifts occur within the fabric of adolescents' cultural backdrop. Whatever the current issues are, the key is not just to observe them but to explore, probe, and analyze them. Skillfully asking "why" to the "what" that you observe takes practice and effort.

Communicating well to a second culture always takes more work than you would expect. It's much easier when you are but one or two years removed from adolescence. But as you age and as you mature (these are not one in the same) you will find that connecting requires more of you and from you. Again, no skill set can replace actual time logged with your students. However, here are four hints to help you stay in tune:

1. **Find a "Bridge Person"**

A "bridge person" is one who is immersed in the culture and who can explain it to you. A youth pastor friend of mine regularly sits down with a student or two who are particularly well informed and asks, "What is the word for 'cool' today?" "How do you say something is 'not good'?" "What musician is everyone listening to?" "What movies is everyone watching?" But he is not just asking about words and phrases. He is seeking an understanding of the makeup of the adolescent context.

A particularly good bridge person will be reflective enough to offer an explanation of the priorities and passions of his culture. She will be able to offer thought regarding the present social, moral, and behavioral context. You will find it helpful to try out your thoughts on this person: "When I tell this story, how do you feel?" "If I approached this talk like this, how do you respond?"

2. **Ask Someone to "Back-translate"**

A technique commonly used among cross-cultural missionaries is back-translating. To be translated well, a message needs to be adapted from one culture to another. A culture is always more complex than merely language: cultural differences consist of more than simple vocabulary. Often, a speaker will talk to people of a second culture and then ask those in that culture what they heard. "Tell me what were the major points. Talk to me about the big themes. What are you hearing me say?" When the hearer back-translates the message for you, the cultural grid will be exposed. You'll hear in his own words how he's thinking and what he understands from your intended message. In the process you begin to catch cultural filters. And with sensitivity of the cultural filters, you'll be much more able to communicate.

Meaning is always in context. Adolescents have a context different from yours and mine that modifies the understandings of young people. When you talk to them, preaching or giving a devotional, you need a feedback channel. If you don't have one, you'll filter through your own grid of meaning. So talk to your encultured kids and ask them to tell you what they hear from you, what they're coming to understand about faith from your instruction, and how they're making meaning of your teaching. You'll learn a great deal about their culture and how to communicate to it.

3. **Study and Imitate a Cue Person**

Find out whom young people respect, and then study those people. Watch the ones they listen to, and then imitate their style, pacing, voicing, rhythm, tone, spirit, posturing—all kinds of "feel" variables. Of course, don't try to be someone other than who you are, and don't adopt attitudes without critically and theologically examining them. But to a great extent, you can learn much about cultural engagement by watching and imitating recognized persons of influence.

Right now, a popular host on MTV has winsomely dialed in the cultural ethos. (I'd tell you who he is, but he'll probably be long gone by the time you read this.) The way he expresses himself, the tone of his communication, the expression of his humor all draw students into his influence. Kids love him. I know it sounds strange to study and take cues from an MTV host, but I'm sure you can find others. And even if an effective person's ethos bears no attractiveness to imitate, studying the reason for his or her connection will lend helpful insight for the relevant youth worker.

4.   Pray for Insight into Cultural Sin

Every culture has it—unique expressions of depravity about which the members are largely blinded. Missionaries understand this. The cultural sin of the Balkan countries is disunity and lack of cooperation (hence the addition to our vocabulary of *balkanize*). The cultural sin of the Czech Republic is a sense of fear and melancholy. Christians from other countries quickly note that a North American cultural sin is independence, arrogance, and self-sufficiency.

Similarly, each generation within a particular geography because they each have distinct cultures, exhibits particular blindness and adulteration. For instance, you will find right now among young people in the Northwest a suspicion of truth; a celebration of messiness, confusion, and despair; and blindness toward right and wrong. These are different sins than my generation's. And these are sins about which these young people are largely unaware. Pray that the Lord will give you insight to see the unique warping that the Evil One has worked on the culture of young people. This sense will make a great deal of difference in how you pastor and teach them.

Clothing an Unchanging Message

When you think of Jesus, you think about his death, burial, and resurrection. You think about his profound and winsome teaching. You think about his miracles. When you think of Jesus, you think about God clothing himself in our culture, with our form and language, so that we could truly behold the divine.

Some of the kids you work with have no parents to model their lives after. They have no church to guide them. They have no religious heritage to draw on. You have to do the hard work of reaching into their existence to communicate the truth of Christ to them. So clothe yourself in their culture, in their form and language, so that when you are with them, they will see Jesus in you. For you may be the only "Jesus" who these kids see.

Notes

1. For a discussion about the developing shape of youth ministry, see Mark Senter III, *The Coming Revolution in Youth Ministry* (Wheaton, Ill.: Victor Books, 1992).

2. Take note of the variety of tones, methods, and approaches used by the evangelists in Acts.

3. Robert Kegan, *The Evolving Self* (Cambridge, Mass.: Harvard University Press, 1982).

4. Elliot W. Eisner, *The Educational Imagination: On the Design and Evaluation of School Programs* (New York: MacMillan, 1985), 219.

11.
Speaking to Youth

CHRIS KAINU

EFFECTIVE COMMUNICATION matters to God. He takes upon himself the burden to communicate in a way that makes sense to his listeners. God's entire personality and character is defined by going to great lengths and stooping to severe lows to tell people about his love. We must do the same for our students. As we prepare our speeches, we must take extreme measures to help them hear what they need and in ways they can actively and passionately embrace. A. W. Tozer endorsed this "speaker-serving-the-listener" responsibility in his preface to *The Knowledge of the Holy:* "True religion confronts earth with heaven and brings eternity to bear upon time. The messenger of Christ, though he speaks from God, must also, as the Quakers used to say, 'speak to the condition' of his hearers; otherwise he will speak a language known only to himself. His message must be not only timeless but timely. He must speak to his own generation."[1]

Most youth workers resonate with the idea of speaking in relevant terms to a specific generation. Yet, too few youth communicators develop their teaching and preaching skills with an intensity that results in consistent life-altering messages. For some, busyness or laziness causes such neglect. Many are simply unsure of where to go for practical help. This chapter is designed to help you in two specific ways: first, to help you understand a few biblical principles related to preaching, and second, to give practical direction for preparing a message.

Principles of Speaking to Youth

Sacrifice before You Speak

Great communication will cost your life. "Who, existing in the form of God, did not consider equality with God as something to be used for His own

115

advantage. Instead He emptied Himself by assuming the form of a slave, taking on the likeness of men. And when He had come as a man in His eternal form, He humbled Himself by becoming obedient to the point of death—even to death on a cross" (Phil. 2:6–8).

It's impossible to imagine what Jesus gave up to communicate to us. He traded the comfort of heaven and the companionship of the Trinity. He embraced the aching experience of humanness—including loneliness, torturous pain, and spiritual temptation. And for what? Certainly, he died as the substitute for our sin. But he also took on human form to communicate to us. The best way to talk to a bug is to become a bug. And in a sense, that's what Jesus did for us. Therefore we must do the same for our students. If we do, their lives will change.

I couldn't understand why a "food vacuum" like Josh wasn't eating his pizza. So I asked. Now before I share his answer, you have to understand the context. Though we took hundreds of kids to camp, we always supplied our own cooks. We had two motives: to cut cost and increase quality. Our goal was to see these students eat the best meals of the year at camp.

About a dozen adults volunteered for seven days of culinary punishment. Most took vacation time and paid their own way so that the students wouldn't have to bear their costs. They slept in mediocre dorm facilities and worked tirelessly for fourteen hours a day. (Most people disbelieve the level to which these cooks sacrificed. But they did it—year after year!)

On the cooks' one day off during the camp, we fed frozen pizzas to the students. This gave the adults a break from the extensive work of preparing food from scratch. When I asked Josh why he wasn't eating, he blankly responded, "I eat one of these every day after school." His words hit me hard. I knew Josh's story. His parents divorced some years earlier. His dad was an alcoholic. His mom was a workaholic. Each night he fixed a frozen pizza for himself and his little sister.

A home-cooked meal communicates love. It's unmistakable. The key ingredient is sacrifice. Who has made the best home-cooked meals you've ever tasted? Someone who loved you enough to fulfill the requirements of diligent preparation. There is power in the culmination of thoughtful preparation. Josh's rejection of that frozen food chiseled a biblical imperative into my perspective of speaking: Life-changing love is imparted through sacrificial work—especially when the laborer considers the person.

When you extend your efforts to studying truth, understanding your listeners, and packing your presentation in an accessible and inspiring manner, people will sense your love. But, if you don't truly love and sacrifice at great length for your listeners, your best sermons will have shallow effect. The Bible says that I can beat out angels in a speech contest, but if I don't have sacrificial love, then my words are like a muffler dragging on the road.

Stoop before You Speak

Great communication will cost your ego.

To communicate the highest of truths, you must stoop to the lowest of levels. Jesus did. The greatest truth a human could ever know is the love of God through his Son. Jesus stooped way down so we could understand that truth. Life-altering communication is an all-consuming passion of the Lord's. That's why he was willing to subject his message (and himself) to significant levels of lowness in order to see lives changed. All too often in preaching, my pride, passions, and traditions overshadow the consideration of my listeners.

You and I must learn to differentiate form and substance. It would seem more natural to carry diamonds around in a bag of cow dung than it would be to pack divine nature into human form. Yet, "The word become flesh and made his dwelling among us." A canyon of oppositeness exists in this dichotomy between form and substance, yet our familiarity with the idea of incarnation leads us to perceive merely a poetic chasm. But the force of Paul's argument for selfless service is fueled by the dissimilarity between God's nature and our fallen human form. How embarrassing for God to take on human form!

I suspect that Paul (in the intellectual and religious snobbery of his pre-conversion days) would have viewed the theology of incarnation a blasphemous claim. After all, don't such ideas accuse God of gross compromise just to get his message across to a group of ignorant, carnal, and thankless pagans? But, when you are dealing with the truth of God, evidently form does not determine or compromise the substance.

As you're deciding how to preach to your students, don't confuse form with substance. Like any small town, every Christian organization has its cultural norms and taboos. And the customs of your church will likely elevate one or two particular forms of preaching. Perhaps your tradition heavily emphasizes expository preaching. So you feel the need to share a lot of the details of your personal Bible study with your students. You are sure to mention the scriptural context, historical setting, some grammatical intricacy, and maybe even a Greek word or two.

By contrast, some of you come from a tradition with a heavy emphasis placed on relevance and emotional buy-in. So you bury yourself in CDs, DVDs, and Web sites to glean the latest values, feelings, or trends. Others may go heavy on application and practical life skills. You read the best self-help and Christian life books you can find. Then you work hard to give students good advice and direct them to helpful resources and opportunities for whole-life development.

Still others may heavily emphasize the experience of the supernatural power and presence of God. You likely spend a lot time in prayer, seeking the Lord's direction for your messages, praying he will lead you to the key issues and Scriptures that will keep your message fresh with the Spirit's anointing.

Which of these forms is the best? They can all be life-changing. But all forms can also amount to the superficial jabbering of a religious salesman. To be sure, the form does matter to God. After all, the boat you choose for life-saving really depends on the water in which someone is drowning. You'll need a Coast Guard cutter if one is going down in the ocean. And a life raft is better suited for one struggling in a river. As crucial as the form is, however, it's strictly the form. It's not the substance. The substance must contain the strong elements that each of those preaching traditions tends to exclusively elevate—biblical accuracy, high relevance, person application, and powerful spiritual experience.

Examine Your Motives

Effective communication to students depends on the recognition that your message is a means to God's end: the life change of your students. Your message is not a means to your end: whatever it is. If you were going to give a message for some selfish motive, what would it be? To be liked by your students, their parents, or your lead pastor? To be the hottest communicator around? To get more guest speaker invitations? To keep your job? To feel important? To appear very spiritual? If you suffer from none of these, then you suffer from denial.

My adolescence peaked in the good old days of modernist thinking—the '80s—and so verifying and proving the Resurrection was a big deal to me. I read *Evidence That Demands a Verdict* and realized that Resurrection was the linchpin issue. Jesus penetrated human history and proved his divine claims by victory over death. His incarnation was not only about atonement. It was also about communication that changes lives.

Your job is not to speak. Your job is not to be impressive. Your job is not to look good. Your job is not to copy your senior pastor. Your job is to be understandable. Nobody criticizes Sunday school teachers for using flannel graphs to teach toddlers. Why do we condemn youth workers for using stories, songs, and visual arts to explain life-altering truth to students?

Where would we be without the historic existence of Christ? Up a transgressionary creek without a redemptive paddle. After all, no salvific death and resurrection means no forgiveness and regeneration. But imagine for a moment that Jesus lived and died among illiterate, mute alpaca herders in Greenland. Would he have been sin-free? Yes. Would his death have paid for our sins? Yes. Would we have known about it? No. We needed a message we could understand.

Listen before You Speak

God, the great speaker, set the ideal for such extensive consideration of the lowly listener. If you want to become a great communicator, then you must become an even better listener. The concept of attentive listening is covered in other chapters (see "Reading Youth Culture" and "Shepherding"), and I challenge you to assess yourself right now. Are you a talker or a listener? Most of us who are communicators by trade are natural talkers. However, the truly effective communicators are disciplined listeners.

Pray before You Speak

God can anoint preparation as much as he can anoint delivery. You may have heard this axiom, but do you believe it? Do you consistently submit your life and thoughts to God's influence as you prepare a message? Or do you tend more toward a do-it-yourself form of message prep such as "winging it," "over-thinking it," or "cranking it out"? The practical elements of preaching, which we will discuss below, are designed to be a functional guide for your thoughts and actions. But they will only lead you to life-changing messages if you also use them as a prayer guide. Message preparation void of spiritual interaction leads to dehydrated sermons. Those messages lack the living water that brings life.

Prayer is not only vital for the preparation of your message; it's vital for the preparation of your listeners. As I mature, I find that my premessage prayers are increasingly focused on the receptivity of listeners and decreasingly on me. Even if one could give the "perfect" message, it would make a difference only to receptive hearts.

A Practical Guide to Speaking to Youth

I hope to practically help you become more effective in communicating to students. But I feel a bit overwhelmed. Using written words to guide someone toward giving an oral presentation is a bit like trying to teach someone to play the trumpet by giving him a manual. Obviously, the better method would be to have him bring his trumpet and you, the teacher, bring your trumpet and exchange musical phrases, conversing all along the way. Therefore, I strongly urge you to find a good biblical communicator to listen to and talk with. I also urge you to listen to (and watch if you can) at least one recording a month of someone else's sermon. As you listen to others, you could use the following thoughts as a guide for your own assessment of the strengths and particularities of any given speaker. Nevertheless, even without a trumpet, I believe much can be gained from the following ideas.[2]

As a teacher-preacher, your job is to get God's permanent truth into a temporary form that makes sense to your students. This process is designed to catalyze maturity in their lives. Each time you prepare a message, consider the Six Prep Questions below to increase the relevance and impact of your messages. These questions, in turn, will allow you to speak to four key areas of a student's life: heart, head, hands, and feet. Excerpts from a sermon to youth are given as an example for each of the four key areas. Read aloud the italicized sentences under each heading as if you were speaking to your youth group. (The subject of the example sermon is God's ability to comfort us in the midst of loneliness.) Following each italicized excerpt is one or two Prep Questions, which you must ask yourself as a part of message preparation. Hopefully, after reading this, you will be able to pick a topic and work through the questions. Having written those answers, you then could order your thoughts to speak to the four key areas of a student's life.

Speak to the Heart

I remember being nineteen and sitting at home alone on my bed. My friends were out partying. I was a brand-new Christian, and I had made up some excuse as to why I couldn't go out with them. But there I sat, alone in my room, reading a Bible and feeling no sense of God's presence. I remember thinking, "God, you better make this worth it." I was pinning my whole emotional and relational life on the fact that God's Word was true, that he would always be with me. But it didn't feel like it was true in that moment. I wonder how many of you feel like that right now. You're trying to hang on to God in the lonely moments, but you're losing your grip.

I talked to one student last summer, I'll call him Brandt. He said it this way, "I really want to stay close to the Lord. It's just that it's so hard to feel his presence when I'm all alone." He then went on to describe how he had tracked down his old girlfriend and got physical in a way that left them both feeling shame. He feels stuck because his sexual interludes kill the pain for a moment but make it worse in the end. Some of you can relate. You're trying to hang on to God in the lonely moments, but you're losing your grip.

Loneliness is a powerful thing, isn't it? It will drive you to do things you never imagined you'd do. Perhaps you kill the pain in a dif-

ferent way from Brandt's. Maybe it's alcohol or computer games or just staying super busy. But many of you know the same feelings. If you can relate to those feelings, you need to know—today—that God longs for you to find comfort in his presence. And he wants you to know he is there for you and that he will never leave you and he will never turn away from you. Listen to what the Bible says . . .

*Prep Question 3:** Why will they care?³* If you answer this heart question well, your students will be engaged from the start of your message. The heart is the emotional and experiential part of life. Jesus' communication was brilliant; he spoke to the heart more than to the head. Accurate thinking, of course, was crucial to his messages, but he was constantly aware of the needs and desires of the people he was trying to influence. We don't need to become worldly or carnal to appeal to the students; we just need to be honest about their feelings.

In your sermon prep, write short sentences that describe their feelings and experiences. If you ask, "Why will they care about this subject?" and then consider their hopes, fears, joys, and pain related to the subject, you will win their trust. You will also disarm their defenses. This will open the door of their hearts to receive God's Word in a way that can change their lives. Furthermore, you will earn a place to speak to their heads in a way that can sustain that life change. Review the heart section of the message again and underline all the feeling words and phrases.

Speak to the Head

One of the greatest themes in the entire Bible is God's faithfulness— that he will stick by us no matter what we do. In Hebrews 13:5, God makes a promise to you; he says, "I will never leave you or forsake you." That seems so foreign to us because there is no human who is always there for us. Parents leave. Friends fail. Dating involves a lot of pain. The closest we can imagine to something always being there is a mountain or a rock or something. But those aren't much comfort when you're lonely. And we tend to put God in that same category of things that are always there, but they're kind of cold and distant. But today, I'd like you to think about this question: Do you believe that God wants to comfort you in your loneliness? The Bible says that he does. Look at these verses . . .

---

* You'll notice that Prep Question 3 is assigned to the heart section of the message. Let me explain. Delivery of the message calls for the heart to come first. But preparation of the message considers the head first. In study, good theology precedes application to the heart. In delivery, you'll need to engage the heart right away.

Prep Question 1: What will they know? This needs to be a single sentence that summarizes your main point and includes your application. For this sample message the main point is this: You can find comfort in your loneliness if you turn to God personally and build deep friendships with his people.

The head is the cognizant, informational part of life. You're speaking to the head when you utilize interesting information, explanation-oriented illustrations, and biblical principles and elements (i.e., history, grammar, context and cross-references). It's critical to speak to the mind so that the students can make truth-anchored decisions and habit changes that are sustainable.

Prep Question 2: How will they know? This question will likely be your biggest brainstorming question. Simply let your thoughts fly. Don't complete your thoughts; just make a long list that may include key Scriptures, personal stories, stories of others, interesting illustrations, movie quotes, song lyrics, Web site articles, and student testimonies. Then go back through the list and determine which of these ideas is really in line with your main point. You may even find that you change how you structure your main point because one of your illustrations led you to a better understanding of what you really wanted to say.

Speak to the Hands

If you want to experience more of God's comfort in response to your loneliness, you need to become serious about a couple of things. First, some of you have never joined a smaller group of students who meet weekly to eat, laugh, read the Bible, and pray. And you're realizing that you need to build friendships that are deeper, more consistent, and more grounded in the Lord. God does use friendships to deal with our loneliness in life. But we've got to be willing to invest in them more and ground them in the Lord. Consider what the Bible says in . . . . So, today, will you let your leaders know that you're ready to join a small-group Bible study? Don't let your pride or your fear stop you from talking to a friend or a leader today.

Second, turn to God himself in the lonely moments. I've asked Becky to share a time when she discovered God's presence in the midst of a very lonely season of her life. (Becky comes to the front and shares her story.) Thanks, Becky. What she just shared with us is an example of how we must trust in God's Word no matter what we feel. The fact is even when we don't feel God is with us, he is. And this is where faith comes in. You need to memorize today's verse. When you're in the lonely moments, read it several times over. Then follow this with a simple prayer, "God will you please carry me through this lonely time." Then sing out to him one of your favorite worship songs, just as Becky did. Some of you have never truly sat in your loneliness and called out to God. Yet he wants you to turn to him. Sometimes, there are pains that only God can deal with. He knows those times, and he longs for you and me to trust him. He will really come through and comfort us. Tonight, will you start memorizing this verse? Will you ask God to make his presence more real in your life? Will you sing out to him, even if you feel a little awkward?

Prep Question 4: What will they do individually? The hands represent the parts of the message that show the application of biblical principles to their individual lives. Students are longing for someone to tell them not just what they *should* do but *how* they can actually do it. Too often a message will leave them all dressed up with nowhere to go. Specific action steps for individual students really do lead to transformed lives. So in your prep time, write out practical steps they can take to become more like Jesus on the subject you're talking about. Too often we think, *They'll never do what I say, so why say it?* That shows a lack of courage and faith. It also reveals our lack of understanding that students want to rise above their selfish habits and desperate situations. Tony Campolo once declared, "We will not loose this generation because we ask too much, but because we ask too little." Very few students will rise above your expectations, though they will long to. So with compassion and realism, set high expectations with specific steps on how to get there.

Speak to the Feet

Finally, tonight, I'd like to present a direct challenge to everyone here: Will we become a group of people marked by a sincere care for others? What would this place be like if every one of us decided to watch out for those who are hurting? Some of you do this so well. You consistently care for others, and you're a part of God's comfort for many. You're the pacesetters for this group. Thank you for your Christlike love for others. What would happen in this place if we all took seriously our responsibility to respond to one another's friendship needs? It would be incredible! Who wouldn't want to be a part of that group? And I've seen it happen before! Many students dream of such a group, but others decide to help make it happen. Does this group matter to you? Do you ever get frustrated that people here are just like the people at school—all caught up in their own little groups? Then change it. Become the answer to the problem, not just the identifier of the problem. Coming up in just three weeks we're going on a weekend retreat. Are you going? And not just to have fun but to grow closer to one another and learn how to serve one another better. This will require sacrifice and a caring attitude from each one of us. This is how God works. And if we're willing, he will work through us. But the answer is up to each one of us. Will you make every effort to be there on the weekend retreat?

Prep Question 5: What will they do corporately? The feet section represents ministry-wide movement. You are speaking to the feet of the whole group. These elements of the message compel students to see themselves as a part of a larger group with a specific identity and mission. With this more-than-just-me perspective, they're challenged to define themselves by the values of the group. They are motivated to participate in the group's spiritual growth and corporate efforts. Unfortunately, the feet feature is missing in most messages. Yet it's easy to do if you just remember to make a group-wide challenge or encouragement. Let them know what they've done right and how that impacts the group. Challenge them where they're struggling. You'll be amazed at how they will rise to a sincere vision of higher values. Keep a list in front of you of upcoming events and of available service opportunities and growth groups. Then after you've written the rest of the message, be sure to add an application for the whole group. A small investment in this area brings a big return, but you need to discipline yourself to review this question or you'll forget to speak to the feet.

Speak to the Barriers

Before we close tonight, I'd like to ask you what it is that could keep you from turning to God and his people for comfort in the midst of loneliness. Consider this upcoming weekend retreat: What's the biggest potential barrier you will face? The schedule? Do you need to schedule time off from work? Do you need to talk to your coach about your faith and let him know how important spiritual life is? You may not be able to leave, but he may say, "Go for it." Maybe your schedule is free, but your friends aren't into church stuff. Maybe you're afraid they're going to think you're becoming a church-freak. The reality is if you're going to grow in your relationship with God, some people aren't going to understand that. But you've got to think on a deeper level about your life.

Consider this question: What does it say about those friendships if God is a threatening subject? I know what it's like to have people think of me as a religious fanatic. But the fact is I can't control what other people say about me. I just need to decide how I'm going to live. Some of you have very tough decisions to make about this retreat. And really, it's about more than the retreat; it's about your life. The retreat is sim-

ply a statement about the shifting priorities of your life: a statement that your spiritual life is increasing in its importance.

May I challenge you very directly? Don't let the opinions of others keep you from pursuing a close connection to God or to his people. As we close in prayer, would you bow your head and ask God a simple question: "Lord, what keeps me from you?" (Have them bow for a moment and pray, then prompt them in another prayer.) *Now that you have that in mind, will you pray another prayer, something like this, "Lord, will you give me the courage to get past this barrier?"*

Prep Question 6: Why will they resist? Strangely enough, students feel really cared for when you compassionately identify the barriers to their change. They're moved that you really understand their lives. Listen to high-impact speakers and you'll notice they identify the barriers to action steps and speak directly to those roadblocks. Often, this knocks the listener out of his complacency and challenges him to take action. When our points of resistance are exposed (fear, pride, doubt, pain, disbelief, lack of trust, selfishness, lack of discipline) we feel not only challenged, but we tend to feel better prepared to make a growth step.

Keep in mind, you can ask yourself the Six Prep Questions every time you prepare a message. I know the time pressures of youth ministry. Most of you are expected to speak every week. Many of you speak two or three times a week. It's very tempting to bypass prep time, but don't. If you learn to ask these questions every time you speak, you'll become much more skilled at preparing truly helpful messages.

A Basic Outline

After having worked through the Prep Questions, you'll be ready to formulate an outline. Following is one outline that reflects a simple progression of thought. I find that this basic approach to messages is very effective with students. It starts by establishing the relevance of the issue (loneliness) and how we deal with it poorly (avoid God and party with friends). It then goes on to explain how this response generally fails (end with shallow friendships and guilt instead of deep relationships with others and God).

In the second major point of the outline, God's ways are presented in such a way that they make sense as the better option. This section starts by recognizing that God cares about our issues and how they impact us (He wants to comfort us in the midst of loneliness). Then you can list your main point and key Scriptures. And closing out this second section, it is very valuable to tell a "success story" about how God's way works (Becky was comforted by God's Word and personal worship).

The third section is a challenge to take action. I suggest you identify a few different challenges, depending on the spiritual maturity of your audience. You can see the examples below.

I. My way of dealing with life

    A. My desire.   *I don't want to be lonely.*

    B. My plan to meet my desire.   *I party with friends. I avoid time alone at all cost.*

    C. My plan to meet my desire fails.   *My relationships with God and friends are shallow.*

II. God's way of dealing with life

    A. God's desire.   *He wants to provide comfort in the midst of my loneliness.*

    B. God's plan to meet my desire.   *He provides companionship through himself and other believers.*

    C. My plan to meet my desire works.   *Becky is going to share her story about God's comfort.*

III. Challenge to live by God's ways

    A. Nonbelievers   *Come back next week and learn more about God's comfort.*

    B. New believer   *Sign up for the retreat so you can grow closer to God.*

    C. Mature believers   *Look out for the lonely on your campus; our youth ministry must be a place of acceptance and care.*

The preceding outline can help you remember to speak to all the key areas of a student's life. The first section speaks to the heart, the second speaks to the head, and the third speaks primarily to the hands, feet, and barriers. Though this is a good basic progression of thought, you'll vary it in each message. At times, you'll speak to the heart during the middle section about God's ways, and you could speak to the head in your opening comments. As you get more comfortable with such a flow of thought, you'll probably insert applications and address barriers throughout the sermon.

I challenge you to work at good message preparation for the sake of your students. They don't need you to be someone other than you are, but they do need you to give the best you can. This involves hard work and intentional development of your skills, character, and spiritual sensitivity. I believe the Lord is greatly honored as we strive to prepare a home-cooked meal that students will eat with a sense of challenge, hope, and joy. And though they may express gratitude to *us* for the messages we deliver, as they mature, they will recognize that the message Giver profoundly outshines the message deliverer. All this adds up to our common goal: students deeply and permanently impacted for Christ.

Notes

1. A. W. Tozer, *The Knowledge of the Holy* (San Francisco: Harper, 1978).

2. In an effort to encourage solid substance and effective form for sermons to students, the last half of this chapter focuses on practical steps. I assume you're devoted to a lifelong study of the Bible and theology, which provides the most solid foundation from which to speak. Many good resources speak to this issue so this writing is limited to the steps that follow a solid biblical foundation.

12.

Facilitating Experiential Learning

BYRON KEHLER

I HAVE AN IMPORTANT QUESTION. What are your goals for the students you teach? Are you satisfied with your students just knowing more: more Bible, more doctrine, more information? Do you want them to know more or live differently? Most of the recorded lessons of Jesus are short, but all call for a change in understanding, attitude, and behavior. The central message of John the Baptist was repentance—once again a change was demanded.

We are often long on information in our teaching and short on change in students' lives. Why? Mark Twain once commented that it wasn't the Bible verses he couldn't understand that bothered him most, but rather the ones that he did understand. James cautioned us against the propensity to simply become listeners and not doers of the knowledge we receive. The blessing comes from doing what we know rather than merely knowing (James 1:22–25).

Learning is a change in the way we feel, think, or behave. For learning to be complete, change must occur. Traditionally we associate learning with rows of students listening to lectures, studying textbooks, and memorizing information. Memorization has often been motivated either by some form of threat (tests) or reward (buttons, recognition, or points). Yet Jesus seemed less concerned with the transfer of information and more concerned with what people did with it. "Not everyone who says to Me, 'Lord, Lord!' will enter the kingdom of heaven, but [only] the one who does the will of My Father in heaven" (Matt. 7:21). Even the rich young ruler understood the lesson of the day but refused to be changed.

Teaching for Change

How do we teach for change rather than simply the transfer of information? Teaching at a Bible college, I find it curious that students spend years in college studying *what* Jesus taught and give so little attention to *how* he taught. How did he teach? Although he often commanded great audiences of people through lengthy orations, he still left people changed after only a single, brief exchange. His presence changed them. They remembered his lessons and applied them to their lives. How did he do it?

If you review the record of his teaching, you see a pattern. The vast majority of his lessons occur in the midst of everyday life. They're propelled by the simplest events of the day. Seldom do we find him scheduling meetings, gathering people for lectures, or teaching in the manner of the formal rabbis. The most common place to find him teaching was the street. The world was his classroom; experiences were his tools. He converted everyday moments into his curriculum. He was the great facilitator of the lessons available around any corner. Every exchange and experience were opportunities for learning. He made lessons hard to miss. He scattered reminders wherever he went—from the nature of doors to the nature of light, from fig trees to sparrows overhead, from places of worship to people's behavior at parties.

An evaluation of our teaching approach is long overdue. A paradigm shift is needed. Why don't we teach as he did? Is this why students are so frequently bored? We line them up in rows, face them all in the same direction, and then proceed to lecture them on what the Bible says, as though they need only information. The most powerful learning seems historically to have happened through experience. Modern research supports this old lesson. People learn most deeply and retain more when they learn through experiences. Hence the danger in what I say. This could challenge our traditional youth ministry.

Think about it: When Jesus taught, if children were distracting from the lesson, they became the lesson (Matt. 19). When Jesus taught, if the lesson was disrupted by some who were putting down or making fun of others, their attitudes became the focus of learning (Luke 18). If someone got in trouble during one of his lessons, he became an illustration of the condition that all of us share, the grace we receive and are to extend to others (John 8). If children were making too much noise in the hall outside, they were not reprimanded. Instead, they became the illustration of how we are to live within the kingdom (Mark 10). When people were being selfish, when they wanted the favored spots, if people raced to the chairs closest to the food, a lesson preceded the prayer of thanks about the order of things in heaven (Matt. 19). His teaching grew out of the life they shared and the experiences they found in common. Today we call that *experiential learning.*

Introduction to Experiential Learning

Experiential education is based on doing—learning by doing, reflecting on what has happened, and applying those observations to the rest of life. Studies in how people learn best are very clear. Modeling and experience are the best teachers. We remember 20 percent of what we hear, 50 percent of what we see, and 80 percent of what we do. Even the old sages knew, "Give me a fish and I eat for a day, teach me to fish and I eat for a lifetime." Confucius identified the same principle in these words: "I hear and I forget, I see and I remember, I do and then I understand." If we really want change for our students, then it's time to explore other teaching approaches that offer greater effectiveness.

If this approach to learning is so powerful, if it was modeled for us by Jesus and we see the results in men willing to die for their convictions, what stops us from following? First, let's look at some conditions or mind-sets that hold us back in more traditional and less effective patterns of teaching, including:

- Lack of familiarity with the approach
- Laziness and loyalty to what we experienced
- Less predictable
- Less "teacher" recognition and control
- Too time intensive
- Requires different and possibly greater skills than the traditional lecture

Certainly teaching through experiences is far less familiar to us. Most of us were taught in the traditional classroom approach, and even though we may have found it boring and only modestly effective, we still subject others to it hoping the outcome may be different. To consider an alternative approach can be intimidating. Yet the potential benefits far outweigh the risks and discomfort, for both our students as well as us teachers. Consider the differences between simple information assimilation and experiential education.[1]

Assimilation	Experiential
Time-efficient initially	Time-consuming but greater change
Speaker-driven, relies on enthusiasm and entertainment	Learner-driven, effect engaging and reinforced
Passive, less retention	Active and better retention
Symbolic medium (excludes some)	Concrete medium, stimulating environment
Less application (know a lot, do little)	Rehearsed, experientially practiced
Less relevant or practical	Cognitively meaningful

Predictable, boring	Unpredictable, inherent risks
Attendance encouraged by threats, guilt, or games	Enjoyable, so self-motivated
One teacher, stands above you	Many teachers, stand among you

The traditional classroom still has important benefits in education for simply conveying information, teaching skills, and helping others acquire knowledge. However, when we want people to learn about themselves, grasp truths about relationships, build character, embrace biblical principles in their living, experiential education offers a powerful medium to realize these goals.

When what we're teaching really matters, notice how it's taught. Consider the fields of medicine, the military, or even car mechanics. Who do you want to perform your surgery, the student who sat in the classroom, listened to the lecture, and passed the exam or the intern who stood by the operating table, held the instruments, and eventually performed the surgery under supervision? When sending troops into battle, they feel safest after long hours of war games and practice. Listening to an engine to diagnose the problem can't be learned by reading the book again. When we really want to feel confident, we trust those who learned by experience. How do students learn to live in the kingdom in your ministry? Jesus invited disciples to share his life and learn as they walked. How do you seek to inspire, train, and equip?

Jesus did have the advantage of living with his disciples. We don't usually live with our students. But what if we could create an environment in which students learn by doing, as Jesus' disciples did with him? What if we were better at identifying teachable moments and knew how to capitalize on them so that potential learning wasn't lost? What if we could create experiences for our students that stimulated them and produced learning moments that we could then use to guide them in their own self-discovery?

I believe we can and must. Part of our responsibility in ministry is to convey the gift of the gospel in the most effective vehicle we have available. How much greater is the demand to deeper kingdom learning and living then that of medicine, war, or car mechanics?

Creating Environments of Discovery

How do you make such a shift in your educational approach? The first step is to create the best possible environment for self-discovery and experiential learning. This begins with creating a space where it's safe to explore. Jesus created an environment where it was safe to approach him, ask questions, wonder how things would work, complain on occasion, impulsively step out of boats, momentarily lose loyalty, and even doubt his word.

Students learn best when they feel safe. Think of when you do your best work. Do you feel most at ease in your performance when your boss is standing over you? Few of us do. Self-discovery, even when guided, involves risk—the risk of trying something new and stepping outside your typical behavior or thinking, the risk of asking questions and exploring different perspectives, the risk of challenging the status quo. In order for students to stretch themselves, they must feel safe both physically and emotionally—safe from insults, embarrassment, ridicule, and harm.

In an effort to provide this type of safety, many experiential and outdoor programs have adopted a philosophy of what they call a "full value contract." Project Adventure popularized this approach during the 1980s, asking groups to agree to a standard of conduct, to commit to one another to work cooperatively, give and receive feedback, and avoid insulting or discounting one another. Such a formal structure or agreement can help create the type of environment in which people are willing to risk in order to learn.

Ask students what would help them feel safe to begin to learn in a new way. Discuss ideas for physical and emotional safety. Ask them to brainstorm what guidelines would they like to use to ensure they could take risks without fear of harm. Below is one version of a full value contract, using the acronym *secret*. We ask students to each make this commitment to themselves and the group.

Full-Value Contract

The S.E.C.R.E.T to Learning Effectively in Groups

1. *Safety:* I will keep others and myself safe.
2. *Effort:* I will stretch myself to try, even when uncomfortable.
3. *Communication:* I will give and receive feedback.
4. *Responsibility:* I will accept responsibility for my actions.
5. *Encouragement:* I will encourage those around me.
6. *Teamwork:* I will work together toward common goals.

After you have established guidelines for your care and conduct with one another you're ready for the next element in the environment preparation.

The Learning Zone

Learning is retained longest when coupled with stimulation. Curiosity, fear, dilemma, new environments, or intense circumstances can stimulate us. The greatest change is realized when students are kept in a particular state—a stretched state sometimes called the challenge zone. Most of us prefer to live within our own comfort zones, where we're familiar and secure. Pushed too far, people find themselves embarrassed or, worse yet, overwhelmed by what's happening, thus resulting in a crisis-zone experience.

We must seek to encourage students to achieve self-discovery and growth. This occurs when we help them first choose, and then stay, in their own challenge zone. We must resist the temptation to force self-discovery, but rather challenge by invitation and choice. It is easy for us to impose our own agenda on others' learning. Our desire for them to be stretched may be so strong that we push them into places for which they are not yet ready. This push can often undo any benefit they derive from their accomplishment. We may believe that we know what is best for them at the moment, but unfortunately all too often we are operating out of our own desires rather than theirs. Notice Jesus' gentle invitational approach that allowed others to decide where he could take them. Here's a description of these three different learning zones.

Comfort Zone

This is where we prefer to live. We most commonly seek this station. Here resides security, predictability, and control. Through these, we try to avoid surprise, embarrassment, and failure. The lower the self-esteem of an individual, the greater the fears, the more comfort is sought and clung to. This zone is too calm and content for optimal learning.

Questions that can help students identify this area for themselves when considering an experience might include:

- What would be easy for you?
- What can you see yourself doing comfortably?
- What would feel safe for you?

Jesus challenged the rich young ruler to move from his comfort zone into a life filled with adventure and self-discovery. He left sad and stagnant, unwilling to be stretched. Jesus asks these same questions of us today, regarding our faith and walk with him.

Challenge Zone

This is where we learn best. When we're stretched, we discover what we're truly capable of. We extend our vision and trust in our abilities and ourselves. We develop confidence and competence. In short, it is here where we grow.

Questions that can help students identify this area for themselves might include:

- What would be difficult for you?
- What would stretch you?
- What would you like to imagine yourself doing?
- What would you be excited to accomplish?
- What would you feel proud of or pleasantly surprised by doing?

This is where Peter met Jesus on the water. Somewhere outside of what we ordinarily might expect of ourselves. Some call it living on the edge, experiencing the adventure of life. Jesus calls us to live this way. It was his invitation to Peter and Paul, and it's his invitation to us as well.

Crisis Zone

This is where we become overwhelmed. Here the danger or our fear eclipses the potential for learning. Helplessness is often the result. We retreat, withdraw, and lose face and confidence. This zone is too much stimulation for optimal learning.

Questions that can help students identify this area for themselves might include:

- What can't you imagine doing?
- What would be too much for you?
- What would overwhelm you?
- What do you consider impossible for you?

Choosing Your Learning Experiences

Once the most suitable environment is created for optimal learning, the next step is to identify the type of experiential learning you're going to employ. Experiential learning takes many forms. Some opportunities occur naturally (the Samaritan woman), while in other situations the teacher may create them (washing the disciples' feet). We can learn to recognize and exploit naturally occurring experiences for teaching moments. We intentionally create designed experiential learning moments to use for teaching moments. Designed experiential learning can be nature-based, service-based, mission-based, initiative-based, and adventure-based.

Using Naturally Occurring Experiences to Teach

Let's begin with those experiences that just occur naturally. We don't plan for them and don't know when they will happen, but when they occur, we recognize their potential for teaching. During my junior high years, my mother, mistaking the mischievous look in my eyes as possible criminal potential, arranged with our pastor for me to act as a janitor for our congregation. I think her hope was that the more I touched holy objects, somehow holiness would rub off on me, similar to osmosis.

One Saturday morning I was sitting with the pastor in his study, avoiding my cleaning duties while he was avoiding his study duties. As we sat drinking a soft drink and sharing a morning candy bar, he wadded his empty candy bar wrapper in his hand and casually pitched it in the direction of the wastebasket in the corner. It barely made it halfway, when it floated to the floor in the middle of the room. We sat and continued to talk. In a few moments a mouse crawled out from under his bookcase and marching across the floor in front of us, began to nibble on the remaining chocolate still on the wrapper. We sat in awe of its boldness. After the mouse retired under the bookcase, we sat in silence.

The pastor finally broke the silence with a smile and these words, "We are that mouse; Hebrews, chapter 4, 'Let us approach the throne of grace boldly, so that we may receive mercy and find grace to help us in our time of need.'" It has been more than three decades since he made that comment and I can still hear it ringing in my ears as I write it. He artfully captured a naturally occurring event and applied it to our lives as we sat quietly one Saturday morning. I felt at that moment in the presence of Jesus. I have never forgotten that lesson.

Think of the opportunities for learning that occur naturally. We get so used to thinking inside the box that when opportunity invites us we easily overlook it. A new youth minister talked to me about his frustration with the church bus breaking down on a mission trip. He complained that it had ruined his carefully laid plans, interrupted his timetable, and created problems for the trip. "Why did God allow such a thing to happen?" he asked. He failed to see the opportunity that the breakdown afforded to illustrate a wide variety of lessons and applications. He could have used the experience to discuss the lack of reliability of systems around us, our plans versus God's plans, how Paul headed in one direction and was taken somewhere else.

The beauty of much of Jesus' teaching is that it was simply an authentic response to life's natural experiences. Can you imagine the thrill and excitement of spending a day with him when any life experience could have spoken a lesson to you? Sick people crying out, little children crowding in, tax collectors spying from above, and women caught in scandal all invited opportunity for Jesus to teach. What opportunities are we missing? Those hidden in what may appear to others as ordinary life. Wouldn't it be wonderful to develop such a perspective? The bee sting on the hike is an invitation for a discussion on pain. The argument before youth group becomes an entry point for how we treat one another within the body of Christ. The distraction by students during the lesson changes the lesson to how easily we become distracted from the important things God has for us.

Such an approach allows the Bible to live in our midst, for God to speak to our lives in the present, and for us to recognize him as he walks among us. How do we learn such a skill? Consider this: Naturally occurring learning opportunities, or NOLOs (rhymes with solos) as I refer to them, are all around us all the time. We first begin by recognizing that lessons are available almost anywhere. We only must have trained spiritual eyes to see them. Because they are naturally occurring we don't have to plan them for our students, but we must learn to identify them, direct attention to them, and apply them to life.

Last year a young person and I were clearing a piece of property of trees in preparation for a new building. The property was small and the trees tall, so we were trying to be careful not to take out all the electrical lines overhead as we dropped the trees into the interior of the property. To aid in felling the trees where we wanted, we tied a rope around the selected tree and attached it to the rear of our pickup truck to pull it in the desired direction. Many of the trees were more than seventy-five feet tall, and the rope we had available was only about thirty feet long. This provided for some exciting moments as we dodged the falling timber.

After pulling a number of trees over without serious incident, we finally had a close call. In our efforts to dodge the tree, we drove over the new chain saw which had unfortunately been left on the ground. Frustrated by the loss of the saw, we cut our losses so to speak, packed our things, and proceeded to drive home. As we pulled onto the nearby expressway, I noticed oncoming traffic giving us a particularly wide berth and many people waving in what seemed to be a friendly manner as they went by. After driving a mile or so, I was stopped by a signal light. At the intersection a car pulled beside us and motioned for us to roll down the window. Frantically the other driver pointed to the back of our truck. Looking now for the first time in my rearview mirror, I realized that in our haste to leave the property we had overlooked the fact that portions of the last tree were still attached to the rear of the truck. We had been pulling a forest down the freeway behind us.

As we headed back to the property to deposit the tree, we laughed at our mistake and discussed Hebrews 12. We talked about how easily we unknowingly are impaired by our earlier histories and our sin and how we struggle so much with unresolved issues in our lives. We discussed the importance of feedback from others along life's highways and the importance not only of perseverance in the race of our faith but in removing the things that hinder our success. The fifteen-minute lesson opened doors of discussion that could never have been opened in the same way within the classroom. My young passenger has shared that experience with others on numerous occasions in discussions of growth and faithfulness. Learning the skill of identifying and translating experiences into life lessons takes time and practice but yields powerful fruit.

This outline is a starting place to help you use NOLOs.

Natural Discovery Model

1. **Identify an opportunity through observation of a situation, crisis, conflict, feeling, metaphor, or example.**

Notice what occurs around you. Bring a sense of anticipation into your perspective on life. Expect that lessons will present themselves and be ready to help others learn from them. Learn to view experiences as teachers, not obstacles, interruptions, disruptions, or distractions from the other "important" planned events in life. An unexpected death in your community, current events, personal mistakes, daily chores, a relational exchange, or crisis all afford opportunity to explore life's deeper issues.

The story of Jesus and the woman at the well in John 4 provides a wonderful illustration of how naturally occurring events can unfold and become teaching tools for those who are prepared. Jesus was simply thirsty, a contact occurred, and a NOLO developed. Listen to him: "Give Me a drink" (John 4:7).

2. **Formulate an application to visualize the potential for learning.**

Train your mind and eye to apply what you experience first to your own life and then in the lives of those around you. Learning the art of personal reflection and observation of others will allow you to see experiences as metaphors, examples, and illustrations of deeper principles and lessons. Personal experiences then act as parables in our lives. How each of us think and respond to life is often revealed in common everyday experiences.

Help people recognize patterns in how they deal with life, from the small to the large and significant. Discipline yourself to build bridges between singular events and larger, deeper applications. The tragedies of 9/11 provided a stark reminder of the frailty of life and the intensity of loss. Jesus wept above the city of Jerusalem because he saw what others could not and then applied that to the lives of those with whom he traveled. With the Samaritan woman, Jesus applied our common thirst to the deeper needs in life. He refers to "living water" (John 4:13–14).

3. **Direct attention to circumstances and open a process by sharing your observations.**

Invite others to notice what you've noticed. Don't preach, don't lecture, but rather let your observation spark their interest as well. Curiosity is contagious. Bait the hook, tug, and then prepare to reel them in slowly. Let them borrow your wonder, interest, or confusion.

Jesus created curiosity at the well by his request, redirected the exchange to more meaningful issues, made an observation about the nature of thirst, and suggested there was something else at stake (John 4:9–14).

4. **Invite discussion through questions and directed inquiry.**

Discussion encourages investigation, which can often lead to discovery. Learn the skill of asking the right question, rather than telling others what you think. Notice how seldom Jesus directly answered the questions put to him and how often he asked questions of others. As we guide others in their exploration of life lessons, learning to find the right question at the right time is much of the skill. Another hint: The shorter the question, the sharper the point. Jesus invited the woman to talk about her life. He showed interest in her circumstances and her condition (John 4:15–18, 21–25).

5. **Promote discovery by helping recognize principles in lessons.**

In the discussion, help your students identify life principles, truths, and lessons. Start with general principles and then get more specific. Teach to the moment; let the experience be your illustration of the lesson.

Jesus' discussion allowed the woman to discover that she was in the presence of someone unique. This was no ordinary exchange. He had something for her. Truth was available. There was the opportunity for self-discovery, if she would only proceed. Admittedly, Jesus had inside information, but the principle for us remains the same: the woman was in need of living water, and he masterfully exposed her true need. We are also capable of promoting self-discovery like this when we bring insight, trained reflection, and knowledge of people and God's Word to bear on any life experience. She proclaimed, "I see that You are a prophet" (John 4:19).

6. **Encourage life application. Connect the lessons to students' lives.**

Herein lies the treasure. What does this truth mean to me right now where I live? Don't let them escape before they realize that the principle applies to their lives today. The process just described is like drawing a dot-to-dot picture. If you connect each point as you move along, the picture eventually is identifiable and distinct.

With the Samaritan woman, Jesus moved from Jewish oddity, to prophet, to Messiah within a single exchange. The dots developed into a picture she could identify as the Christ. With practice we also can facilitate face-to-face exchanges between Christ and our students through day-to-day experiences. Jesus stands at the well still today, waiting for us to intentionally and skillfully bring young people into an exchange with him where they can be changed and their deepest needs met for all eternity. The Samaritan woman came to understand. "Could this be the Christ?" (John 4:26–30).

The story of learning in John 4 doesn't end here. The woman couldn't contain her learning. She passed her experience on to others, just as your students will when their learning is exciting, spontaneous, insightful, and relevant. Changed by her encounter with Christ, the woman returned to town and urged others to share in a similar experience. After a brief lesson on food (NOLO) with his disciples, Jesus continued his ministry to the Samaritans. Notice the conclusion, "We no longer believe because of what you said, for we have heard for ourselves and know that this really is the Savior of the world" (John 4:42).

Personal experience is a powerful teacher. Self-discovery promotes belief. We have heard for ourselves, he is the Savior of the world. Whether through an inviting environment, safety to explore, or observations you share with those around you, experiential learning changes people. The Samaritan woman could testify to his power, but when others came to hear him themselves, they moved from believing to knowing. Such is our task as youth ministers—translating our experience with him to others. Through experiential learning we can help those we serve "hear" his voice themselves, and in such an encounter they can then "know" who he is. And in knowing, they also will be compelled to serve.

Notes

1. Simon Priest and Michael A. Gass, *Effective Leadership in Adventure Programming* (Champaign, Ill.: Human Kinetics, 1997).

13.

Designing Experiential Learning

BYRON KEHLER

IN THE PREVIOUS CHAPTER, we discussed the power of using naturally occurring learning opportunities to promote lasting transformation in the lives of young people. Although these natural and spontaneous experiences are effective, they also are limited because we don't know when they may occur, how long they will last, or who will be present. Consequently, we find it difficult to plan a lesson around them, hoping they appear at just the right time as youth group begins.

How can we bring this same impact or power into planned or scheduled events? How do we build experiences that shape people within the confines of a predictable, scheduled youth program? We again have biblical examples of various types of this learning.

Designing Learning Experiences

Jesus faced the same need for designing experiences. At times, Jesus wanted to teach lessons for particular needs or situations, so he gathered his disciples and the lesson began. In experiential education we would describe this example as *initiative-based*. Let's look at an example from his ministry in the Gospel of John, chapter 13.

Jesus had an agenda. As his time drew near to leave, there was one more important lesson to teach—leadership. His disciples were graduating. He wanted them, future leaders of the church, to understand the very nature of leadership, the importance of servanthood, and the expectation of sacrifice for the sake of the kingdom. It would be easy for them to argue about leadership, status, and the desire to call the shots after he left.

How would you have taught the lesson? How would you have prepared them for what was to follow? Would you have lined them up in chairs, lectured them on how leaders are to behave, cautioned them against infighting? Instead, Jesus created an experience that would resonate within them as they carried his message to a hurting world. He chose an experience reinforced by touch, sensation, activity, atmosphere, and even confusion. He chose something familiar and common and infused it with new meaning. Instead of simply *telling* them how to lead, he *taught* them about leadership.

Years ago as a youth minister, I was looking for a way to convey the importance and interconnectedness of each young person within the youth group as an expression of the ideas in 1 Corinthians 12. I wanted the students to understand that when they were absent they were missed and each brought something unique to the group dynamic.

The week before the lesson I bought a wooden puzzle of the face of Jesus and sent out a single piece to each member of the group. I asked them to bring their puzzle pieces to youth group the coming week. When they arrived, they were blindfolded and sat together on the floor. Their task or "challenge" was to assemble the puzzle as a group without the benefit of sight. Eventually they put it together even though some pieces were missing because some who had received puzzle parts didn't attend that evening. The discussion that followed allowed them to see and understand how we make up the body of Christ, how we each play a significant role, and the loss or gap created when one is missing.

Let's look at the elements of designed teaching experiences and how to build them. Use the following outline as a guide.

Designed Discovery Model

Design of the Learning

John 13:1–3: "Jesus knew that His hour had come to depart from this world. . . . He loved them. . . . Jesus knew that the Father had given everything into His hands, that He had come from God, and that He was going back to God."

At the beginning of each step, you will need to ask yourself several questions. To identify the purpose, ask:
- What are you trying to accomplish?
- What lesson is to be taught?
- What needs are you attempting to meet?
- What change are you encouraging?

The process begins with identifying the goal. What do you want your students to learn from the experience—the importance of honesty, the value of prayer, placing others first, or making good decisions when faced with temptations?

Think in terms of what you want to change in their lives, not only what you want them to know. Experiential learning is best applied to promote change. Whatever your target lesson, you want to be clear about your objective. Moving targets are hard to hit.

Delivery of the Exercise

John 13:4–5: "So He got up from supper, laid aside His robe, took a towel, and tied it around Himself. Next, He poured water into a basin and began to wash His disciples' feet and to dry them with the towel tied around Him."

- What exercise is best to accomplish the purpose?
- What resources do you have available?
- What limitations does your group present?

Once you have identified your lesson objective, brainstorm about what type of activities might best convey that lesson. This can be tricky. As you become more acquainted with experiential application, ideas will flow more easily, but at first you may want to consult various books on learning exercises. Check Internet Web sites where you can do searches for books about adventure-based or experiential-based learning. I have at least a dozen books on this topic.

Notice the surrounding natural resources. Different environments offer different options and limitations. Can you use the outdoors? Is your youth group room large enough for the activity? Are there trees, water, tables, and adequate staff? Each environment has benefits. Don't overlook them. What physical limitations exist within your group membership? These may include height, weight, gender, strength, and physical disabilities.

Dilemma of Resolution

John 13:6–8: "He came to Simon Peter, who asked Him, 'Lord, are You going to wash my feet?' Jesus answered him, 'What I'm doing you don't understand now, but afterwards you will know.' 'You will never wash my feet—ever!' Peter said. Jesus replied, 'If I don't wash you, you have no part with Me.'"

- What problem are you presenting?
- What rules will guide the exercise?
- What is your solution? What solutions may be offered? What will you allow?
- What problems may arise in accomplishing the task?

As you design your experience, keep in mind the learning potential of intensity. People retain best what they struggle with. If you've ever labored over a decision, you understand how unlikely it is that you would forget the experience. When we struggle, the emotional charge involved cements the experience into our memories. This is why trauma has such powerful long-term effect on people. Lessons learned amid emotional, active, or sensation-laden experiences stay with us. What dilemma will you present to your group? What challenge will you introduce? Challenge, struggle, dilemma, or problems create energy that holds your audience attentive and reinforces the lesson in their memory. This is one of the reasons the media and television seek to create tension through presenting opposing sides and conflicts; they know people will watch and remember. It holds us captive. We desire to know the solution, the outcome. That's why we'll finish even a bad movie, just to know how it ends.

As you develop the challenge aspect of your experience, decide on the rules that will guide the activity. Make sure your rules are complete. Consider the various ways people may attempt to solve the puzzle. Keep the rules simple. It's often easier to describe what you will allow, rather than what you won't. For instance, say, "You may touch only one another and the red squares as you cross the floor," instead of saying, "You can't lay sweatshirts down to walk on, or coats, books, or other things." Try not to add new rules after the exercise has begun or students will feel as though you're working against them rather than for them. Postulate various solutions beforehand and decide what you will allow, what you won't, and what might pose a safety issue.

Development of Strategy

John 13:9–12a: "Simon Peter said to Him, 'Lord, not only my feet, but also my hands and my head.' 'One who has bathed,' Jesus told him, 'doesn't need to wash anything except his feet, but he is completely clean. You are clean, but not all of you.' For He knew who would betray Him. This is why He said, 'You are not all clean.' When Jesus had washed their feet and put on His robe, He reclined again."

- What interactions do you anticipate?
- How do you expect individuals to react? What group reactions might you expect?
- What conflicts do you anticipate? What do you expect the exercise to evoke?
- What safeguards do you have in place for containment?

The next step involves anticipating what relational issues the exercise might evoke. Because safety isn't limited to only physical aspects, you want to make sure people are protected emotionally as well. Think through what type of reactions you may get from both individuals as well as the group as a whole. Be prepared to intervene and talk about what's occurring to ensure emotional safety as well as personal and group growth. Only open what you can safely close. Reactions from people can be part of the learning, but you must know what to do with the reactions as they occur. Notice that Simon Peter objected to having his feet washed and could have sabotaged the learning had Jesus not responded as he did. Prepare for a wide variety of responses and know what you'll do with them before they occur.

Debriefing of the Process

John 13:12b: "Do you know what I have done for you?"
- What will you look for?
- What questions will you ask?
- How will you guide the process?

Learning can occur without discussion of the experience, but it depends on each individual's ability to reflect. Debriefing of some sort will occur, whether we do it or not, if the event is effective at all. Debriefing allows you to guide the reflection and reactions toward your particular goals. Facilitators act as guardrails to keep the group on the road to discovering the truths they've identified and targeted. Mark Twain exhorted, "We should get out of an experience all the wisdom possible; lest we be like the cat that sits down on a hot stove-lid. We will never sit down on a hot stove-lid again; but he'll never sit down on a cold one either!" You need to help students grasp the lessons of the experience. Gently lead them toward the particular goal of the exercise.

The experience itself is only the vehicle through which learning is transported. Much learning occurs through reflection afterward. *Debriefing* stimulates reflection and thought about the experience and directs reflection toward learning and life application. *Transfer* is the process of integrating the learning from structured experiences with daily living at home.

As experiential teachers, we try to help students apply (or transfer) what they've learned in our planned experiences into permanent change and growth in their lives. What questions do we ask, how do we stimulate insight based upon the experience, how do we help them transfer or translate this learning into change elsewhere in their lives? As you facilitate or debrief, the goal for your lesson must guide the direction and choice of your questions. If your goal is team building, your questions must direct the discussion there. If your goal is serving others, your questions must focus attention in that direction. Sometimes our goals are broad and more process oriented, other times very specific and lesson focused. The diagram below gives examples of typical process goals and common content goals.

Process objectives are reached by focusing on the interaction and application between members of the group and the individual and corporate lessons of growth. Content objectives use experiences to illustrate or enhance learning related to particular and specific themes.

Sample Process Goals	*Sample Content Goals*
Team building	Learning about prayer
Group cooperation	Learning about giving
Personal insight and growth	Learning about honesty
Conflict resolution	Learning about self-control
Trust	Learning about the value of others
Leadership	Learning about character qualities
Communication	Learning about reliability
Roles in groups	Learning about setting priorities
Developing confidence	Learning about any biblical truth

Discovery of Insight

John 13:13–17: "You call Me Teacher and Lord. This is well said, for I am. So if I, your Lord and Teacher, have washed your feet, you also ought to wash one another's feet. For I have given you an example that you also should do just as I have done for you. I assure you: A slave is not greater than his master, and a messenger is not greater than the one who sent him. If you know these things, you are blessed if you do them."

- What individual and group insights are you striving for?
- How will those insights be used to build deeper understanding?
- What applications will you encourage?

In this final step, you help students transfer learning from the experience to their daily lives. The key to learning is their daily application of the principles. In Jesus' words, "If you know these things, you are blessed if you do them." As teachers we must not be satisfied with an experience that went well or was stimulating or that students enjoyed if it doesn't result in change.

Lasting change happens when we help them see what this means after the experience is over—or how their experience is a lens through which they can review their behavior and attitudes elsewhere. The designed experience provides an example for them to observe and study. It's a piece of how they conduct their lives, an opportunity to view themselves through the microscope of the exercise.

The forms experiential learning can take are almost endless. The table below lists biblical examples of several types of experiential learning forms.

Experiential Learning Activities in Scripture

Natural	*Designed*	*Service-based*
Samaritan woman	Foot washing	Feeding five thousand
Woman caught in adultery	Cleansing temple	Choosing the seven
Widow's mites	Transfiguration	Paul sending Timothy
Little children	Triumphal entry	Barnabas and Paul sent

Nature-based	*Mission trips*	*Adventure-based*
Temptations of Jesus	John the Baptist	Jesus walking on water
Calling of Peter while	in wilderness	Peter's walking on
fishing	Sending out the	waves
Jesus calming the sea	disciples	Jailing of Peter and John
Consider the sparrows,	Ananias sent to Paul	Shipwrecks of Paul
lilies	Paul's journeys	

Here are suggestions of how a youth ministry could apply similar natural, designed,[1] service-based,[2] nature-based,[3] mission trips, and adventure-based[4] experiences to help students learn and grow.

Youth Group Activities or Experiences

Natural	*Designed*	*Service-based*
Spontaneous teaching moments	Group initiatives and teaching games	Serving children
Observations that illustrate lessons	Team-building activities	Serving elderly
Examples of biblical attitudes or behaviors	Object lessons and illustrations	Serving disadvantaged
Examples of problem areas or conflicts	Teaching activities and experiences	Serving environment
		Serving community

Nature-based	*Mission Trips*	*Adventure-based*
Day hikes	Local trips that	Spelunking (caving)
Wilderness trips	expose your kids to	Windsurfing
Navigation	different environ-	Snow skiing
(compass exercises)	ments, economies,	Exploring
Camping	or cultures	Rafting
Fishing		Rock climbing
Solo experiences		

Twenty-five years ago I began my counseling practice. I specialized in working with adolescents and I was seeing about a half dozen for weekly counseling. I struggled with how to get through to them, how to help them see the consequences of their choices, and how their choices affected others. A friend who was into outdoor activities suggested that we take them into the woods and present them with various physical challenges similar to boot camp as an adjunct to traditional therapy. He thought we could use those experiences to teach them principles I was struggling to convey in the counseling office. At the end of my therapeutic rope, I agreed to give it a try, even though it was somewhat unconventional.

After planning our activities and lessons, we contacted parents and arranged for the young people to be brought to the office one Saturday morning. The teens didn't know one another and had no idea what the day would hold. As they piled into the van at 6:30 that morning, they grumbled, then sat in silence as we drove for two hours to the activity site. They were not happy campers, to say the least. Upon arrival, we immediately launched into the initiatives and activities. As the day progressed, I witnessed a rare transformation. After about eight hours of climbing, falling, jumping, pulling, and piling on and over things, we headed home. I was awestruck at the change in the ride home from the ride there. They were laughing, discussing, sharing openly about their problems, and making plans for getting together for a reunion in the near future.

I left that day with a newfound awareness and appreciation for the power of experiential learning to effect substantive, long-term change. Not long afterward, I began a search for property to build a permanent outdoor, nature-based learning facility. Since then, more than thirty thousand young people have been through our program, developing self-confidence, building leadership, and gaining insight into themselves, others, and God.

I encourage you to experiment with this teaching approach. Begin by first becoming a student of life experience around you, then practice sharing your observations with others so they can benefit from your insight. Start including more activities in your regular meetings to help illustrate your lessons. Intentionally look for experiences that provide teaching opportunities. Experiential learning is a powerful medium.

Jesus modeled for us a life in which lessons grew out of experiences, and from those experiences change and conviction grew. Expand your classroom and prepare for an adventure in learning!

Notes

1. See Karl Rohnke and Amy Simpson, *On-the-Edge Games for Youth Ministry* (Loveland, Colo.: Group Publishing, 1998).

2. See Peter L. Benson, *Beyond Leaf Raking: Learning to Serve, Serving to Learn* (Nashville, Tenn.: Abingdon, 1993).

3. See John Graham, *Outdoor Leadership: Technique, Common Sense & Self-Confidence* (Seattle: Mountaineers, 1997).

4. See Simon Priest and Michael A. Gass, *Effective Leadership in Adventure Programming* (Champaign, Ill.: Human Kinetics, 1997).

14.

Creative Programming

THE THEME OF A weekend retreat was "The Kingdom." For two days, we described, experienced, visualized, and celebrated the kingdom-oriented life to which God calls each of us. On the final night during a "knighting" ceremony, we called students to surrender their "crowns" that represented a part of their life not yet under control of the King of kings.

We set up the room to resemble a castle. Students approached by crossing a "drawbridge" leading into the room. They could see candles surrounding a cross in the center of the stage. Two adult leaders stood on each side of the cross with a sword in hand. We invited students to respond to what God was doing in their lives by laying down their crowns at the foot of the cross and then moving to the side of the cross to be knighted.

One by one, hundreds of students knelt at the foot of the cross to lay down their crowns. Crown after crown was placed at the cross. These crowns represented relationships not yet surrendered to the King, thoughts that needed to be transformed by the King, activities pursued for the sake of another king, and hearts that were coming to the King for the very first time.

Students then approached one of the adults who stood ready to knight them. Some of the students came to me and as they knelt, I spoke the King's truth into their lives: "You are a child of the King, and because of what Jesus has done for you on the cross, the King is pleased with you. He is calling you into his service. I knight you because you are set apart for him. You are his ambassador. Don't let anyone look down on you because you're young. But set an example. Let God expose others to the beauty, the majesty, the splendor, and the joy of his kingdom through your life. Don't waste a moment. Don't belittle his splendor. Let his light shine through you so that all others around you would be drawn to all that's good and lovely. Let his kingdom come and his will be done in and through your life as it is in heaven."

I was amazed. As students heard words of truth they responded wholeheartedly, some with blazing eyes, others with soberness, brokenness, and tears. These young people were called to the life of the kingdom that night. Each student responded by celebrating and praising the King, worshipping and adoring him, lifting their hearts in song.

I don't think any student present that night will ever again be able to read Jesus' descriptions of the kingdom in the Gospels without remembering the knighting ceremony. I'm pretty certain that not one will again quote the Lord's Prayer and not remember that God's heavenly kingdom and heavenly will are to be experienced and realized here on earth, today, as in heaven. These students may never again watch a movie or television show that has to do with kings or knights and not remember that they are part of God's kingdom and are called as servants of the King of kings.

Seeing spiritually, thinking theologically—*feeling* a part of the kingdom is powerful. Every time I witness the development of spiritual awareness in an adolescent's life, I'm reminded of our privilege and responsibility of exposing students to the truth of God—not only by *what* we say but *how* we say it and through how they *experience* it.

The power of this experience cannot be explained simply by our choice of retreat location. It didn't happen because we had talented musicians and artists or gifted teachers and leaders or because we had a good theme. The force of this experience resulted from creative thinking, planning, sound teaching, and the collaboration of a team committed to truthfully and creatively representing God throughout the retreat.

As teachers, shepherds, and disciple makers, we carry the mantle of teaching God's truth in all that we do. We need to expose students to the truth about him, not only in our words but in the experiences we design for them. Our God is creative—he *is* the Creator—and he loves to reveal himself to us in creative ways.

He also created us as image bearers. We, then, are creative beings as well. That means none of us are one of those noncreative types. We all were designed in the creative image of the Creator. However, some of us have learned how to settle for noncreativity. We've learned to accept the standard and expected. Some of us even crave control and order at the cost of creativity. Others avoid risk taking for fear of rejection and have chosen the redundant, repetitive, or safe at the expense of adventure, exploration, and the unchartered.

Throughout the Bible we see displays of God's creative means to communicate who he is to his people—Noah and the rainbow, Moses and the burning bush, the complex design of the tabernacle, the sacrificial offerings and the sacred festivals. Sometimes God used a particular creative means only once, never to repeat that experience again. Yet God continued to communicate in creative ways through the prophets, using metaphor and pictures. Then Jesus arrived. And John 1:14 reminds us, "The Word became flesh and took up residence among us. We observed His glory, the glory as the One and Only Son from the Father, full of grace and truth."

God spared no expense to ensure that we had access to the full expression of his glory, part of which is his creativity. Jesus said, "The one who has seen Me has seen the Father" (John 14:9). God didn't just tell people the truth. He showed them in creative ways, even taking on flesh to do it.

Our Creative Model

Jesus' teaching was like no other. It amazed, perplexed, inspired, challenged, and changed people. Jesus stepped fully into the creative when he taught. Take his kingdom teaching in Matthew, for example. How many different pictures can we find that describe what the kingdom is like? Or look at the variety of places Jesus taught and the different ways he taught in these places. He drew word pictures using the fields that surrounded them, the birds above, the fish in the water by the fishermen's boats, the bread they had just eaten, and all kinds of common experiences. Think about the events around which Jesus communicated his truth—the woman caught in adultery, the rich young ruler, and the Last Supper. Jesus spoke out of the venue of common circumstances or he created new circumstances from which he spoke.

If we're going to follow him and take seriously his words—"As the Father has sent Me, I also send you" (John 20:21)—we must become students of God's creativity, especially as it has been expressed in Jesus Christ.

So let's get back to our roots, our creative roots. It's time to accurately reflect the creativity of our God through the creative expressions he wants us to explore. If we are going to take seriously the call to make disciples who are baptized in (immersed in, saturated throughout, and identified with) the Father, Son, and Holy Spirit, we must call them to follow and experience the creative God of whom we are disciples.

The Journey

One of the mental shifts I've made in my creative approach to youth ministry is from providing a delivery service to a travel service. A delivery-service approach sees the students as the recipients of a product or package (message, event, retreat) bound up in a neat package (script, outline, schedule) to be delivered at a particular address (place and time). The students as stationary observers passively receive the product. Whether the product is a message, an event, or a retreat, the students are seen primarily as receivers or consumers.

A careful observation of the whole of Scripture as well as several creative entities (Disney, Pepsi Co., Hollywood, the Internet) leads us to a very different approach of how we ought to express the image of God creatively in our ministries. God called his people to a journey with him, not just to watch or receive an event. Jesus called people to join him in the adventure of turning the world upside down, not just to view a presentation.

For example, Disney invites you to join an adventure and provides you with an experience. From the moment you arrive at Disney World to the time you leave, the journey grabs you. In a way, you even get to shape and interact with the adventure. The Disney company provides much more than a show. It takes you on a journey. Similarly, we need to take students on a spiritual adventure to direct them toward the point of entry to the journey, and to creatively craft opportunities and experiences so they may interact with and personalize them along the way. These experiences can take place through an event, retreat, or activity, but the point is not to just deliver a message, an event, or an activity. Our focus is to go on a spiritual journey together. And our role resembles more of a travel guide than a pure dispenser of information.

Knowing Your Traveler

In order to create spiritual journey experiences we have to pay close attention to the travelers. We must continually be aware of the factors that shaped their life journey so far. Where have they already been? How are their families shaping them? What affects has culture had in their journey so far? What kinds of dreams have they dreamed, or stopped believing in? What presuppositions do they bring to the journey? What information are they lacking in order to understand the nature of the journey? What would motivate them to get on board for the journey?

Another aspect of the traveler that we must keep in mind is the way God designed us, both in general and specifically. Generally, God made all of us sensing beings. He created us to understand and experience truth through our senses. We hear, see, smell, touch, and taste. When God revealed himself, he didn't just tell people about himself. He gave them visuals to see. He filled their ears with sounds and their noses with aromas. He called people to *taste* and *see* that he is good.

First John 1:1 tells us, "What was from the beginning, what we *have heard*, what we *have seen* with our eyes, what we have observed, and *have touched* with our hands, concerning the Word of life" (emphasis added). Jesus invites us to remember him by *hearing* his last words at his last meal with the disciples, *seeing* him touch the eyes of a blind man, *smelling* the aroma of food at a meal with tax collectors and sinners, *touching* the hand of a young girl healed of her diseases, and satisfying our spiritual hunger by *tasting* the bread and drinking the wine.

My creative team (made up of adults and students) recently designed a multisensory journey inviting students to experience and engage in new forms of worship. I asked them to create several opportunities for students to worship through additional formats to singing. Before we began our brainstorming, I wrote each of the senses on a different color card and encouraged them to think in terms of senses as we created a journey together. As we thought through each sense, creative ideas took form. We wrote them on the cards associated with the senses. Our desire was to design a journey that allowed students to experience worshipping God through all the senses.

I was very encouraged with the outcome. In our plan, students could go to the offering station and write down what activity, resource, or relationship God was leading them to offer to him as an act of worship. They could visit the light station and acknowledge God as their guide through seeking his counsel in a particular area of their life and lighting a candle to represent their faith that he would give them guidance. The creation station challenged them to read through examples of praise in the Psalms and to write their own psalm to God or design a piece of art that reflected their personal psalm to him.

In the Communion station, students could worship God through remembering what Jesus had done for them on the cross by breaking bread and dipping it into a large cup of grape juice. At the prayer station students could receive prayer, pray alone, or pray for someone else who needed prayer. And for those new to this, there was a question station, for those who needed more information to take the worship journey.

The room was full of sights, sounds, tastes, aromas, and textures. The students journeyed to a significant place of depth and sincerity in their worship that night. And I remembered again why creatively crafting a spiritual journey is well worth the time and effort.

God designed each of us to be multisensory beings. We learn best when our whole being is exposed and engaged in truth. Because our purpose for learning is never just to be better informed but, rather, to be fully transformed, we must engage students in fully transforming experiences that involve the whole person and not only the head.

The Traveler's Style

In God's creativity, he also designed us in specifically unique ways. Each one has a unique personality and temperament that lends itself to different learning styles. If we're going to expect that the majority of our students get on board for each journey we provide, we have to open the doors wide enough to each learning style. There are four different learning styles that we should take into consideration for the journeys.[1]

Thinking: Just Give Me the Facts

Thinkers are interested in information, details, and accuracy. Their motto could be "Just give me the facts." They enjoy reading, researching, and memorizing. This type of student listens to lectures and takes careful notes to make sure nothing is missed. When designing a journey for *thinkers,* remember they enter into the journey best if they're given carefully prepared and relevant information that challenges their minds and spurs them on to think and study more. Creativity disconnected from well-constructed truth will fail to engage the thinker. They'll find it difficult to get on board if you don't speak to their minds. For this student, our preparation in study and research helps them enter the journey.

On our worship night, I taught about what true worship is before we walked through the worship stations. I spent some time in Job 1, letting the message of Job instruct us about the heart of worship. I also explained how God reprimanded Israel for worshipping through the activity of sacrifice even though their hearts were far from him. Then, I brought them to the place in John 4 when Jesus instructed the Samaritan woman that the Father seeks worshippers who worship in spirit and in truth. I gave my *thinkers* what they needed to take the journey with the rest of the group and to help them mentally prepare for the worship stations.

Intuitive: Connecting the Dots

Some students have a strong intuitive sense. They tend to anticipate what we're going to say or do before we do it. They get bored if we continue to give them all the facts, leaving no room for personal discovery. This type of learner often puts a book down before they've finished it because they've already drawn their own conclusion partway through. They do the same thing when we approach events like delivery sessions instead of journeys that they're invited to shape. Their motto is "Let *me* connect some of the dots."

These students go from apathy to full ownership of the journey when they have the space to draw their own conclusions. That's what they need—space, freedom, and an invitation to make their own sense of the pieces. If we take a close look at Jesus' style of bringing people to truth, we see that he often withheld answers in order to draw people in. At other times he told parables without giving a translation. His desire seemed to be to get people to think for themselves. I know my tendency, if I'm not careful, is to answer all the questions, fill in all the blanks, and leave no stone unturned in the minds of students. But this only sends our intuitive types away to find another journey they have some part in shaping. So I have to leave room for them to connect the dots.

A question-and-answer time can be helpful as long as you're the questioner and students get to provide the answers. Keep in mind, we need to ask open-ended questions (questions with answers other than yes or no or predetermined answers) and ask questions based on their answers. This allows them to start shaping the direction of the journey.

Other catalysts like video, drama, song, poetry, or game can help open the door for intuitive students as well. They connect the dots best when these elements precede clarification and explanation instead of succeeding instruction by way of illustration or application. Recently, we taught about the value of inclusivity in our youth ministry versus exclusivity (cliques that have no room for new people to join). We played a game of ultimate Frisbee at the beginning where we seeded the teams with pickers (those who picked only the fastest, strongest, most likely to dominate). We restacked the teams several times using this approach. All the intuitive types started drawing their own conclusions once we started talking about including others in the body. They felt honored by the opportunity to discover and think for themselves.

Sometimes, props set up as visuals create an opportunity for discovery. One week I taught on listening to God and I had a phone off the hook, an answering machine, and a cell phone all sitting on separate stools in the front as students walked in. *Intuitive* students drew their own conclusions about listening to God from those images.

Feeling: How Does This Affect Me?

Students who are *feelers* are motivated to take the journey because they feel connected to someone else taking the journey (making the journey *our* journey). They value the community of travelers, anticipating how growth can make a group of people better. Feelers often have more tolerance for poor preparation or loose planning once they feel connected to those inviting them on the journey. That's why many in youth ministry continue to see students stay with them regardless of their creative effort. Once the feelers sense the connection, they're in. However, no youth worker can continue to be the relational hub for every student. If we're going to invite more students who are feelers into the journey, we must not only recruit and develop more people to be connection points on our team, but we also need to provide creative opportunities for connection points to be made during our journeys.

Feelers join in the journey when we use life stories to illustrate spiritual truths. They especially connect to real-life stories from their peers. They also connect when the whole group joins together in physical, emotional, and spiritual activities. At one of our student gatherings, we were exposing students to the idea that God loves to redeem the past and lead us into new futures. To connect with feelers, we had an open-microphone time when students could share how God had or was presently redeeming their past. At one point, Jacilyn came forward and began to share her very painful story that God was turning around for good. She shared through tears, and many of our feelers shed tears as well (I was one of those feelers). At the end of her story, I asked if some students were willing to pray for Jacilyn. Immediately, all the students rushed forward, surrounded her, laid hands on her, and began praying. Afterward, we joined in a circle, held hands, and thanked God for his work in Jacilyn and in our group that night. All the feelers were on board for that journey and would have stayed all night if we didn't shut down the place.

Doing: How Do I Practice This in My World?

Some students won't understand the purpose of a journey unless you give them practical ways to take the journey into everyday life. They're the doers, and they want to know how they can experience a particular truth in their world. They may seem more pragmatic to us, but they just want to live out truth in real ways. They understand James when he said, "But be doers of the word and not hearers only" (James 1:22). They may take a few journeys when we don't give practical application, but they have a low tolerance for truth that seems to have no place in everyday life.

Doers need to hear or see examples of how this has been lived out. They need to be given opportunities to experience the truth we're examining. And they need to be given additional steps to take when they leave. In just a couple of days, we're going to challenge students to become world-class Christ followers. We want to call them to care for the globe and not just our little part of the world in Seattle. So we're going to provide computers with Internet connections opened to mission organizations in other parts of the world. We will give them cards on which they can commit to pray for and research another country. Then we'll ask them to help us create a world ministry board over the next couple of months. They will develop this board through prayer and research.

We anticipate that our doers will want to stay on the journey of world missions because they didn't only hear about it; they did something about it.

A Travel Plan for a Great Journey

Creating life-changing journeys for students requires a diligent attention to the travel plan. Certainly, we need a theology and philosophy that motivates us to put forth the effort to enter into the creative realm. We also need to understand the traveler well and design journeys that appeal to their senses and learning styles. But a few other elements are necessary to create an inviting journey.

Time

I have seen ministers with amazing talents design journeys that captivate students, inspire them to live compelling lives, and stamp eternal memories on their souls. I've seen these same ministers design journeys that paint a picture of a mundane and boring God. In most cases, the difference was time.

We must invest time in preparation and planning if we're going to think creatively and develop and execute creative ideas. If we think we can most effectively design creative journeys the night before an event, we're fooling ourselves. Think about songwriters who took a year to pen a song. A recent cinematic blockbuster was in creative development for ten years before coming to the screen. Creativity takes time.

I've found that time gives me more creativity and gives me more freedom to improvise on the spot because my mind is freed for creativity during an event. Spontaneous creativity happens only when we have well prepared ahead of time. That's why I generally aim for a two- to three-week creative window for an event that occurs weekly and two- to three-month window for a weekend or week-long event.

Also, time is necessary for creative expression within the journey itself. Too often we pack our schedules so full that we leave little or no room for the activity of the Holy Spirit and the inspired, creative responses he breathes into us. I'm convinced that we need to leave more time and space in our journeys to allow for his inspiration and our creative expression as we respond to what he's doing in our midst.

Team

I did youth ministry in isolation for quite some time in my early years. I don't mean I didn't have adult and student volunteers that I shared ministry responsibilities with. I just kept most of the creative stuff to myself. And my ministry was limited in both its diversity and quality. Eventually I embraced the idea that if I wanted creativity and diversity in our expression and experience of truth, I would need creativity and diversity in the development process. That's when I began to develop a creative team.

I now refuse to expect that diversity and creativity will take place in our ministry unless I have a team. And each team I assemble to create spiritual journeys is made up of a diversity of age, experience, talent, and perspective. I've also learned that creative teams need to be allowed to shape the journey together, and they need freedom to take the journey together before they shape it for others.

This process may look different for each group. But it should include these elements:

- spiritual preparation through prayer and mutual discussion and study of a passage
- creative brainstorming based on spiritual preparation
- identifying the best ideas that should be considered for this journey
- shaping the experience
- ownership to identify responsibility for idea completion

Talent

God has given a variety of gifts and talents to his body, the church. This, too, is an expression of his creativity. The creativity of each journey we design is connected to our faithfulness in employing the gifts and talents he's given to us. In other words, there is a parallel between creativity and gift-based, talent employed ministries.

I was privileged to grow in my understanding of this dynamic while I was involved as the director of Student Impact, Willow Creek's high school ministry. We created opportunities for a variety of expressions of the spiritual gifts and talents in each of our journeys. We had roles for those who excelled in the visual arts (video, photography, painting, graphic design, lighting, staging), dramatic arts, and musical arts (voice, instrumental, songwriting, dance choreography). We had opportunities for those more technically inclined (computers, sound, operating video cameras, grips). There were roles for those who had administration and leadership gifts to ensure that our creative energies would come together in a realized journey, not only a dream. Also, those with administrative gifts who loved behind-the-scenes work made sure the details were in place. Without this talent pool, many of the journeys we experienced together would have never been fully realized.

Now, many stop at this point and say, "Yeah, but how do you expect me to be creative when I don't have the talent you just described?" My answer to that question is simple. You will never see that kind of talent join you in your work if you don't value it, build it into your ministry framework, recruit it, and give freedom for the creative expression of the image of God within your ministry. In many cases, this kind of talent chooses to go outside the church to express the image of God in creative ways because the church has failed to value creative expression. If you value expressing the full image of God, including his creative image, God will provide you with talent. Then be faithful with the talents he brings your way (Matt. 25).

So let's do everything in our power—our creative power—that God has instilled within us to bear carefully and fully his image in all we do. Our students need to see us model creativity in the way we teach, through the gatherings we design and throughout the experiences and journeys we invite them to join. We must also encourage them to express their God-given creativity. If we're going to be serious about making disciples who bear Christ's image, we will call them to the creative image of Christ while we call them to bear his truth, love, and grace.

The young people of this world are dying to know the Author and Designer of the creative works they see all around them every day. We can shape this generation to recognize that what they see and experience is the expression of God's handiwork. And we can help them see their role in following God to become a creative artist.

Notes

1. For further reading see Cynthia Tobias, *The Way They Learn* (Colorado Springs, Colo.: Focus on the Family, 1994) and Marlene LeFever, *Learning Styles: Reaching Everyone God Gave You to Teach* (Colorado Springs, Colo.: Cook, 1995).

15.

Good Group Dynamics

STEVEN PATTY

I WAS SO FRUSTRATED. Discouragement clung to my heart like the oppressively hot, muggy air of a late August day in the Midwest heartland. I could not escape a deep and pervasive disappointment with my youth group.

Working with this group of American military kids out of the basement of a chapel in Ramstein, Germany, was actually my second job as a youth pastor. I was right out of college, but I had taken a year off between my junior and senior years to start a youth group for a small chapel in another military community.

That first ministry experience was unbelievably fun. Students were excited. They loved the Lord and one another with abandon. They would rip off the doors of our youth room with their raucous singing. If I planned an event—even obviously ill-conceived and clumsily managed from such a rookie—students joined in enthusiastically. My teaching fell on receptive hearts. They certainly had ears to hear and courage to apply my lessons to their lives. And my teaching, looking back now, left much to be desired. Yet, kids fell in love with the Lord in ways and numbers unimaginable.

In contrast to that first experience, I couldn't figure out why my new group was so difficult. I had a little more experience by this time. I was a better planner, a more accomplished worship leader, and a more effective teacher. But no one wanted to dive in, very few desired to sing, and my teaching seemed to skip off the tops of their heads like a flat stone spun onto a placid lake. I was so frustrated!

I had to get to the bottom of this. But it didn't make sense. I was the same leader, if not slightly more skilled by this time. The conditions were about the same—students are students and military communities are military communities. The teaching of Scripture, the songs, and the events were all better. So what could be keeping this ministry from taking off?

I could think of only two variables: the blessing of God and the unique atmosphere of this group.

I knew what to do about the blessing of God. I needed to search my life and make sure that all was well with the Lord. Then I needed to start praying that God would pour out his blessing on this ministry and establish his work among the youth of Ramstein. And so I did. And the other staff and even some of the parents began to do the same.

Also, I needed to attend to the climate of the group. I had no idea what to do at first. It felt cold and hard and impenetrable. It wasn't chaotic or uncontrollable—I was able to keep unruly kids to a minimum. The group just had no center, no direction, and no shared sense of anything. Even though the group at this time was small, it felt big—as if no one knew each other.

In looking back, I think it felt like a dinner party among insecure acquaintances or a network meeting among disinterested professionals—those meetings in which people go through the motions of talking, nodding, and listening but look suspiciously absent. These students seemed to be only in loose association and have even looser commitment. They related to one another and to me and to the Lord but only on the surface. As a group, they had no heart.

Group Dynamics Are a Living Thing

So much of ministry looks like life. It's no wonder that Jesus used many living illustrations when he talked about God's kingdom. He has truly given us life—spiritual as well as biological (1 John 5:11–12). And it is not only our spiritual nature that looks like life. Life is also the functioning piece of our togetherness as the body of Christ. The expression of a group that meets together in the name of Jesus is also a living thing.

The nature of living things is different from nonliving things. For instance, you can shape an inanimate object quickly by bending, forcing, or pushing. In contrast, true shaping for a living thing must be done delicately and over time, through careful efforts of coaxing. It can't be forced. Furthermore, most inanimate things—like machines or engines—basically run alike regardless of the mood or any other peculiarity of the operator. If you have the right pieces connected in the right order, no matter what the conditions of the day, machines run dependably. The animation of living things, however, is quite unpredictable at times. Sometimes you have no idea why people act as they do or feel as they seem to feel. Inanimate things, once put into place, stay basically where you've set them. Living things have a tendency to move, wander, change, and slip away.

The dynamics of a group are more living than not. There is no foolproof method for developing a good group atmosphere. Forcing or pushing rarely helps. Also, conditions outside your control can greatly impact and erode a carefully laid foundation. Group climate constantly changes, like those early spring days in Oregon when the only thing consistent about the weather is the inconsistency. But some practices create the environment for growing a good group sense. You just can't think mechanistically about it. Developing good "groupness" is an art.

Understanding group climate is challenging. Sometimes you have a collection of really great kids who meet together, but you just can't seem to develop some group momentum—the kind that pulls individuals into a strong relational core and draws them into the purposes of the group. Sometimes you have a group humming along nicely, showing great energy and authenticity, and so you relax and tend to other responsibilities only to find that the group atmosphere erodes with frustrating speed. And other times, for no apparent reason and from no intention of your own, a group will come together magically and you find yourself leading a tight-knit family.

The life of the group atmosphere can be confounding. But the living nature of a group can be a wonderful thing too. When living things are robust and healthy, they flex and adjust to new variables easily, they overcome obstacles and gain strength from the challenge instead of losing energy, and they grow and develop in even the most hostile environments. A group that's functioning well is a powerful context for the ministry of the gospel of Jesus.

So what can you do to gain this art of developing good group dynamics? What methods can you employ to nurture the kind of group you feel will enhance learning and be honoring to the Lord's idea of the family of God? Before we tackle those questions, we need to try to understand the dynamics of a group's personality.

The Personality of a Youth Group

Three elements make up the personality of a youth group. Each of these elements is dynamic, not static. They're always flexing and changing—either for good or ill. These elements can't just sit, so they are always either growing or degenerating, gaining momentum or losing it. And then, to complicate matters, they interact with one another. Each set of interactions produces its own unique personality.

Like the personalities of people, each group displays an atmosphere, a "feel" that's unique. There are as many group personalities as there are youth groups. Certainly, a number of different kinds of group personalities can be healthy. But some dynamics cause groups to feel unhealthy. And some personalities are less conducive to the kinds of youth groups you and I dream of leading.

Let's look at features of group personality:[1]

Element 1—Connection

What is a youth group without good relationships? It's difficult to over-estimate the importance of interpersonal connection. Relationships characterized by generous love among students and among students and leaders give a group vitality, warmth, and energy. When individuals experience deep love from those in a group, they open up and receive so much better the gospel of Christ. The gospel is about love, and the hallmark of a group of true believers is the expression of love for one another (John 13:35).

Element 2—Purpose

Groups of people oriented around a shared sense of purpose exhibit all kinds of wonderful characteristics: vitality, momentum, engagement, direction, stability. With purpose, even a disparate arrangement of individuals coheres. Without purpose, even an impressive array of individuals can easily and quickly fall apart. Purpose gives a youth group movement. And groups are like bicycles; they are amazingly stable if they're moving and amazingly unstable if not. A bicycle that's not moving is difficult to balance. So is a group. A group needs to have some sense of *why* they are meeting and *where* they are going. This is purpose.

Element 3—Safety

Safety is an index of variables like predictability, familiarity, and security. When kids can predict what will happen in a group, when they have an understanding of what's expected of them, when they can anticipate what will happen when one disregards the group's norms and can foresee accurately how they'll be treated, they feel safe. When kids are familiar with the practices of a group, when they feel at home with the people, the leadership, even the room, and when they're familiar with the leader's or group's expectations of them, they feel safe. When kids are secure, secure from the threats of exposure, embarrassment, or any kind of emotional or physical assault, and when they know that someone trusted is in charge and able to take control when needed, they feel safe. Most students will not relax and truly engage with their hearts when they feel unsafe in a group.

The combination and interaction of these three elements provide a group with its personality. For example, a high degree of connection and safety with a lower degree of purpose will give a group a warm, inviting but slightly stagnant and ingrown feel. Over time, this group begins to feel like a bad therapy group. It may feel healthy and genuine, respectful and nurturing, but over time tends to be "boring" to the participants.

A high degree of purpose and safety to the exclusion of connection will

Stagnant Group

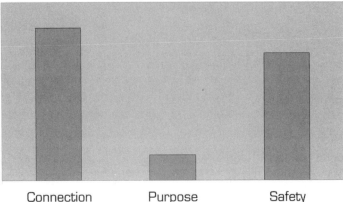

Connection   Purpose   Safety

give a group a missional feel. It will tend to feel choleric and driven. Kids who need only to be loved and to belong and to feel a sense of rest in their hearts will experience discomfort. They will know the systems but will tend to feel disconnected. Groups like this tend to feel pushy, preachy, and slightly coercive.

Driven Group

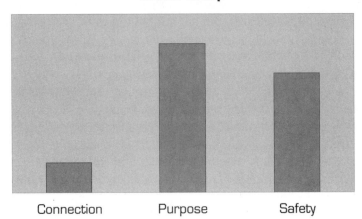

Connection   Purpose   Safety

A group with a high connection and purpose but low safety will exhibit an underlying reluctance among students. Those with tough skins will be fine—they'll tend to show off, in fact. But the rest of the participants who are slightly less brave will hold back. The more outspoken, brash, gregarious, and aggressive will dominate, but they are usually the minority. The others will withdraw into the safety of smaller groups of close friends.

A dangerously low degree of any of these three elements will sabotage a group's feel. Miss one and you'll have your hands full. You can give the world's

Reluctant Group

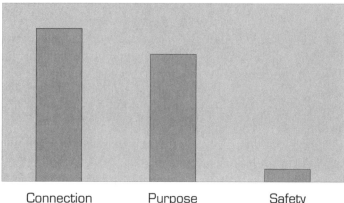

Connection   Purpose   Safety

best talks, write the most insightful devotionals, or even develop the most inspired worship band, but without connection, purpose, and safety your group will languish. Pockets of students may respond well, and a few individuals will connect with either you or the material. But a wholesale welling-up of excitement, support, and unity around the group's work will elude you.

The dynamics of a group's personality need to interact in balance. An overemphasis on one element can also lead to difficulty. Overzealousness in one element is probably not as immediately dangerous as an element's absence. However, consider what happens when a leader takes safety to the extreme, for example. One could so lock down a group, make it so predictable, familiar, and secure, that all spontaneity is squeezed out. Group traditions are important for students to feel secure, but sometimes you have to break out and do something novel. Sometimes you need to let things go chaotic for a bit in order to be spontaneous and fun and to let kids be kids.

Safety is important but not too much. So it is with connection and purpose too. If you overemphasize relationships, students will believe implicitly that worship is all about them and their feelings of connection. Too much emphasis on the mission and students will begin to implicitly believe that what they do for God is all that matters.

Even though each group will have a different and distinct personality, the goal of a leader is to nurture these elements so each is robust, growing, and in balanced interaction with the other two.

Group Glue

Looking back now at that frustrating experience with the youth group in Ramstein, I think I understand now more about what was going on then. I remember trying to push the group to grow before we had healthy elements of connection, purpose, and safety in place. I remember expecting the group to respond as a group beyond its experience and strength as a group. My inattention to these factors caused mushiness. No wonder we couldn't get the group moving.

A group needs to congeal before it's taken anywhere. Have you ever tried to push a group before it's ready? It's like trying to use a fork on jello before it has congealed. It's like an eager child playing with a model before the glue has taken hold. Trying to move a group without the glue of a group's coherence can actually set you back. It burns through your account of goodwill and, more often than not, places you in an adversarial role with the students.

But once a group develops connection, purpose, and safety, a kind of glue sets. And then you teach, and if a couple of students are moved, the whole group moves. And you challenge them to activity, and if a couple of kids capture the challenge, the whole group inches forward. And you love on the students, and if a few of them receive your love, their experience affects the entire group.

Group glue multiplies your efforts and places them in a ripe context of receptivity. Without it, even the best expression of youth ministry skills is thwarted.

Common Dissolvers of Group Glue

Many variables can dissolve group glue. Just as your biological body has to continually fight bacteria and viruses, so also the life of a group must resist a barrage of harmful elements. The problem is not just with outside variables. Well-meaning but unwary youth ministers can also undermine a group's atmosphere. Take these for instance:

- Poor meeting room (too large, poor lighting, too bright, poor acoustics, etc.)
- Not enough infrastructure for large numbers (too many students for the support staff can crush the feel of a ministry)
- Too much structure for low numbers (a youth meeting during a vacation period that takes many of your students out)
- A troublemaker left unchallenged (or a group of troublemakers who sabotage your best intentions)
- Lack of forgiveness and broken relationships left unmended
- Exclusive relationships (in dating or friendships)
- A spectator attitude among key students (just watching from the side, instead of participating)
- Leaders who don't like the students (a staff member who is annoyed or feels bothered)
- Pushing a group in a direction before it has jelled (asking for things too risky before students are ready)

- Lack of challenge
- Misplaced expectations by students or staff

The list could go on. Many reasons for a good group atmosphere to go bad are uncontrollable and unpredictable. Others are avoidable and can be minimized with some forethought and planning. In any case, threats to a healthy group have to be faced. A youth leader can't afford to go on blithely while something is compromising the feel of a group.

It's like the advice you give to parents of unruly kids or to parents of kids who are sullen and withdrawn. You tell them that even if they don't fully understand what's going on and even though they may not feel fully competent to address the issues, they still need to get in there and do something. "Become a student of your son or daughter," you tell them, "and then try something. Keep watching them all the while so you can stay responsive." Similarly, to develop and maintain a healthy group climate, you will need to watch your group closely and then try something.

Here are four common dangers to the health of a group, and some thoughts about how to respond:

Change

After you've worked diligently to get your kids to change, it's difficult to think of change as a detriment to good group climate. But it can be. You know what adolescents go through when a beloved staff member changes churches or moves to a new ministry. Think about the difficulty you have trying to corral a group in late summer after a group of especially vibrant seniors graduates and heads off to college. Changing worship leaders, choosing a different location for winter camp, or dropping your traditional missions trip in favor of a different program all cause the insecurity of change.

In each of those cases, everyone—students and staff alike—experience loss. Even when it doesn't seem to be a big deal, this grief at the loss of something familiar and loved throws a group into uncertainty. People need to process, to redefine, to re-create, and to bond. If they don't, they will withdraw and a good group atmosphere will erode.

How do you handle change? Recognize it. Admit its effects. Be in touch with your own loss (because you will feel it too). Call other students to fill in the holes. Challenge the group to redefine itself and its purposes. Provide extra amounts of bonding activities (retreats, affirmation circles, group projects). Commemorate the past as the people of Israel did by piling up stones during the time of Joshua. Talk liberally about the future with a heart full of faith.

I remember one particularly difficult transition at a church where I served in Chicago. A special group of seniors graduated, and we couldn't have missed them more. The group had no chance of feeling the same without them. We loved them so much. And so we all gathered one night and told stories of all the wonderful things that God had done among us, laughing and crying as we reminisced and gave glory to God. We then reminded the students of God's continued faithfulness to his children. We then talked about the future, setting goals and casting vision, praying that God would bless us into the future. We changed our fall kickoff retreat to incorporate more group bonding activities and to cast vision more clearly. We called the next generation of our student leaders to carry the torches of leadership. Soon the group was feeling like its old exciting, robust self again.

Criticism and Negativity

Nothing eats away at the fabric of a group's disposition quite like the cancer of criticism and negativity. Typically, this poison flows from two sources: particularly pagan kids who don't know any better and particularly cynical church kids who do. In any case, the poison of critical spirits spreads much more rapidly than one would expect.

· Criticism and negativity has many faces—complaints about all kinds of uncontrollable things; insults of less athletic students during games or of the musically challenged during singing or the less attractive during hangout times; or sarcasm and slightly disrespectful humor. It can be a blatant frontal assault on the safety of the group that sidetracks the group's agenda, as when a student gets up and walks around in the middle of worship.

My youth group was once returning from a spring-break trip. Two of our most solid girls began to complain on the bus about the lateness of lunch. After serving the students for a week, the exhausted leaders were wounded by their words. We had to gently remind them of the privilege of being positive. We couldn't let their complaints go unaddressed. We've all seen the consequences of unchecked cynicism.

In effort to maintain good group glue and a healthy atmosphere, hold kids accountable for relating positively. Exercise leadership to create a positive environment, even if it feels a bit artificial and exterior. Correct those who will receive correction. If you're doing an activity together and it turns negative, stop the activity and graciously but firmly hold the standard. It's fine and appropriate to speak freely about your vision for the group to be characterized by love, affection, and support. Defining the group positively sets an important expectation and one that may be unfamiliar but eventually welcomed for some students.

Broken Relationships

Discordant relationships spell big trouble for the development of good atmosphere. This has been the complaint of youth pastors since the very early days of youth groups. One clique can't seem to get along with another. One age can't graciously welcome another. A dating couple breaks up, and the youth group takes sides with one faction hating another. Students take offense with other students and the group atmosphere spirals downward.

Broken relationships can easily surface between staff as well. Discord is a constant stress for ministry teams. Expectations, roles, communication, accountability, commitment levels, inequity in work loads, and other variables can drive wedges within staff relationships and stir stress between team members.

Remember that our theology about the human condition warns us of the propensity to develop interpersonal antagonism. We all tend to be proud, independent, and self-consumed. By nature, we're still a fallen people, even though we enjoy a gracious regeneration and a progressive sanctification. Just don't be surprised if your gang can't get along from time to time. This is normal.

So what do you do about broken relationships? Certainly, if left alone, dissension can ruin a group. That's why youth leaders need to pay attention. They need to have an ear to the ground, not to join in the gossip but to be aware of interpersonal trouble that could be brewing. They need to look for underlying issues that cause discord and then address those. And they need to have the courage to jump into the fray and work on relational difficulty until it's resolved. Sometimes it takes courageous confrontation. And sometimes it requires educating your group in how to handle conflict and deal with it productively along with gentle but persistent coaxing to get people to talk, apologize, forgive, and reconcile.

Compromised Trust

Any breach of trust undermines the effort to create good atmosphere. Unfulfilled promises eat at the foundation of trust and safety. Inconsistent behavior from the leaders keeps students' hearts in a self-protected mode. Impure motives and interests or any other conflict of intention within the leader-student relationship destroys all three of the key elements of a group's atmosphere.

Trust can easily be broken. Misrepresenting yourself or someone else during a message can do it. Forgetting to call a student when you say you will can do it. Using students—their growth, dependence, affection, and so on—to make you feel better or fill some need within yourself can do it. The importance of personal integrity can't be overestimated.

The apostle Paul took great care to maintain propriety and integrity in his ministry behavior. Listen to these words:

> For our exhortation didn't come from error or impurity or an
> intent to deceive. Instead, just as we have been approved by God to
> be entrusted with the gospel, so we speak, not to please men, but

rather God, who examines our hearts. For we never used flattering speech, as you know, or had greedy motives—God is our witness—and we didn't seek glory from people, either from you or from others. (1 Thess. 2:3–6)

We, too, need to be careful, for the enemy would love to discredit the ministry.

How to Get Group Atmosphere Humming

Let's say that you've cared for the big issues that can destroy the group's vibrant feel. You've set a hedge around your ministry. Still, you wonder what you can do to help a group develop a good feel more quickly. You recognize that group atmosphere can't be forced or demanded. It has to be coaxed. You are working with the feelings of people, the source of intimacy, conviction, and passion. Feelings can't be legislated or bullied into place. They are nurtured.

Youth leaders have employed various practices in order to develop a healthy climate. Not all of these are appropriate for every setting. And for some settings, maybe none of these are. Still, they may start you thinking in the right categories and spur you to try what may benefit your group. Here are a few examples:

- Provide activities that force people to touch one another (appropriately, of course).
- Act as if there is group glue—your expectations have a way of affecting the climate and behavior of students.
- Teach about love within the body of Christ.
- Affirm students yourself and give them opportunity to practice affirmation of one another.
- Pass on positive comments you've overheard said of students by students (positive gossip goes a long way).
- Offer bonding activities and time together (trips, performances, fundraisers, adventures).
- Publicly remember common experiences together.
- Celebrate individuals by showing pictures and telling stories about people.
- Talk about the group as a "family" and "body."
- Pray aggressively and specifically that the group will bond together.
- Pay attention to things that affirm the value of people and relationships (cards, birthdays, care packages, encouraging notes).
- Regularly give students a vision for reaching out to one another, loving one another, and building friendships.

- Above all, worship together. Nothing brings together a group better than a corporate focus on God.

Group Dynamics in Perspective

Good group dynamics are a powerful force. Many youth leaders experience moments of intense joy when they're at the helm of a group of young people who deeply and passionately believe in the group, are committed to the group, and engage with their whole hearts in the group. A good group can make you heady. It can powerfully move your own heart. A good group can meet your own needs for belonging, appreciation, respect, adoration, and passion. It is probably not too strong to say that a good group can make a leader experience euphoria.

The allure (even sometimes addiction) of a vibrant group for a youth leader can sidetrack the ultimate efforts of youth ministry. Even though love between people is a strong theme within the Scriptures, it is not the whole counsel of the Word of God. Even though church doctrine and instructions on how the body of Christ should relate are powerfully presented in the Bible, a well-functioning group is not the ultimate point. And even though the mission and purposes of Christ are so compelling as to draw generations of followers into the vortex of his vision, the gospel of Jesus is about more than just the sharing of purpose by a group of people.

A good group climate should enhance the effort to develop a generation of worshippers of God, not worshippers of a group. We should not get pulled into an effort of developing a good group feel at the expense of causing adolescents to love the Lord with all their heart, soul, and mind. The group should aid in the strengthening of a student's convictions and the straightening of his or her trajectory of holiness. It should not elicit unhealthy dependence or misdirected worship or naive, cultlike attachments to mere mortals.

God alone is to be worshipped and not a youth group. The extent to which a healthy group feel serves the effort of making true disciples among young people is the extent to which we should attend to the group climate. So attend to the climate of your group, but don't lose sight of your disciple-making mandate in the process.

Notes

1. Steven R. Patty, *Affective Characteristics of Adolescent Church Ministry Contexts: Case Studies in the Development of the Youth Group Climate Index,* Ph.D. dissertation submitted to the faculty of Trinity Evangelical Divinity School (Deerfield, Ill., 1993).

16.

Connecting through Small Groups

JEFF VANDERSTELT

I REMEMBER FEELING STUCK at the forty mark for far too long. I had been in my first youth ministry for a little more than two years, and we just couldn't seem to get beyond forty students consistently. I tried doing events that appealed to nonchurched students. I encouraged students to invite their friends. I worked on my communication skills, sharpened our promotions, and improved program creativity. But nothing seemed to change. Sure, we observed numbers increases in brief spurts. Invariably, the group steadily slid back to the forty mark. I wasn't interested only in numbers. I understood that numbers represented lives, and I hoped to see more lives connected to Jesus and transformed into followers as devoted to Jesus as were his first disciples.

It was around this time that I met Bill Clem. He was leading a university ministry in Bellingham, Washington, where he'd built an effective small-group ministry. By multiplying small-group leaders he watched that ministry grow from four hundred students to sixteen hundred. I began to see through my times with him that almost every ministry's growth is limited by the relational capacity of its leadership. Jethro, Moses' father-in-law, observed this same truth in Exodus 18. He watched Moses' foolish attempts to care for everyone's needs alone. He instructed Moses to divide the people under leaders of tens, fifties, hundreds, and thousands. Jesus did the same with his followers. He had three disciples whom he spent more intimate time with, twelve whom he closely developed, then seventy, one hundred twenty, and the five hundred.

After observing students cycling in and out of our ministry, I realized that my relational capacity to connect and care for students reached its limit at about twenty-five. The other fifteen students came and went. Granted, I couldn't truly develop and disciple all twenty-five, but I was able to stay relationally connected to them enough to shepherd and care for them. So they stayed. At this point I began to see the importance of adding people who would share shepherding responsibilities of our student ministry. If we were going to see spiritual influence grow beyond my relational capacity, we had to recruit and develop shepherds who could oversee smaller segments of students. Our first small-group ministry had begun.

Spiritual Transformation

As I stepped into my second ministry, I noticed my predecessor was a highly creative and talented leader who developed strong programs for his high school ministry. Students met twice weekly in large gatherings, once for spiritual growth and once for evangelistic outreach. The programs had been well attended, and the ministry had the reputation for vitality and numerical growth.

However, as I began to get to know the students, I discovered that many who were part of the ministry team had learned to put up the façade of spirituality. They faithfully attended the programs, participated in activities, and often carried the responsibility for implementing program elements such as drama, music, and competitive events. Yet their lives beyond programmed activities carried very little likeness to a disciple's. I suspected they had learned to equate spiritual maturity with activity—especially visible activity—within large group events.

What these students needed was a safe, spiritual community in which the façade of their performance could be set aside and the real self could emerge and interact with truth.

So we replaced one of the large programs with a night set aside for small groups. We wanted to create a consistent place where authentic community was fostered and spiritual transformation experienced. There is a vast difference between being spiritually informed and spiritually transformed. One of the keys to that difference is the context of loving and honest relationships through which truth can work. This may be one of the most significant differences between ministries that develop students with the façade of following Christ and those that develop true, authentic followers of Christ. It's possible to look spiritually impressive at a distance yet remain empty in one's heart. But it's impossible to fake authentic community.

Ministry Mobilization

When we started small groups, we had no one trained to lead them, so my wife and I took the first groups. She led the girls and I led the boys. We soon identified some students as apprentices and began developing them to lead a small group in the future. For six months we shared increasing responsibility with our apprentices. Occasionally, we offered formal training meetings to equip these students in small-group leadership skills. After six months of training and experience, we invited these students as well as some adults who were catching the vision for small groups to attend a weekend retreat on preparing to lead a small group the following year. That fall we started the year with six student-led and six adult-led small groups.

Each of these small-group leaders had an apprentice they set out to develop, just as we had. The next fall we started the year with thirty small-group leaders in place—sixteen students and fourteen adults. And because of what I had learned about relational capacity and the need to multiply shepherds, we began implementing a coaching structure as well. We identified and appointed an adult coach for every two to three student small-group leaders to ensure that each student continued to get the accountability, support, and development they needed as they led their small group.

Like Moses, we multiplied our ministry's relational capacity by dividing our ministry into segments that could be shepherded. We created environments in which true spiritual transformation started to take place. We developed and mobilized more students and adults into relational ministry. And we created an expectation in our ministry that students would be engaged in authentic, transformational community, using their spiritual gifts in ministry to their peers.

The disciples pursued an intimate, authentic, small group as they led the first church:

> And they devoted themselves to the apostles' teaching, to fellowship, to the breaking of bread, and to prayers. Then fear came over everyone, and many wonders and signs were being performed through the apostles. Now all the believers were together and had everything in common. So they sold their possessions and property and distributed the proceeds to all, as anyone had a need. And every day they devoted themselves [to meeting] together in the temple complex, and broke bread from house to house. They ate their food with gladness and simplicity of heart, praising God and having favor with all the people. And every day the Lord added to them those who were being saved. (Acts 2:42–47)

We would be wise to follow their example in our own ministries as we seek to multiply a ministry through spiritual transformation and ministry mobilization.

An Environment for Transformation and Mobilization

Observing how Jesus' development of his disciples was reproduced in the early church, we see an environment with four transformational dimensions: vertical, circular, internal, and outward.

Vertical

Jesus lived upwardly dependent. He said, "I assure you: The Son is not able to do anything on His own, but only what He sees the Father doing. For whatever the Father does, the Son also does these things in the same way" (John 5:19). When Jesus taught his disciples to pray, he started with "Our Father . . . ." Then, he instructed them to hallow or set apart and make holy his name. After that, he called them to pray "Your kingdom come. Your will be done on earth as it is in heaven."

He continuously modeled a life of adoration and submission to the Father's heart. When he spoke to the Samaritan woman, he instructed her that the Father is seeking worship in spirit and in truth. When the disciples were unable to cast out a demon, Jesus stated that dependent prayer was the key—not creative methods. He spent an entire night in prayer before appointing the twelve. He shared a meal of remembrance and worship with the twelve, what we now call the Lord's Supper, and he called the disciples to pray with him in the garden before he went to the cross.

This vertical dimension of our environment must seep through all we do together. And if we're going to see students mobilized for ministry through our small groups, we first need to ground them in the priority of spiritual dependency on God through adoration of and submission to him.

As I lead small groups, I'm mindful of the vertical dimension of our environment. I regularly direct us to pray when we bring up a need. I lead our groups to express worship in a variety of ways. Sometimes we do it through singing. Other times we praise God using his names or attributes. I invite students to write out prayers to God and read them out loud. We create worship art together. Sometimes we put a chair in the middle of the group and one by one have a student sit there as we exercise our dependency on God by praying for the student. This vertical aspect can take many different forms, but it must be a regular part of the worship environment.

Circular

Jesus shared his heart with his followers. They saw him weep, rejoice, suffer rejection, experience betrayal, and wrestle with facing the cross. He created environments safe for others to be known and accepted, regardless of their failures or pasts. He modeled for the disciples a heart of serving by washing their feet and then calling them to do the same for one another. The environment he created with the disciples was a circular flow of caring and sharing that intersected the hearts of those in the circle of his influence.

The early church reflected this circular flow of authentic community. Look at the descriptions of the kind of relationships they shared together: "And they devoted themselves . . . to fellowship . . . all the believers were together and had everything in common. So they sold their possessions and property and distributed the proceeds to all, as anyone had a need. And every day they devoted themselves [to meeting] together." Later, Paul told the Thessalonians, "We cared so much for you that we were pleased to share with you not only the gospel of God but also our own lives, because you had become dear to us" (1 Thess. 2:8).

The church God imaged is not one of distance and disconnection. Our small groups must have this circular flow of authentic community so we share our hearts and lives with one another if we expect to become the kind of people God dreams for us to become.

This kind of community doesn't just happen. It's the result of intentional leadership that begins by modeling appropriate transparency and authenticity. Each small-group leader must lead by example. Students won't feel free and safe to share their personal stories, struggles, and doubts if the leader hasn't honestly shared his heart first. If we wear a face of perfection, we'll lead students in our groups toward hypocrisy and deceit instead of authenticity, repentance, and dependency on God. We must not only model these qualities but also create opportunities for students to share their hearts with one another and serve one another.

Internal

Jesus didn't waste much time with the external part of a person. He went straight to the heart. He said adultery, murder, hatred, and lust weren't just outside behaviors but were rooted in the heart of people (Matt. 5). He taught that out of the overflow of the heart the mouth speaks (Matt. 12:34; Luke 6:45). And he reminded his hearers that the greatest commandment was to "Love the Lord your God with all your heart, with all your soul, and with all your mind" (Matt. 22:37).

He did the same with his smaller group of disciples. He pushed Peter to identify who he believed Jesus was. He challenged the brothers' request to be seated at his right and left in the kingdom. He taught Martha the value of time with the Savior when the tendency is to be just busy for him. He was always paying attention to their hearts. The writer of Hebrews picked up this theme, saying that transformation happens as a result of God's Word dwelling in the internal parts of our being (Heb. 4:12).

Small groups should not become another Bible study with a curriculum or a guide that we need to get through externally. We need to do more than download information to students. Too often I've observed small-group leaders look at their small group as a classroom. They identify with the teacher, and the students are the observers and receivers. In these situations, students may learn truth. They might even walk away with more knowledge. However, it's rare that the information alone translates into transformational living. Transformation needs truth. But transformation is the result of truth meeting real life in the context of authentic relationships.

I encourage students to read the Bible on their own during the week (if they don't know how to, we spend time in our group learning to do this together) and come together and share what God is saying to each of them. We share areas of our lives where we need God to intervene. We discuss what we see him doing in us and through us. Then we let the Word inform our response to each of these things. If someone needs instruction on how to deal with a relationship, we look together at passages on that topic. If someone is discouraged, we look to passages that offer encouragement and hope. Whatever we're experiencing in life or in our personal study shapes the interaction we have together. And most often, what we studied before we arrived to the group informs our interaction.

The challenge then for the leader is to be attentive to the Spirit's promptings, discerning enough to see the needs of the heart and prepared enough to know where to go in God's Word to address the need. The long-term challenge is to develop students well enough so that the leader is not the only one who carries this responsibility, but so the group is equipped enough to carry it together.

Outward

Jesus' life was the seed of a movement that transformed the world. He knew he was on mission from the Father and had been sent into the world. He also informed the disciples that just as he was sent from the Father they, too, were being sent. As Jesus' ministry impact increased, he shared more responsibility with his disciples to minister to the crowds. Before he went to the cross he sent the disciples out in pairs to share the good news. Then after his resurrection he commissioned them to make disciples of *all* nations (Matt. 28:18–20; Acts 1:8). As a result of this outward movement, the early church had "favor with all the people. And every day the Lord added to them those who were being saved" (Acts 2:47).

If our small groups are to reflect God's heart and his call of the church, we must build into them the outward flow of missional living. If we fail to mobilize students toward reaching a lost and hurting world, we will only compound the ineffectiveness and impotency of the church's influence for future generations. The church is not called to only send missionaries to other places. The true church is filled with missionaries who live missional lives everywhere the church exists. The only question for every follower of Christ is, "Where am I called to be missional?" not "Should I be a missionary?"

Mobilizing students in small groups outwardly as those who live missionally starts with teaching them about their calling: They are also "sent ones." There is no other kind of follower of Jesus. Next, we must help them understand that their mission field is in front of them—the community, school, and job. Then we need to talk about mission fields together in our groups and pray that God would open doors for the gospel to be seen and heard in our lives.

At some point, we need to help students understand how God has uniquely designed them to reach their world. This includes helping them identify their spiritual gifts, talents, passions, personality, and unique style of evangelism. Finally, we need to get out of our comfort zones and go together into our communities to build relationships, serve others, seek to understand our culture, and engage in conversation as the active listeners and learners.

Small-Group Life Cycle

Start-up

A small group doesn't easily become what I've just described. To begin an effective small-group ministry, you must recruit and develop qualified, gifted, and trained small-group leaders. I have seen too many ministries that began with ill-prepared or unqualified leaders and their small-group ministry flopped. Then, too often, the youth ministers falsely concluded that small groups with students don't work. They missed that in order to see effective ministry take place, they need effective ministers in place.

Qualifications

It's important to identify qualifications necessary for effective small-group leaders. Each of our ministries may have different qualifications, but I believe some qualifications are nonnegotiable. They need to be led by adults or students who are Christians not in word only but as observed by the fruit of their spiritual lives. They need to be able to call students to the kind of lifestyle they are already living out, which should resemble what we've just examined (upward, circular, internal, and outward). They need to know how to study the Bible and how to teach others to study it. They need to know church values and doctrine well and be able to articulate it to someone else. They should have a growing love for God and others and a commitment to living out the Great Commission.

Gifts

In terms of spiritual gifts, people with the gifts of leadership, shepherding, encouragement, teaching, wisdom, or discernment tend to do well in leading small groups. Whatever the particulars, each small-group leader will need to learn to use her gifts to facilitate discussion and interaction instead of taking over the group. For instance, a teacher may tend to spend time lecturing instead of facilitating a learning and caring community. A leader could easily make the group pursue a cause at the expense of community. And a shepherd may build a strong community but have no connection to a cause that keeps the community focused on something other than itself. Whichever of these gifts, the small-group leader will need to be careful not to let personal spiritual gifts set the direction of the group, but instead find a good balance of truth intersecting with community and cause.

Training

Finally, it's our responsibility to prepare small-group leaders through a variety of training venues. First, they should have experienced a well-led small group personally for some time before they lead one. You can't reproduce what you haven't experienced. Each new leader should first be an apprentice under a leader who can equip and share ministry with the apprentice leader. Each should also attend training sessions or a retreat to be immersed in your small-group values, trained in skills, and prepared for your ministry season.

<u>Ideas for Training Sessions</u>
- Small-group leader skills
- Environmental development (upward, circular, internal, and outward)
- Teaching inductive Bible study
- Small-group dynamics
- Active listening skills
- Facilitating discussions

- Leading different personality types (the talker, the wounded, the dominator, the debater)
- Knowing when to refer to counseling
- Building a safe community with a cause
- Sharing the gospel and training others to share
- Identifying and developing an apprentice
- Designing small group outreach opportunities
- Intentional shepherding (shaping the head and heart, redeeming one's history, etc.)
- Planning and preparing for small-group multiplication (splitting)
- Creating environments for spiritual transformation
- Time management
- Leading through the small-group life cycle

Show Up

Once you have qualified, gifted, and trained small-group leaders in place, they will need to get students to show up. The saying "Build it and they will come" tends to represent how most small-group leaders think the small group works. But this isn't the case. The leader needs to be very intentional about getting a group of students to commit to a regular meeting. The initiation of the small-group's life cycle must not be overlooked. At this point, the *upward* dimension of adoration and submission needs to be a priority as students pray for the beginning of their group's life together.

Small groups need promotion. Pathways into groups must be made clear. Students must be pursued through personal invitations. Reminders and follow-up calls need to be made to students weekly for the first month or two. After students make the small group a regular part of their week, a leader will be able to back off a little, but regular phone calls or personal contacts will still be necessary throughout a small group's life cycle.

During this time, it's important to talk together about a group covenant, a set of standards the group formulates and commits to uphold. (Consider including such elements as attendance commitment, preparation for meetings, listening while others share, praying outside the group, getting together outside the group.) A covenant assists in building a group image and in solidifying the sense of belonging to a community. Just as the first gathering of believers in Acts 2 had "everything in common," a covenant enables students to commit to a common set of convictions. After a covenant is written you should encourage each student to sign it as a commitment to the group's values.

Shed Skin

During the initial month, give students the opportunity to let one another see them for who they really are. Here, the circular dimension of your group should be emphasized. If you intend to lead a small group toward spiritual transformation, participants will need to go beyond the surface level to the heart. You can initially facilitate sharing through a variety of discussion starters and creative activities (for example, favorite something, most embarrassing moment, biggest fear, etc.).

At some point you need to encourage students to share their stories with one another. The leader should lead by example and share how God has been at work in his life to lead him to faith in Christ. He can share about his family, his faith, and the things he's still learning and struggling with. The leader will set the standard by how he shares, so it's very important for him to shed his skin first and to remove as many layers as possible and as appropriate. After the leader shares, invite students to ask questions. Then follow this same pattern with each student, encouraging the students to ask one another questions. This could take several weeks to complete if done well so don't rush this process.

The leader's goal during this phase is to (1) learn everything she can about the students' families, history, and spiritual health so she can intentionally shepherd them well, (2) create a place of safety and familiarity within the group, and (3) give students the opportunity to express their present spiritual status. Keep in mind that this exercise will set the tone of the group in terms of safety and openness to share in the future so work hard to protect the environment by not allowing any insults or negative talk. Each student should walk away from this sharing experience eager to share more as the group proceeds.

Shape Hearts

At some point in the groups' life, to encourage life transformation you need to move beyond getting to know one another to caring about one another. At this point the internal and upward dimensions need to be implemented. There is no set time line for when this should start, but don't wait too long to begin interacting with God's Word and moving them upward in their adoration of and submission to him. As you encourage students to study the Bible and share what God is teaching them and as you express together adoration and dependency on God, you'll be able to see how far along your students are.

The focus at this time in a group's life needs to keep going to the heart. The job of the small-group leader is to lead students toward spiritual transformation. And true spiritual transformation is not only behavior modification. It takes place in the heart. So a leader will need to be a spiritual heart surgeon. This work is supernatural and takes sensitivity to the Spirit and a huge dependency on God. The leader needs to pray for students and be attentive to cries of their hearts. The leader needs to (1) encourage students to read the Word of God regularly, seeking God's direction and guidance, (2) ask questions that get to the heart of the matter with students (don't just focus on behavior, but on the motives of the heart), (3) address needs and motives with Scripture, and (4) pray with and over students for the areas where they need God to transform them with truth and by his Spirit.

Share Lives

Finally, as a group interacts with God's Word—experiences authentic community, adoration, and spiritual transformation—it needs to be spurred on toward the outward dimension of the group's expression. The missional call of our students as sent ones needs to be made clear early on in gatherings. However, the expression of this may take some time as they need to be personally transformed in order to take the message and hope of transformation to someone else. If, on the other hand, we wait too long to experience missional living together, we can easily become inward focused and our group will gravitate toward selfishness, safety, and apathy. The identity of being sent ones needs to be in the group DNA. The sooner this language enters the vocabulary of the group the better.

It is the leader's job, as soon as the group is ready, to expose the small group to missional activities together. This can take place as a progression. Here are some suggestions:

- Do a group activity in the community or at school, then discuss observations of the culture together.
- Pray for the needs of that community.
- Meet a need in the community by service.
- Go together into the community and ask questions that lead to discovery of the spiritual heartbeat of the people.
- Pray for the real spiritual needs of people in the community.
- Return and engage in spiritual conversations with the hope of learning their stories and each student sharing his or her own story.
- If it hasn't happened yet, encourage each student to identify his or her own mission field and the individuals the student is loving, serving, listening to, and sharing with.
- See someone come to faith in Christ as a result of being missional and invite the person to join the small group. (You may find the person wants to join the group before expressing faith in Jesus.)

Envisioning Small Groups

Although I've described the life cycle in terms of a linear process, it is more cyclical than sequential. You will find that because of the nature of life and the fact that students will come and go in a small group you will have to go back and forth between the phases. Sometimes, because a new student joins the group, you need to return to shedding skin together. Other times, because of a significant event or situation, you may need to back off on sharing your lives with others and work on caring for hurting members of the group. And at times you have to do the start-up phase again because of a group split or only needing to take a break. The same is true for the environment of the group. A healthy small group that experiences spiritual transformation and ministry mobilization needs to have a balance of upward, circular, internal, and outward dimensions. At times, however, you will need to emphasize one over another.

Ultimately, there is no step-by-step, foolproof formula to creating a perfect small group. The leader of a small group needs to be a shepherd who knows the sheep, leads them toward spiritual transformation, and cares deeply for them as they grow toward greater dependency on Jesus Christ. If leaders do this, the small group will not only be a place where spiritual transformation takes place and students are mobilized to be missional, but they will multiply other shepherds to lead small flocks of students to experience authentic communities of spiritual transformation as well.

17.

Handling a Difficult Group

DAVE PATTY

IT WAS AN AWFUL RETREAT. A nightmare, but worse because I couldn't wake up and pretend it wasn't happening. I felt caught and unprepared, especially because the reality stood in such stark contrast to what I had prayed and planned for.

We needed a strong kickoff for the fall program, and an August getaway seemed like the perfect plan. I had found a rustic youth facility on an island, complete with a beach, dunes, and a quaint village nearby. The elders voted to subsidize the trip so we could offer it at a price that encouraged young people to invite their friends. This was youth ministry heaven! I could hardly contain my excitement at the opportunity to draw in non-Christians and begin to expose them to the claims of Christ.

My excitement must have been contagious because the registrations started rolling in. Somewhere along the way, we noticed a series of names no one recognized. After poking around, we realized that a linebacker on the football team had invited all his friends. Though not a believer himself, he had started attending our programs in the summer and managed to recruit his "gang" en masse for our event. My heart skipped a beat. What if God was opening the door to penetrate this rather rough crowd with the gospel? If some of them turned to Christ, it could have a huge impact on the entire school!

It wasn't until we got on the bus that I realized the full picture. Of the fifty students who had joined us, more than half were nonbelievers, and most of those were new. On top of that, they knew one another and had already built a strong culture among them.

The bus immediately segregated with the rowdy crew in the back and our core group of Christians in the front. Clearly our students felt threatened, and from the furtive glances, I guessed they secretly wished the "pagans" hadn't joined us.

These Christian kids have no idea what an opportunity this is, I thought as I made my way to the back and began trying to learn names. Though they seemed a bit distant, I did get a name out of each—let's see, Fatima, Tracy, Edward, Jodi. I had never met a guy named Jodi before. But from the look on his face, I guessed he had never met someone like me before either.

Despite the palpable tension, we arrived on the island without a mishap and began assigning students to their various rooms. "Evening program at seven o'clock!" I called out, as kids hauled their bags off the bus. Then I went to set up the room. At seven o'clock I cranked up the music and stepped up to the front for a rousing kickoff. Instead of the sea of faces I expected, my gaze was met with several clumps of our ministry team students—and a room full of empty chairs.

"They must not have watches," I muttered as I headed out for a sweep through the cabins. In the first room I saw Jodi and Fatima, engaged in conversation with a couple of girls I vaguely remembered from our bus introductions. "Hey, guys," I called enthusiastically, "it's time to start!" They looked up, nodded, and then turned back and continued their conversation as if nothing had happened. "Meeting's starting, guys," I said jovially. "You won't want to miss it!"

"Yeah, we heard you," one of them said coolly before reentering his conversation. They were treating me like a commercial break to their own program. I froze, not knowing what to do. *Maybe they just need a minute,* I thought. *Sure wouldn't want to lose them over a little thing like this.*

"OK, I'll go tell the others. See you there!" I said, my voice sounding a little plastic.

I swung through the other rooms and managed to round up at least part of the crew. We started the meeting without Jodi and his friends. Unfortunately, it was as if we started without anyone. The singing was a bomb. The new kids started snickering at the words, and the Christians withered under their pressure. Who wants to sing praise songs with the defensive line of the football team laughing at you?

Then I stood up to talk. That seemed to be the cue for everyone to catch up on the latest gossip. I felt I was speaking in the school lunchroom, trying to break through the background noise of three or four conversations between people who had no interest in listening to me. Every time I would ask them to quiet down, the most I got back was a polite nod and a momentary lull, which lasted only until I turned my head to look at the other side of the room.

At one point something in me broke. "I want it quiet right now!" I lashed out in anger. "You are all being rude and insensitive!" The church kids were taken aback. They hadn't seen that side of me. On the other hand, our guests seemed to be quite at home with yelling. Though there was a cautious silence for a couple of minutes, soon the volume started creeping up again. I tossed the rest of my talk.

"Refreshments are in the next room," I said. "Lights out at eleven."

You can imagine what happened at eleven o'clock. Our adult sponsors were happily in bed with the lights out. The rest still hadn't found their watches.

The next morning the charade continued, and the next afternoon and into the evening. We were in a constant tug-of-war. For me, this was a losing battle. Two retreats were going on, the one I was trying to lead according to my plans and preparations and the one that the football team decided to have in the same facility. The problem was I was responsible for both of them.

Soon it was clear that the second retreat was gaining momentum. Some of our weaker Christian students were being sucked up into the negative peer pressure that was beginning to dominate. Feeling overwhelmed, our ministry team began to disappear into the catacombs. Soon some of them began to skip meetings, on the pretense of needing to talk to someone or pray. The atmosphere was so unsafe they withdrew rather than engaging, leaving us leaders standing alone. On top of that, it started to rain, and all of our plans for the beach and the dunes were drowned in an unending downpour.

It was the retreat from the dark side.

I thought I was prepared because the games, music, and talks were all in line. I thought we had everything we needed because the facility, bus, and food were all arranged. But I had never prepared for the rebellious students and their agenda or for the disruption. My failure to stay in charge cost us the entire retreat—and a great deal of momentum as well.

I'm convinced that the skill of staying in the driver's seat is one of the unsung secrets of healthy youth ministries. A little leaven can ruin the whole lump, and a couple of bad apples can cause the entire bushel to rot. If we don't know how to control disruption and weed out problems without destroying the overall spirit, we'll continue to be held hostage by the immature. On the other hand, if we walk the halls with guns loaded, we may create resentment and distance and ultimately lose our influence. What do you do when you feel the youth group bus driving somewhere you don't want to go? Here are tips for staying in charge.

Expect Problems

I shouldn't have been surprised when our guests behaved like pagans—they were! But even the best kids from solid Christian families can be downright sinful at the most unexpected times. Here is where we can't forget the theology of man. Even at its best, the human heart is "deceitful and desperately wicked." As long as we work with sinful students, we will regularly find ourselves face-to-face with their sin. Rather than be shocked, we should expect it and prepare for it.

Of course, theology also tells us that every man, no matter how rotten, is made in the image of God and is infinitely valuable. And we know the power of redemption is miraculous and deep, able to transform the darkest situations into good. We must treat all students with incredible dignity and deep hope but at the same time count on the sinful nature that's still embedded in each one of us. That sinful nature is in you, too, by the way!

Practically, this means planning sessions need to not only build contingency plans for rain but also for the kid who sneaks a bottle of Jack Daniels in his bag and gets his whole cabin drunk, or the couple planning a rendezvous with more than just a quick kiss in mind. We need to keep our eyes open for the subagenda going on in the back of the room and the destructive conversation in full swing at the back of the bus. This isn't done with the suspicious posture of a vigilante but with the knowing gaze of someone who's been around the block and knows what a gutter looks like.

Deal with Problems Quietly and Quickly

The camp director paced sternly back and forth across the front of the room. "Now we have had some problems here in the past," he said gravely, "and we will *not* have them this year. Some of you hung underwear from the flagpole. That will *not* happen again. Others of you went swimming in the pool in the middle of the night. That is *not* acceptable. There were even guys raiding the girls' cabins. We *will not* have that as part of our program this year."

The students listened politely. But he didn't realize what was going on in their minds. "Hey, underwear on the flagpole, what a great idea! Wow, we've got to find out how to top that and not get caught!" What the camp director didn't know was that a number of campers were taking notes, and he had just helped them plan their free-time activities.

Others were just turned off. Why was this guy mad at them? They weren't at camp last year. Why were they getting punished for someone else's mistakes? Here they were at their first day of camp and already in trouble. Better stay away from this guy—he is liable to get mad at everything!

In the end the kids planning to behave withdrew and the ones looking for fun on the fringes emerged with a whole new set of ideas. Like the cat in the hat, the camp director's attempt to clean up the problems just spread them further.

Discipline was in order, but it should have been applied directly to those who failed to keep the rules, not to the rest who were not part of the problem. Not only that, but it should have been applied immediately, not twelve months later. A basic principle of discipline is to applaud publicly and reprimand privately. As much as possible, the resolution of problems should include only those who participated. That way, the disruption is dealt with quietly and doesn't have the opportunity to mark the entire environment.

Too many times we do the opposite: we applaud privately and reprimand publicly. Soon it seems as if there is nothing but problems, and the discipline process begins to mark the spirit and culture of the entire group. Those who are in the wrong bury themselves in the crowd and walk away unaffected, while those who aren't troublemakers end up feeling discouraged and guilty.

Here's a practical application: If you have to reprimand the entire group for not paying attention during the program, first take note of who is misbehaving. When the meeting ends, your first task is to find them and quietly and directly engage them in conversation about what went on. Tell them how you feel and what you expect in the future. Stand close to them and look them in the eye. Be direct and clear, but keep a loving, gracious tone. Let them know exactly what you want from them, and then make sure they know you're saying it because you care.

Generally, people are caught off guard by the fact that you came directly to them and did so immediately. A young person who's insolent and hard in a group often becomes pliable and responsive when it's just the two of you. And the information about the problem is not fuzzy and distant when you deal with it immediately. If the problem happened only minutes ago, it's much easier to get a clear read on the facts.

Discipline Communicates Love

Counselors suggest that every young person is asking two questions. The first, "Do you love me?" The second, "May I do what I want?" These questions are asked as a pair, and the answers must be "Yes, I love you," and "No, you may not do what you want." If the answers are yes and yes, a kid grows up with no sense of boundaries, no capacity for self-discipline, and often no sense of security because they feel they live in a fenceless world.

On the other hand, if the answers are "No, I don't love you," and "No, you may not do what you want," a young person struggles with a sense of identity, with self-acceptance, and often with deep anger from not being valued as a person. Of course, the worst situation is when the answers are "No, I don't love you," and "Yes, you may do what you want." You can imagine what a double dose of this kind of irresponsible parenting does for the soul of a young person.

Discipline shouldn't be applied just to keep your program under control. It's also one means to help students answer a basic life question—one with profound implications. The discipline process is for their good and is an expression of love. That's why the writer of Hebrews stated, "The Lord disciplines the one He loves, and punishes every son whom He receives" (Heb. 12:6), and "If you are without discipline—which all receive—then you are illegitimate children and not sons" (Heb. 12:8). You're ministering to a deep need in their lives when you communicate, "No, you may not just do what you want!"

It also means that you must see the two questions as an inseparable pair and always answer both of them, even if only one is asked. Recently, I was teaching a college class and had to correct a student for his disruptive behavior. Because another class followed afterward, I didn't have the opportunity to touch base with him immediately. The next morning I spotted him at a table and sat down beside him. As we began talking about what happened, I suddenly realized he had taken my correction as a rejection of himself as a person, not just his behavior. I had answered only one of the questions, and because of that the no had bled over into both, communicating that he was unloved as well. "Tony, let me tell you what I see in you," I said and began to affirm his gifting as well as our relationship. I could see the words heading deep into his soul.

Later in the week he came up and apologized for his behavior. With the pressure removed from the first question, the focus was back on the second and the no began to penetrate. Strangely, I felt much closer to him because I had to discipline him. I sensed somehow that the same was true for him as well.

Love and discipline are closely intertwined and must function as a symbiotic team, each supporting and strengthening the other. You can't fully love if you don't discipline, and you can't discipline effectively if you don't love.

The Destructive Power of Anger

Too many leaders practice the rubber band method of discipline. They stretch and give, letting their boundaries be pushed as the pressure builds. At some point, it becomes too much and they snap, releasing the tension in an angry stream, like a rubber band cutting loose. Then, flushed out, they go limp and the stretching process begins again.

Remember my angry outburst during the retreat from hell? It created silence and compliance for just a bit but actually lost me ground in the long run. When a leader explodes in anger, the focus becomes his anger rather than the behavior that needs to be corrected. Some are hurt and wounded by the emotion and automatically kick into self-protection, defending themselves at all costs. Others are accustomed to anger and write the person off, discounting the message because of the medium through which it came. In any case, it becomes hard to respond productively—for everyone involved. Often, the end result after an angry outburst is that two problems replace one.

This doesn't mean we should never be angry. Anger is a legitimate emotion that may motivate us to action when we would otherwise be passive. But the Bible warns us that we must not sin in our anger and that anger should be quickly resolved (Eph. 4:26–27). It also clearly teaches that "outbursts of anger" are not in keeping with what God desires (2 Cor. 12:20).

If anger is present, it must either be kept under control so it's not flowing to the other person through the channel of discipline, or else we must pause to deal with our anger before the discipline process begins. This takes alertness and self-control, and avoiding damage is well worth the extra effort. Discipline must be carried out with all our energy focused on the other person's good. Anger can easily cause our discipline to be selfishly energized by an unconscious desire to punish or even hurt the person for how he's wounded us. This kind of outburst does not bring about "God's righteousness" (James 1:20).

Discipline to Correct Not Punish

What is the point of discipline? If it's to somehow make the students pay for what they've done, we miss the truth of the gospel—that we don't have the resources to redeem the past. In fact, the price is more than we can bear. The only way to satisfy the demand for punishment is through the redemptive work of Christ.

If, on the other hand, the point of discipline is to restrain evil, we have a better goal. This still has limitations though. If a student complies only because of immediate pressure from you, the old patterns will most likely emerge again the minute pressure is removed. Outward conformity keeps the student from causing problems for others but doesn't build lasting maturity in his life. We may keep unruly students quiet in the meeting but still not help them grow.

The point of discipline should be correction—a change of direction and a molding of the heart. Correction starts with behavior but continues into mind-set, attitudes, habits, and beliefs. Discipline is a tool of disciple making to turn students to a different path, to mold young lives for lasting change.

How is this done? We've talked much of the beliefs and goals of discipline, but what are the nuts and bolts of how it works? If we need to expect problems, how should we get ready for them and what should we do when they occur?

How to Discipline

At times it helps to develop models based on examples from other arenas of life. For me, the picture of a referee in an athletic game helps. When a game is refereed well, the players can throw all they have into the competition, confident they're operating in a fair and controlled environment. When the referees are poor or missing altogether, endless disagreements and side agendas sabotage the game. For referees to function well, three crucial pieces must always be in place.

Clear Lines

Imagine a football game with no boundaries, no markings, no end zone, and no goal. You might toss the ball back and forth a few times, but who's to say if you're making progress or even playing on the right patch of grass? The official's first responsibility is to make sure the field is clearly marked and the rules of play are clear and agreed upon *before* the game begins.

This is a classic error in discipline—trying to bring the game into control with no agreed upon lines or clearly communicated expectations. How can I expect students to be responsible if I haven't clearly spelled out what responsibility means? How can I hold them to my expectations if they don't know what those expectations are?

If the lines on a field are fuzzy or unclear, there will be endless discussions about which side the ball landed on. Tempers flare and accusations fly. On the other hand, if the boundaries are clear and each has agreed to play by the rules before the game begins, disputes can be dealt with quickly and objectively.

It's best if there are not too many lines and that the ones in place cover big areas of the field clearly and logically. If you've ever played in a gym where the floor is littered with lines from five games (not to mention the Awana club that meets there Wednesday night), you know what I mean. Too many lines and people get confused.

The line needs to be objective as well. If we agree that when one person is talking up front, no one else does, all know when the boundary is being crossed. But if the standard is that the background noise cannot surpass the tolerance level of the teacher (who randomly responds when that level is surpassed), the standard is quite relative.

Once expectations are agreed on, they must be communicated to everyone. This has always been difficult for me. I never liked starting a retreat with a description of the boundaries or opening a meeting with a quick list of my expectations. My gut feeling was that it ruined the atmosphere. What I found over time, however, was that the opposite was true. If I failed to communicate at the beginning, I invariably had to put boundaries in place halfway through the event. This impacted the atmosphere much more than if they had been presented right away at the start.

Consistent Calls

Once the lines are in place, you can be sure they will be tested. Some testing will be motivated by a desire to see if your expectations really are firm. Other testing is because the boundaries haven't yet been adequately fixed in people's minds. In any case, if a boundary is crossed and nothing happens, students soon learn it doesn't really exist. Or, if it's randomly enforced, no one knows what to expect. What would happen if a ball crossing the finish line meant six points in some cases and ten in others, for no apparent reason? Without consistency the boundaries lose their meaning and the players begin to make up rules of their own.

This is another classic mistake of discipline. The youth worker establishes guidelines and then assumes they will enforce themselves. Rather than noticing and responding when the line is crossed, he hopes the new behavior will come automatically. Once a new guideline is in place, the leader must monitor it, especially in the beginning. After students learn where the boundary is and that it's firm, they begin to look out for it themselves. A new way of relating can become woven into the group culture, and students will even monitor themselves. At the beginning, however, it takes considerable effort from the leader to put the boundaries in place.

Consequences

What would happen if a referee simply ran around the field, naming the various infractions, but doing nothing about them? What if the ball never changed directions, if out-of-bounds simply meant playing in deeper grass, or if it wasn't possible to remove a player from the game? If there were no consequences, the clear lines and consistent calls would simply be an exercise in futility.

This is not to say that all consequences must be earth-shattering. Many can be quick and simple, not even particularly painful. However, consequences remind players that a line has been crossed and that actions produce outcomes. The referee also needs to know that he has the ability to remain in control of the game by removing a player from the field if need be. The red card is always in his back pocket. Though not often used, the fact that he carries this authority gives the referee the ability to enforce the other calls as well.

In youth ministry, the consequences are often simply a quick conversation, a direct request, or a reminder of how this is impacting others. As the stakes get higher, the consequences can include the loss of certain privileges, a conversation with parents, or even particular assignments such as clean-up duty. In the end, the youth worker needs to remember that he carries the red card in his back pocket. The power to remove someone from the activity gives authority to enforce the other rules as well.

This shouldn't be used lightly. Generally, consequences should start light and increase as the instructions are ignored. It should be clear that if a student continues to disobey the leader, the consequences will increase. At times, the youth worker must remove students from the game. I've driven an unresponsive student home from a retreat to waiting parents. And I've escorted a disruptive student out of the youth room to wait in the hall until the end of the meeting. This is never pleasant. But if the lines are clear and fair, it doesn't have to be done in frustration or anger. Because the student knows ahead of time what's expected and how you'll respond, removal from the game is a consequence they themselves have chosen.

Remember the retreat from hell? Because I was unprepared, I carried all the consequences for the students' misbehavior. Their actions actually produced pleasant outcomes for them, such as longer nights' sleep and freedom to do whatever they wanted. The negative consequences, however, were born primarily by me. This wasn't healthy for any of us! On top of that, my lines were not clear and my calls certainly not consistent. I was afraid of losing the new kids, afraid of what they would think, afraid of what they might say about me.

The bottom line is this: We must love students enough to not give them everything they want. We must love the students more than we love their approval, our reputation, or the lack of tension. We must love them enough to stay in charge, even when competing agendas threaten to hijack our youth ministry. "No discipline seems enjoyable at the time, but painful. Later on, however, it yields the fruit of peace and righteousness to those who have been trained by it" (Heb. 12:11).

Part 3

Leading
the Ministry
Effectively

18.
Planning

STEVEN PATTY

HOW DO YOU KNOW what to do?

In ministry, when you sit down with your youth staff to plan a retreat, how do you know what to do? When you plan a message to give or a devotion to present, how do you know what to do? When you draft your calendar for the next quarter's activities, how do you know what to do?

Do you know how you know what to do?

There is a crisis of planning among youth ministers today. I'm not suggesting that youth ministers don't plan. The abundance of youth activities carried out weekly across North America, even around the world, proves the productive capacity of creative and energetic youth leaders. Youth ministries can't exist apart from planning. Without it no ministry, except spontaneous, spur-of-the-moment activities, would run. And spontaneity can take you only so far. Every youth leader knows this.

Strategic planning, however—the kind that's sensitive to the place of the group, that reflects the long-range vision for students, that captures the best imaginations and creativity of the present—is difficult to find. Hence, the crisis. Take the following examples, for instance.

Youth Pastor 1

One reason Kevin entered youth ministry was because an effective youth minister had a positive impact on his own life. His leader pulled him aside during high school and invited him to participate in a discipleship small group. That group changed Kevin's life. The group members read Scripture together, memorized verses, tackled a week-by-week discipleship workbook, learned how to share their faith, reported on accountability issues, and experienced the encouragement and fellowship of a tight-knit community.

When Kevin imagined youth ministry, he pictured this kind of committed, high-intensity discipleship group. In fact, he found it difficult to envision any other model so effective.

When Kevin took charge of his first ministry, he immediately applied his values of ministry programming to growing these students. He talked his kids into signing up for after school small-group slots. He recruited adult leaders and quickly trained them to work through the discipleship manual. He then disbanded the primary meeting, dived into a small group himself, and watched the magic of disciple making unfold.

Nothing unfolded, except, perhaps, chaos. In a matter of weeks, students began to disappear.

Adult leaders became discouraged. He watched the ministry fall apart in front of him. Why? He had a plan. The plan was executed skillfully. But it was the wrong plan.

If left to ourselves, we will plan from what worked for us.

Youth Pastor 2

Sometime during high school, Matt realized he had a gift for speaking. Growing up in a large youth group, he watched speakers mesmerize crowds of young people with power-packed messages. The best youth speakers cycled through his groups. Their influence and the power of their messages on the hearts of young people astounded him. And so whenever he had a chance, he spoke.

His opportunities multiplied quickly because of his skill. He commanded attention easily. Turning a phrase came naturally. Communicating the truth of the Bible to adolescents seemed effortless. He quickly gained a reputation because of his gift, securing roles of leadership in just about every group of peers to which he belonged. Through high school and college, he frequently preached with powerful results.

After college, Matt took a full-time position as a leader in a start-up youth ministry for a military community. It didn't go very well. He had twenty kids or so, sitting in rows, listening to his profound and wonderful speeches. No matter how good his preaching, those students were unmoved. Why? He had a plan. The plan was executed with brilliance. But it was the wrong plan.

If left to ourselves, we will plan from what we do well.

Youth Pastor 3

Sharon's commitment to seeing the girls in her group grow to maturity impressed everyone around her. So it was no surprise to anyone when she announced a new small group. Her girls looked forward to the program with

great expectation. They all rearranged their schedules to be free to meet and spread the word so that as many as possible could attend.

In thinking about her plan, Sharon became excited about studying the Minor Prophets. She was just finishing a Bible and theology degree at the local Christian college and thought the study of books like Hosea and Malachi would keep her challenged and hold her interest. Certainly, she believed any study of God's Word would produce dramatic impact in the lives of these girls. After all, she reasoned, this was God's Word. The challenge of the Minor Prophets would be good for anyone.

The group went fine, but it never really sang. Girls came, studied, and were loved week after week, but they never really locked into a group as everyone had expected. Sharon reported that those who had strong Bible training dominated the discussion and the others were surprisingly quiet. Even with Sharon's passionate and gifted heart, the group never did very well. Why? She had a plan. The plan centered on the Word of God. But it was still the wrong plan.

If left to ourselves, we will plan from our own interests.

Errors in Orientation

We could go on with story after similar story. Leaders provide the same kind of winter retreat year after year but see a gradual decline of impact over time. Leaders look around at the latest new youth program, a concert of prayer, or a mission trip, and apply it to their group with less effectiveness than they expected. Leaders take their cues from former pastors, from seminars, or from books and then wonder why their students seem strangely untouched and the stories less exciting.

All of these scenarios illustrate errors in orientation. And each of us, even the most seasoned youth ministry professionals, falls prey to this crisis.

The place from which you plan makes all the difference in the world. What worked for you may not be the exact fit for the students in front of you now. What you're good at and gifted in may not be the next step for the kids in your care. What you're learning and going through may not be the right well out of which you should draw water for the young people in your group. What you've heard may be a great idea for a different group or for your group at a different stage of development. Even the programs that God faithfully used in the past, to great effect, may be the wrong ones today. God rarely performs encores.

I'm not suggesting that youth leaders disregard these sources. Many program resources are rich for the plunder. For example, a heritage of personal experience enriches a minister's imagination. But it may be in some cases that past success clouds current thinking. The power of a full quiver of ministerial gifts can give a minister amazing ability. But in some cases personal giftedness gets in the way of seeing clearly the need and the next step for a group of young people. Consider these possible liabilities for your current ministry:

- Your past successes
- Your own giftedness
- Your training
- Your own needs

We need to plan carefully, diligently, and with discipline in order to use these resources instead of being misled by them.

The Rookie Mistake

Here is a common occurrence at a youth staff meeting: "OK, guys, we have a retreat coming up. What do you think we should do?" What usually comes next? One person suggests a repeat of something that went well last year. Another mentions a creative activity he heard about from another church's retreat. A third says he's been studying the book of Ephesians and has some great things he'd like to share. Another mentions a speaker she heard about who may be available, but she'd have to check to make sure.

The conversation goes like this for awhile until the meeting time is covered. Then the pieces are collected and tied together, a plan is devised, and a retreat is born.

Have you ever been there? In this kind of planning meeting, the attention goes straight to the plan. "What should we do?" is the functional and prominent question. Do you see the difficulty? All eyes are on the development of a *plan.*

A more thoughtful youth minister, discontent with the quality of the aggregate-plan approach, decides to come to a planning meeting prepared with the latest ideas. And so he attends ministry-training conferences that teach about the latest and best practices. He reads articles and books to keep up-to-date on the cutting-edge techniques of the most creative ministries.

This youth minister comes to a planning meeting with a revised question: "OK, guys, we have a retreat coming up. Let's get the best ideas and make them happen." You can anticipate the turns in the ensuing conversation. "How can we pull together this funny-man skit?" "Can we find the materials for the world's largest Slip 'n' Slide?" "We only have time for either the affirmation circle or the concert of prayer. Which one do you want to do?"

Have you also been here? This meeting feels slightly better. The primary questions focus on the best ideas and how to do them. You still see difficulty though, don't you? The focus is on the *ideas* to the *plan.*

Both cases reflect an underdeveloped view of planning. Here's a better method.

NOIPE[1]

Needs → Objectives → Ideas → Plan → Evaluation

Before any ministry activity, a minister needs to carefully examine two things. These are twin thoughts, and they ought to happen simultaneously in the first step of planning. Without a good look at these, the starting point is skewed.

1. Where are my students right now?
2. What is God's vision for them in the future?

The answer to these two question provides the *need* piece of NOIPE. The difference between where students are and where they should be defines their need.

Maybe this seems simple. And maybe you think this starting place is automatic for any reflective youth minister. But consider how many times we start planning by asking questions like these, "What is possible?" "What can we do well?" "What did we do last year?" "What are we scheduled to do right now?" "What's the latest and best idea we've heard recently?" We could continue asking great questions that may improve the program but have little to do with determining where students are and where they need to be taken.

The need in any student's life—and the need in the life of any youth group—defines the facets of Christlikeness that have yet to be developed in the student's heart. Remember, the aim as youth ministers is not to have a great program but to raise true disciples. The goal of our labor is not to have an impressive group but to grow true lovers of God. And so often the first step in the mind of a planner is more reflective of a concern for a good program, not for a good disciple.

How do you answer these two questions? You shepherd more than one or two students. Can you truly know where they are?

The task challenges every minister. Pray for God's insight into their lives. Listen to how they talk, to what they say, and why they say things. Watch their actions. Observe their emotions. Ask them questions: "I've noticed there are usually people in this group you don't seem to like very much. Can you tell me about that?" Think through the individuals in your group if you find that focusing on the whole group seems overwhelming. You'll need to be close to them.

At some point, to answer the second question, a youth leader must search the Scriptures to determine what he or she believes to be God's vision for these students. God has communicated. He's told us what his children should look like. We need to sit down and capture this picture of what the Lord would have students know, feel, and do and what heart change must happen for them to reflect the presence of Christ in their lives.

When these two questions are answered, the true need will be much easier to decipher. Be careful not to get sidetracked by a perceived need. These can mislead you into believing that caring for an immediate concern—fixing a discomfort or fulfilling a temporal desire—is tantamount to making disciples.

Needs → *Objectives* → Ideas → Plan → Evaluation

When you compare students' current spirituality and a picture of mature, adolescent spirituality, the needs feel overwhelming. There are so many truths to teach, so many skills to train, so many feelings to evoke toward the Lord God before they're mature. Where do you begin? You need objectives.

Remember that defining objectives is the second task of planning. It can't be the first. To develop objectives without first examining needs leaves you subject to referencing off the wrong feature. Once a sense of need is explored, the objectives step asks, "What is the next step?"

The next step should be captured in your objective. Determining the next step requires that you think carefully and theologically about the process of sanctification. With all that these students need to learn, what is the next piece they must have? What primary sin currently undermines their growth? What is the next challenge of obedience they must face?

The next step for a group of students will look at their path of growth. Keep in mind the various uses of Scripture. Second Timothy 3:16–17 says, "All Scripture is inspired by God and is profitable for teaching, for rebuking, for correcting, for training in righteousness, so that the man of God may be complete, equipped for every good work." Any of these uses for Scripture—teaching, rebuking, correcting, and training—could respond to the present and unique objective, the particular next step, for your students.

A good rule of thumb regarding the next step, a way to tell whether you have the next step as the objective, is to anticipate the student's response. Barring rebelliousness or callousness in their hearts, can you picture them taking this step if you challenged them to it? If you can, this probably is a great objective. If you can't, an intermediate step may be a better objective.

Take, for example, a group of middle school students who've never shared their faith. You want to teach them how to share the gospel, but you suspect that merely knowing how to speak about their faith will do nothing to get them sharing it. And so you consider an intermediate step. Maybe your students don't truly know and believe that their lost friends will spend eternity

apart from Jesus. Maybe they have no good concept of heaven or hell. If these students were instructed in this theology, they would then hear about and be able to understand sharing their faith. In this way, you adjust the objective to the true next step, then run hard after that.

Needs → Objectives → *Ideas* → Plan → Evaluation
After needs are identified and an objective or two determined, comes the task of exploring possible ideas. If ideas are explored too early—before needs and objectives—it's difficult to keep them in perspective. A good idea can lure a youth leader into a poor plan. Why? Because an idea is only as good as it meets the objective to fulfill the need. Great ideas can show off a ministry but get students no closer to being disciples.

Ideas can be gleaned from all kinds of sources. Think through experiences. Attend good conferences filled with great ideas. Read about the newest and the most imaginative strategies currently employed in youth ministry. Get on the phone and ask other youth leaders for ideas. Collaborate with those outside your denomination or theological tradition. Fill your library with good books.

Perhaps the most fruitful idea-generating exercise, however, can be achieved with your own staff. Brainstorming together can produce creative ideas. Let your minds go, imagine, and reach for the innovative. Refuse to judge, limit, or contain your conversation at first because premature judgment stifles creativity. Build off one another's ideas and let your conversation freewheel. Often during the last bit of brainstorming the best ideas surface. So when you feel you are all tapped out, keep at it for a little longer. You may be surprised at what you create.

One of my mentors in graduate school was fond of saying, "A plan is only as good as its options." Think about that. To go straight from objectives to plan makes a minister miss the opportunity to explore other possibilities. To go straight from objectives to plan skips the question, "Is there a better way to get there?" The ideas stage opens up possibilities. And the quality of your plan depends highly on all the possibilities that you explored and turned down in favor of your chosen path. Even if you come back to your traditional way of doing things, generating ideas will remind you why you're doing what you do and infuse your tradition with new meaning.

Needs → Objectives → Ideas → *Plan* → Evaluation
Now, finally, we come to the plan. When you NOIPE a program, it feels like a lot of work to reach your plan. The plan is what you need—talks, retreats, and calendar deadlines bear down on you all the time. Consequently,

youth leaders feel huge pressure to skip the first steps and get right to the plan. Rushing to the plan sells the program short. Resist the temptation. Don't get impatient. The first three NOI steps will pay rich dividends for your plan.

When needs, objectives, and ideas have been developed, selecting a plan is easy. Take the best of the ideas and fashion them into a program. Craft the pieces together into movements. Make assignments. Develop time lines. Schedule contributors. Do all the things necessary to plan a winner.

An effective plan is even better than a flawlessly executed plan. Consider this oft-quoted conundrum: "What is more important, to do the right things or to do things right?" We could devote a whole chapter to discussing this tension and the difficulties it presents for a minister. Suffice it to say here, however, that a "right" program is better than the wrong program done "rightly." Many skilled youth leaders design high-quality programs but to no disciple-making avail. Even clumsily executed, the "right" plan can achieve huge benefit among the students in your ministry.

When you've shaped the plan, take another look at it. Does it capture the best of the ideas? Will it meet the objectives of the next step for your students? Will this fulfill the need of moving students from where they are to where they should be in their relationships with God? Then, check it again. Sometimes in the planning process, the ultimate purpose of a program gets lost in the excitement of the possibilities or the difficulties of the challenges. And the ultimate goal, again, is to contribute to the making of disciples.

Needs → Objectives → Ideas → Plan → *Evaluation*

Why is evaluation part of planning? You may argue that planning, by definition, is an activity *before* the program, not in response and in reflection and *after* the fact. Strictly speaking, you're probably correct. However, evaluation is such a key factor in the next planning cycle that it would be negligent to miss it here in the planning sequence.

Evaluation illuminates the strengths and weaknesses of a plan and its execution. Through evaluation and reflection youth ministers learn, grow, and refine their programming skills. Evaluation is a crucial discipline in the planning processes.

Very few ministerial disciplines create as much stress, insecurity, and distaste as does evaluation, however. For many of us, sitting down for an evaluation of a program requires a monumental act of the will. We're tired. We've opened our hearts and given all we have, and so we feel exposed. We feel pressure to move on quickly to the next item on the agenda or task of ministry. But pausing with others to examine and reflect brings to the surface wonderful insight. Ultimately, habitual evaluation will hone and refine your planning efforts.

Experience alone holds little power in renovating ministries. Just because a leader has years of experience designing programs doesn't mean he or she has been learning from each event. Instead of developing skill, nimbleness, and responsiveness over the years, perhaps the youth minister has fallen into a rut with few possibilities of fresh perspective or practice. Only experience *accompanied by* evaluation promotes ongoing development of a leader's skill.

NOIPE in Action

Most of us who have done ministry for awhile felt clumsy when we first began to plan. The NOIPE process took all the effort and creativity we could muster. But over time, having continually worked through NOIPE, ways of thinking begin to change. The process becomes more familiar and more generative with practice. Don't be discouraged if the first few times through NOIPE feel uncomfortable, unnatural, and perplexing. After awhile, NOIPE becomes second nature.

NOIPE is best done with others to achieve the maximum wisdom and creativity for the group. Furthermore, then the entire staff understands the program purposes and strategy. (The people who run a program generate many of the program's goals anyway.)

NOIPE can be applied to just about any ministerial activity—a message or sermon, a weekend retreat or summer camp, quarterly schedule of activities, and personal-growth events for you and your staff. No, it's not the panacea for all that ails a youth program, but its use will serve you well.

Notes

1. NOIPE was developed in Malachi Ministries, directed by Dave Patty.

19.

Building a Staff Team

GENE POPPINO

THE LONE RANGER never led a cattle drive.

Although most people who read this book will have never seen an episode of *The Lone Ranger,* the story is familiar. The masked Texas ranger and his sidekick Tonto were a combination law enforcement and emergency response team, with a little Batman and Robin thrown in. Each week the Lone Ranger would rescue ranchers and catch bad guys. No possess, no paperwork, no chain of command to work through to get the job done. Charging in with guns blazing, the bad guys were no match for him. In the final scene he rode off into the sunset with people asking, "Who was that masked man?"

I have to admit the Lone Ranger style of ministry has appeal. I would love to charge in, be the hero, and quickly ride off to the next adventure. That *sounds* exciting. Youth leaders who approach ministry with flawed motives can act like the Lone Ranger, doing everything by themselves. But God designed ministry to look more like a cattle drive than a Lone Ranger episode. Rounding up the cattle, a team of cowboys drove the herd hundreds of miles. Keeping the herd together required vigilance and legendary toughness. Rustlers, wild animals, and rough terrain were constant threats. And because cowboys were paid by the head, every animal was important. Even though they were tough and independent, they knew a successful cattle drive was a team effort. The Lone Ranger could never run a cattle drive.

Youth ministry isn't exactly a cattle drive, but it does have a clear parallel: *You can't do it alone.*

Shepherding Is a Team Job

Shepherds worked in teams. Jesus described a good shepherd: "Suppose one of you has a hundred sheep and loses one of them. Does he not leave the ninety-nine in the open country and go after the lost sheep until he finds it?" (Luke 15:4 NIV). Can you picture this? One sheep gets lost and the shepherd leaves the ninety-nine in the *open country* to go and find it. Keep in mind, a flock that size was never left under the care of a single shepherd, especially in open country. To protect so many sheep from danger, an owner would hire shepherd teams. When the head shepherd went after the lost sheep, the flock was not abandoned to danger—a team continued to care for them.

The strong pattern of teamwork in ministry is seen throughout Scripture. God built teams of people to work together, except for a few Old Testament prophets. Jesus invested in the disciples. Moses had Miriam and Aaron. God brought David and Jonathan together in the early years and a host of advisers for David later on. The apostle Paul worked variously with Timothy, Barnabas, Silas, and others. Disciples were sent out two by two, Barnabas teamed up with John Mark even after he and Paul separated, and Paul immediately linked up with a new partner when Barnabas left. In each case, the work was stronger because of the team.

Ecclesiastes says, "Two are better than one because they have a good reward for their efforts. For if either falls, his companion can lift him up; but pity the one who falls without another to lift him up. Also, if two lie down together, they can keep warm; but how can one person alone keep warm? And if somebody overpowers one person, two can resist him. A cord of three strands is not easily broken" (4:9–12).

Youth ministry, like other ministry, requires a team. A youth pastor working alone limits how many students he can shepherd. Many leaders find they will be effective with twenty to twenty-five students and after that the group's attendance plateaus. Even if a ministry is small and easily handled by one leader, you need staff for growth. One pastor said, "God doesn't put newborns in an unhealthy nursery." Build a team so that when God opens the door and expands your ministry, you'll have the staff to shepherd every student.

The Pastor—the Key to Developing a Team

Have you noticed that some youth pastors seem to be surrounded by quality people with amazing ministries, while others are left doing everything themselves? Looking closer, you find that team-building pastors encourage the growth of a team around them. Good leadership does more than attract followers. Good leadership produces more leaders. Team-building pastors have characteristics that draw and motivate emerging leaders.

Have Vision

Don't desire to be significant, desire to do significant things. A leader with a vision to do great things for God and one who doesn't care about getting credit has a vision others will want to join. No one signs on to help a man build his own kingdom, but a vision to build God's kingdom captures imaginations and draws people in.

Be Confident

Knowing who you are in Christ, confident of your calling and direction in ministry, is attractive to emerging leaders. An insecure leader lacks the confidence to give significant responsibility to others, fearing that failure may reflect poorly on himself. His insecurity and fear hinder people from joining a team that will have few opportunities for real ministry. A strong worker doesn't want to give his life to do busy work.

If you're going to attract strong people to serve with you, you can't be easily threatened. The lay staff in one high school ministry had the superintendent of schools, an engineer overseeing part of NASA's Mars mission, the international convention planner for a major pulp and paper company, and several men who owned their own businesses. These workers managed major projects and dealt with sophisticated people. But they also wanted to work on a team doing kingdom work. A leader who knew where he was going and what he was doing gave them that opportunity.

Be Weak

Weakness is good. A team leader should be transparent about his weaknesses. A leader perceived as all-competent will discourage people from volunteering. If you're not needed or if you feel you can't do nearly as well as the leader, why join the team? A leader who's clear about his own weaknesses and limitations creates room for others to partner and make significant contributions.

My value as a person and as a youth leader used to depend on my success in every job. I began a new ministry at a medium-sized church in Portland, Oregon, following the sudden departure of the previous youth pastor. The church secretary came to me and said, "We have a retreat facility booked next weekend. Can you lead a high school retreat?" Even for youth ministry, this was less planning than usual! In those days, the idea of team was foreign to me. No other adults went on the retreat—I did everything myself. I drove the van, cooked, spoke, counseled, led games, and nursed injuries. It was a rowdy group with a history of misbehavior—a reputation the group lived up to on this retreat. I slept little and came home exhausted.

Planning the next retreat for this group, I knew something had to be different. I approached the parent group and asked for help. My appeal went something like this. "I'm sorry to have to ask you this, but I need help. I can't cook worth beans, and if we do another retreat where I cook, kids will come home sick. Can anybody come along and help me?" Notice, I still said "help *me.*" I couldn't bring myself to ask someone to actually do the job. After the meeting, Jan, one of the parents, said, "Gene, I would *love* to help you cook. It's one of my favorite things to do in life." I thought, *Oh, she is just being gracious. No one* loves *to cook.* That next retreat was much better with someone else in the kitchen. I checked in on Jan from time to time, but it was plain she really didn't need me. As I watched, it hit me. She was having fun! It was an epiphany. I finally grasped that others love to do what I hate. It was my first lesson in building teams—I realized I could be bad at things and others would help.

See People in Process

People are in process. A good team builder appreciates and affirms people on the journey. People without experience may fail in early attempts. If they sense failure isn't tolerated, they won't try again. Their self-image may also be rooted in success and so when their work isn't perfect, they feel they've failed. Leaders who inspire others affirm people in process and remind them of their progress.

Trust People with Room to Work

When you ask someone to do a job, you must give them freedom to work. Give clear direction and boundaries and then release the person to do the job in her own unique way. Micromanaging or controlling every detail robs personal motivation. Great leaders exercise confidence in people to release them to ministry. They encourage innovation and creativity.

Lead by Example

Do any job that needs to be done. Your willingness to serve wherever needed teaches by example. The corollary to this is also important: Don't do a job that someone else can do. If he's capable, don't jump in and take over. Demonstrate your trust in his ability and affirm his role on the team by thanking him, then get out of the way.

Help People Find the Right Role

There are adults who *minister* to students and adults who act like chaperones at a school dance. In developing a good staff team, we want to understand people's different gifts and personalities and help them learn to minister.

Leaders versus Workers

It's common to refer to any adults involved in youth ministry as "leaders." Lay staff are not all leaders although they all do minister. I consider staff members who are responsible to oversee a segment of ministry and make decisions leaders. Staff who care for students, discipling them, or leading a small group, are workers, not leaders. The distinction becomes important when you assign team responsibilities. Asking someone with *worker-level* skill to take on a *leader-level* role will hurt the worker and the work. Just because someone is a faithful, godly person does not mean she can lead.

Scott, who is forty-five, runs sound and lights for a large youth ministry. Technically skilled, he is constantly praised for his hard work and attention to detail in setting up microphones and mixing sound for the worship team. It was only natural to put Scott in charge of the student team that would work with him as sound techs. After several months, Scott's youth pastor noticed that fewer and fewer students were on the team. Checking it out, he found many had quietly dropped out because Scott wasn't using them. He still did all the work himself. A look at Scott's skills revealed he was a great worker, but he lacked the ability to direct the efforts of others.

Making Disciples

If you ask a typical youth worker, "What do you do?" he'll probably tell you "I lead a small group" or "I am a worship leader." His first answer will be the *tasks* he does. God defines our job in the Great Commission in Matthew 28:19–20: *Make disciples.* Every staff person, regardless of his tasks, is about making disciples.

Margie is our head cook for camp. She and her team feed 250 students and staff at our water ski campout every summer. Cooking great meals outdoors, all week, for that many, is a big job. But if you ask her, "What do you do?" she won't talk about menus or meal prep. Margie will say, "I'm making disciples by feeding kids. When their physical needs are met, they're better able to hear about God's love when the speaker talks." She isn't a cook. She's a woman on a mission. She knows we're about making disciples.

Sharing the Work

The Lone Ranger never led a cattle drive. No one can connect to every student as groups grow. Team ministry is the best way to carry the load, multiply effectiveness, and use people's gifts.

Recruiting and Training Staff

You're convinced of the value of team ministry; you're the kind of person people want to work with; you've set a pattern for significant staff involvement. Now, how do you recruit and train staff? A good strategy is crucial.

- Don't give a blanket invitation from the pulpit or church newsletter asking for volunteers. Have a job description, a selection and screening process, and clearly stated expectations for staff in place before you invite people to apply.
- Recruit parents of preteens. Invite parents of younger children to consider working on youth staff before their own children reach that age so they can learn how to work with adolescents and become more aware of typical adolescent characteristics.
- Teach students about family from Scripture—talk about parents with honor. Build up and affirm the role of a parent. Ask students to nominate their parents for student ministry staff. (We also ask parents applying for our staff to have their teens' permission and blessing before we accept them.)
- Have specific jobs with structure and clear responsibility. A lay staff person with undefined responsibilities may offer to speak in situations for which they aren't trained or volunteer to work in areas outside of their gifting. Staff without clear structure can be loose cannons, rolling around the deck at the worst moments.
- Learn to lead, not just do. This is one of the greatest challenges many youth workers face. Most of us go into youth work because we love the actual ministry to students. Consequently, we love to step out and connect with students, lead Bible studies, and generally be "the life of the party." Many adults lack the charisma, enthusiasm, or confidence to relate to students in the way a professional youth worker might so they drift into the background. For them to really step up and take a shepherding role in the lives of students, you must lead them into positions of real responsibility and ministry.
- Help people discover their gifts, abilities, and limits. Many people have a heart for ministry but lack skills or understanding of what needs to happen. Because of this they can't contribute all God designed them to. Our role is to equip them to do the work for which they're called. To be successful several things should take place. We use a personality profile called the *Disc Test* to help staff members understand their own personality type and how they interact with others. We also give a spiritual gift inventory, helping them better understand their gifting and how it

can be used to minister. Finally, we try to help people be practical in their commitment. Our staff expectations are very clear, so people can decide in advance how much time they can devote to the ministry.

• Be liberal with affirmation and encouragement. People thrive with affirmation and wither without it. A youth worker who leads by constantly pointing out what his staff has done right, thanking people for their contribution to the work and reviewing significant accomplishments of the team, builds momentum, vision, and passion.

Over the years, I've been deeply grateful for the stability, maturity, and depth parents have brought to our youth staff. An advantage of having an older youth staff is they add both credibility and protection to your ministry because their maturity and judgment give other parents confidence. Kids can exaggerate risk factors while excitedly telling a story about something that happened at a youth activity. Parents may jump to conclusions and assume a young youth pastor took an unnecessary risk. But when they ask, "Who was there? Who was watching when that happened?" and the teen mentions several forty-year-old parents who were part of the activity, the worried parents conclude it was OK. With all those mature adults around, it must not have been as great a risk as their teen described. Over the years I've had very few complaints or even questions from parents about things we've done because they knew that more than half our staff members were forty or older and had maturity and judgment on their side.

Parents and older adults provide the foundation of a good staff. But without younger staff, teams will lack important strengths too. College-age or twenty-something staff bring great energy and enthusiasm. During high-activity camps, retreats, and outings, younger staff will play hard while older adults cheer from the sidelines. Closer in age to the students, teens will relate to younger staff more naturally. Consequently, young staff members tend to hear more openly from students.

Recruiting a variety of ages is important to build a healthy staff. Regardless of staff age, good training will ensure workers are equipped to reach students.

Grow Old(er) as a Team (Keeping a Team Together)

We joke about putting wheelchair ramps in the youth room so our staff can get around more easily. Although we're not really that old, the median age of our lay team is well older than forty. Our oldest worker is sixty-eight. Several on our team have been working with junior highers for more than twenty years! A dozen of us have done youth ministry together for more than a decade. This team is the reason our students are growing in Christ. Our staffers are godly, mature, and invested in student's lives for the long haul. Earlier in this chapter we talked about the qualities of a pastor that open the door for people to want to join staff. In the same way, the leader creates an environment for a staff to want to serve together for a long time.

Six keys for keeping a staff happy:

1. *Communicate.* People need to understand the leader's vision, goals, passion, and even the style to stay invested and energized to serve. During staff meetings, tell the stories of ministry successes. Talk about how team members reflect the values of the ministry. Brief the team regularly about how they're accomplishing goals. Be liberal with praise. Remind them of their significance in making disciples.

2. *Keep your word.* Do what you say or don't say it. Don't overpromise and underdeliver. Remember, your staff's reputation is tied to yours. If you start on time, stop on time, and bring the kids back when you say you will, the team will trust you. If you play fast and loose with the details, your staff will be frustrated or embarrassed. Integrity in the small things builds trust.

3. *Prepare well.* When you show up for a meeting, a Bible study, or any other team event unprepared, it causes others to question your competence or your commitment. A style of leadership that is too casual won't inspire confidence. Few people will be willing to sacrifice if you don't appear prepared or ready for each challenge.

4. *Honor and respect others' judgments.* There are times when a team may disagree about an activity or event. Learn to respect others' judgments and understand their points of view. Make your staff a safe place for people to say what they truly believe.

For years, a regular part of our annual water ski camp was a favorite event of mine called the "wipeout" competition. It had simple rules—a student got on water skis behind the boat and while skiing past the rest of the camp performed a spectacular wipeout. We got great videos of kids doing violence to their bodies. After a number of years, several of my boat drivers came to me and said they were uncomfortable with the wipeout competition. They didn't want to do it anymore.

I pulled out my best persuasive skills and explained that no one had gotten seriously hurt and that it was really not much of a risk. They didn't refuse to do it, but they made it clear they were uncomfortable. I was faced with a choice. Did I continue doing something I thought involved very little risk and cause them to question my respect for their concerns, or was I willing to respect their judgment and cancel the event. With a tinge of regret, I took their advice and the wipeout competition is no more. Whether it was a good or bad decision is irrelevant. What was important was to maintain the great relationship I had with boat drivers.

5. *Train them regularly.* Good youth staff members are shepherds, not chaperones. In order to shepherd, whether it's leading a Bible study, a small group, a discussion, or an activity, the average layperson needs regular training. We devote forty-five minutes of our monthly staff meeting to communicate vision and do skills development. We also have an annual staff retreat to do more significant training and team building.

6. *Be honest when you fail and quick to apologize.* Let's face it, we all do stupid things from time to time (some of us more often than others). When you make a bad call, pull a foolish stunt, or disregard your staff in some way, quickly acknowledge your error. Be honest about your failure and apologize to those involved. I've failed way too many times to be comfortable confessing my mistakes in print. Rather than hurting my relationship with the staff, many workers recount a few of my failures and my contrite apologies and see those times drawing us closer. I don't particularly take delight in their recalling times I said something stupid, had a major error in judgment, or lost my temper. But the fact that they remember not only the event but also the apology and look on it as a positive thing says a lot about the process of God developing grace in our lives.

Everyone Gets Front-Row Attention

I love the kids who voluntarily sit in the front row when I'm teaching. They're eager, motivated, and involved, and also easy to see, sitting right down in front. I can count on them having Bibles, answering questions, and making eye contact. I know their names. I like them.

We have a back row too. Students in the back row don't bring their Bibles, don't listen, and usually look bored. They often talk among themselves, occasionally disrupting the group with their noise. They are way at the back of the room and hard to see from up front. I haven't met many of them and know fewer of their names. I find it easy to ignore them.

Who loves the back row? Front-row kids are easy to love. They're right there with you. Back-row kids—they're harder. A couple of guys on our staff, Steve and Jeff, love the back row. They sit with them, endure the attitudes, and persevere in the slow process of getting to know them. Recently, the back row has been less disruptive and a little more interested. They were actually in a Bible discussion one morning. Why? What brought about a change? It's because Steve and Jeff are building relationships that show God's love. It wouldn't happen without team.

20

Coaching a Ministry Team

DAVE PATTY

I'VE ALWAYS THOUGHT ACTION was much more exciting than study. So when our youth group headed on its first ski retreat, I skipped the lessons offered for beginners and headed straight for the chairlift. *It can't be too hard,* I thought, and in some ways it wasn't. The skis headed straight down the hill with little or no effort from me, and it was easy to change directions—once I had fallen and managed to rearrange those planks so they pointed toward the opposite stand of trees. It was heady stuff—all about passion and speed. "Look at me, Mom! I can ski!"

But self-instruction has its down side. Not many years later, I was ready to quit the sport, frustrated with my inability to take a slope without at least one spectacular wipeout and discouraged with how much work it took to wrestle my body and those long boards around each turn. I began to read books on the sport and watch other skiers, trying to pick up why it seemed so effortless for them.

Still my improvements were incremental, no matter how hard I tried to make those fluid turns. My standard mode when something didn't work was to give it more force and energy. But this time even that didn't help. At the end of the day, my legs were burning with pain and my body bruised from numerous encounters with the ground.

"What you need is a coach," my brother said, as we sat around the fireplace at the end of the day.

"What do you mean?" I asked.

"You need someone to watch you and give you custom feedback, input that hones in on the key mistakes you're making. And then you need them to work with you until the problems are corrected." It was hard to take this kind of advice from a younger brother, but I was desperate. Swallowing my pride, I signed him up as my personal coach for the next day.

He stood at the top of the slope and watched closely as I huffed my way down. Then we went at it again, this time with him skiing next to me. All of a sudden he broke into laughter. "I knew something didn't look right," he said. "You're planting your pole on the wrong side of the turn."

"What do you mean?" I said.

"The skis are designed to turn easily," he replied, "when your weight is placed on them in the right place. Because of that, the pole should be planted on the downhill side. As you ski around it, your weight shifts naturally, and the skies practically turn by themselves."

"So what am I doing?" I asked, still a bit confused.

"You're planting your pole on the uphill side and then pushing on it to force yourself through the turn," my brother explained. "This puts your weight too far back and requires you to actually lift the skis off the ground to make them pivot. No wonder you were so tired!"

A pole plant on the wrong side. Could my problem be as simple as that? Now I could see my error, but correcting it wasn't easy. I had years of patterns to break, and it took intense concentration to flush the old way of doing things out of my system. For a time I was demoted to the bunny hill, where I practiced nothing but the pole plant for several days on end. Once the right pattern was established, however, the learning curve took off, and in no time I was hot on the tail of my brother. The best part was how much easier it was once I began working with the natural design of the skis rather than against them.

A good coach can make all the difference between success and failure, between hitting the ceiling in our growth or breaking through to the next level. I've experienced this many times in ministry. Just last year I flew all the way across the country to spend one day with a gifted ministry coach. What he gave me in just a few hours had more impact on my ministry than all the books I'd read in the previous nine months. It was tailor-made feedback, input that honed in on the key moves I needed to make in my life and ministry. Most importantly, he saw patterns where I saw only activity and was able to expose several "pole plants" positioned in the wrong place.

Coaching is time-consuming, and we won't be able to do it with everyone we work with. Certainly, teaching, training, and group experiences can significantly move people down the road of growth. But I'm convinced we won't produce top leaders without investing focused time and attention in skillful coaching. Coaching is essential for anyone interested in multiplying top leaders.

Coaching is an art. Intuition, connection, and heart all play a big part in the coach's impact. The role of the Holy Spirit in guiding and revealing is essential as well.

At the same time, even an art can be improved through a deeper understanding of the structure that undergirds it and with careful practice of the skills that make it fluid. Though truly great coaches seem to be born with some kind of coaching "sense," anyone can improve his coaching skills.

The Goal of Coaching

First, we need to fix firmly in our minds the purpose of coaching. In sports the primary focus is the upcoming game or winning the next competition. For a believer, the end of coaching is not to best the opponent or match the competitor. Neither is it to simply improve the players' skills and abilities. Our ultimate end is the glory of God. Spiritual coaching must be energized by God and result in praise, honor, and glory going to him.

We know, however, that one of the ways he's glorified is when people look more like his Son, when they're more completely his disciples. Another way he is glorified is when we produce fruit that springs from the source of the vine and that lasts. Considering John 15:8, we could say that our primary goal for the person we coach is that he glorify God by bearing much fruit, showing himself to be Christ's disciple.

The Core of Coaching

Every art form has a relatively simple underlying structure on which complexity and variation are built. The beautiful music we hear on the radio all comes from a simple set of scales and standard patterns of chords, put together in endless variations. A layperson hears only the overall effect, but a musician senses the patterns and can at times listen, then pick up another instrument, and reproduce the song in a simpler form. The underlying structure is simple enough to store in his head and even translate to another setting.

The art of coaching is similarly complex and yet built on a set of simple patterns. In my observation, the weight-bearing structure of coaching can be summarized in four main activities that need to be done skillfully and in concert, over and over. A coach needs to *see, engage, shape,* and *support.*

The Coach Needs to See

In spite of growing up in Colorado, known for its winter sports, I never had much interest in hockey. Then I moved to the Czech Republic, where hockey is a national obsession and a passion for most teenage boys. I remember the first game I attended with my Bible study guys in a stadium near our house. It was loud and chaotic, but I didn't even know when to cheer. The puck was moving so fast that half the time I couldn't follow it, and the entire game seemed a whirl of activity. It made no sense to me and about the only thing I could follow was the scoreboard—at least the numbers were something I recognized.

My guys, however, were chattering excitedly among themselves, pointing out strategies and mistakes, well-executed plays and failures. All of a sudden, I understood the difference. Where I saw a blur of activity, they saw patterns. Where I could discern only movement, they could see structure. Within these patterns they could spot deficiencies or particular skills and strengths. An ability to see patterns where I saw only activity gave them a totally different perspective on what was happening, even though we were looking at the same thing.

A coach must be an expert at seeing patterns, both those that should be and those that are. When my brother evaluated my skiing, he had a picture in his head of how a well-executed turn should look. When he compared my performance with that picture, my misplaced pole plant jumped out at him. The pattern had a fatal flaw, one that had to be corrected.

Good coaches study the patterns of the game and develop pictures in their heads. They interpret activity in the light of these patterns and often develop simple ways to communicate these pictures to others. The locker room has a whiteboard, a flip chart, or an overhead projector, which are periodically filled with Xs and Os or arrows and diagrams. Some of these drawings explain what's currently happening. Others describe what should be.

Over the years I've collected a set of basic pictures that help me evaluate various aspects of ministry. When someone speaks, I check to see if they are holding the listener's attention through *pitch, pace, pause,* and *power.* If believers don't seem to be growing, I hold up the picture of the early church in my mind and use it as a grid to evaluate if the youth group is providing a balance of *God's Word, prayer, sharing, mutual care* and *concern,* and *worship* (Acts 2:42–47). If a junior high leader is not keeping control of his group, I ask if he has *clear lines, consistent calls,* and *consequences.*

A number of helpful patterns can be lifted from various training materials, and the experienced coach develops some of his own in response to repeated problems and careful observation. My purpose isn't to provide all of these patterns but to help a coach be able to see patterns. A coach needs to see and evaluate three kinds of patterns.

1. Momentum patterns.[1] When I walk, I'm using a momentum pattern. My legs go through particular moves in a certain order, and the result is fluid movement in a certain direction. If I skip a part of the pattern—for instance, lifting my left foot off the ground—forward motion immediately slows down. My right leg has to expend significantly more energy to compensate for the failure of my left leg to do its work, and I may even fall and damage my body. All of the other parts of the walking cadence may be in order, but if one essential element is missing, I loose momentum.

If I want to experience forward movement, it is also essential that the parts of the pattern be executed in the proper order. If my right foot takes two steps before the left foot has a chance to take one, the cadence is broken. In a momentum pattern the order of events is very important because each builds on another and transfers energy to the next part in a smooth handoff. If one of the pieces is missing, a hole forms in the pattern, and forward motion may grind to a halt.

When I observe activity in the life of a youth group but little forward motion, I look for a momentum pattern that's being broken. Generally, an essential piece is missing, or steps are executed in the wrong order. Recently, a gifted youth leader shared with me his discouragement at the lack of fruit in evangelism. In spite of two or three evangelistic camps every summer and numerous outreaches throughout the year, his youth program hadn't seen any young people from the world trust Christ and become integrated into the youth group. His first reaction was to conclude that the camps were ineffective, and look for another evangelistic tool. I wondered if he was trying to hop forward on one foot.

We talked about the fact that evangelism is like gardening. A mix of activities done in a certain order provides the optimal conditions for spiritual growth. I shared how the momentum pattern of *cultivating* (building relationships, gaining trust, removing prejudices), *sowing* (communicating God's Word, developing an understanding of the gospel; hearing testimonies of changed lives), and *reaping* (challenging people to respond) help people move from a position of unbelief to faith and trust in Christ. Of course, salvation is a sovereign work of God, but a wise farmer can prepare optimal conditions for his work.

As we talked the lightbulbs began to come on, and this youth leader realized he was viewing evangelism as an event instead of a process. There was little preparation in the relationships before the event, and minimal follow-up with students afterward. Rather than stopping the evangelistic events, his youth program began to work

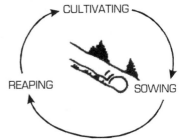

toward filling out the rest of the evangelism cadence, working to understand the order of the various parts and how they all work together to build momentum.

2. Health patterns. Every living thing needs a certain mix of essential elements to stay alive and growing. My body needs oxygen, food, water, and a certain range of temperature to function. If any one of those is gone, in only a matter of time my life will be gone as well. In the same way, spiritual life and living organisms such as youth groups require the ongoing presence of essential elements for them to stay healthy and flourish.

When I observe a youth group with no life, or with obvious signs of ill health, I examine the group's environment and its patterns. Often, an essential item is weak, draining health from the whole.

The difference between patterns of health and patterns of momentum is that in patterns of health the order is not as important. I can eat before I drink or sleep in the afternoon rather than the evening. What is most crucial is that all of the key elements are present and that the proper balance is maintained.

A book by Christian Schwarz, *Natural Church Development,*[2] has helped me understand patterns of health. He described eight essential items for the health of churches, drawing on a study of churches that are growing and those that are stagnating or declining. He used the picture of a wooden bucket, made of various staves.

In stave buckets there are certain essential items. Because every piece affects the others, even if one is missing the entire system won't function. This is true even when all the other elements are strong. If water is poured into a bucket with a missing stave, most of the water will run out. The shortest stave determines the capacity of the entire system.

In a growing system the greatest return will be found in strengthening the weakest element. Because this element limits your overall capacity, even a small change there will immediately increase the function of the entire system.

A good coach is always testing the balance of essential elements to see if the ministry is providing the proper environment for growth. The five essential activities of the early church (p. 224) are a good example of this. Keeping this basic structure in mind, a coach can identify the missing or weak element in the ministry and help the leader bring it back into balance.

3. *Destructive patterns.* Often, a particular problem in a youth leader or youth group functions like a poison, destroying health and wreaking havoc in an environment that would otherwise be producing much fruit. Every youth group has problems and deficiencies, but the nature of a destructive pattern is that it repeats itself. Such reoccurring problems, or chronic diseases, can suck the life out of everything around them, leaving everyone feeling empty and used. Unless they're resolved, other efforts will have limited results because of the destructive nature of this tenacious illness.

To find these patterns, look for a repeating problem. Often everyone will know about it, but no one will know how to get around it or solve it. People will think about it regularly but feel powerless to change it. This problem will sap their hope for the future and make them relate to the people and to the ministry in defensive ways.

The key is to see this problem as a pattern rather than an event. Generally, it's a set of interconnected problems, each reinforcing and energizing the next. If you see the pattern as a whole, there's more chance you can break the cycle and generate true change.

A destructive pattern in ministry, similar to a whirlpool, has a repetitive action and power to pull other aspects of the ministry into its vortex. Here's an example of a personal whirlpool that centers on an area of sin a believer is unable to break free from.

<u>The Whirlpool</u>

- Builds negative momentum.
- The same problem returns again and again.
- It takes continual investment of energy to keep it from getting worse.
- Each part feeds the others.
- It draws other things into its vortex and pulls them down with it.

The coach needs to see repeated behavior as a pattern rather than random events, in order to respond in a focused and productive way.

Using More Than One Set of Eyes

One of the inherent dangers of coaching is subjectivity. Coaches' own experiences, biases, and vested interests can skew their perception. Every vantage point has its limitations. If I sit in the stands, it's easier to follow the big picture, but I'll most likely miss some of the fine points that can significantly affect the outcome of the game. The perspective of the player, on the other hand, is much richer in information but can be skewed by the part of the competition he's focused on.

That's why every good coach relies on more than one set of eyes and more than one perspective as he seeks to guide his players to victory. He gathers information directly from the team, makes his own observations from the sidelines, and studies films made from the stands. Each perspective brings a different emphasis, but the combination of the three offers the most accurate and objective picture of the game.

Television producers know this, too, and in recent years have mounted cameras in players' helmets. As the game unfolds, the viewer is treated to an ever-changing point of view, from the big picture to the sideline shot, and then directly in the game from a player's vantage point. The end result is that the viewer "sees" much more clearly because his viewpoint is not limited to only one set of eyes.

A ministry coach must also work hard at gathering information from more sources than his own eyes. The best "seeing" happens when the coach deliberately looks at the person or ministry from three perspectives and then combines that view into a three-dimensional picture. The picture is most clear when we look at it through eyes of an objective third party (generally our own), through the eyes of others engaged in the game (second person), and through the eyes of the leader we're coaching (first person). Often we use a tool called the "window," which is simply a piece of paper divided into four sections, like a window with four panes, to help us gather information. In three of the panes we write observations from the three perspectives. Then, in the fourth pane, we jot down patterns we see or questions that come up as we compare the different perspectives.

The Window

First party—personal observations

Second party—other participants

Third party observations

The Coach Needs to Engage

It took me a year away at grad school before I had enough distance to see destructive patterns impacting my ministry. I hadn't been offering healthy habits of recharging and renewal for myself and the team, and because of that we often ran out of momentum, worn down by weariness and exhaustion. From several steps away, I was able to see it clearly, but I was sad because it was too late to correct the patterns, at least in that setting.

After I shared this with a coworker, he nodded knowingly. "I knew that several years ago," he said, "and even thought about talking with you about it. But in the end I didn't. I don't know exactly why."

I was angry with him—not for his criticism of my ministry but for his silence. I could have been spared a great deal of trouble if he had taken the initiative to tell me what he saw. Perhaps he was afraid and wondered if I would respond. But in any case, he failed to engage.

I've seen this problem repeat itself in people who would otherwise be good coaches. They make insightful observations, are capable of keen evaluations, but for some reason keep their insights to themselves and fail to take action.

On the other hand, coaches who have powerfully impacted my life always possessed an ability to jump right in and tell me what they saw, often with a candor and openness that's both surprising and disarming. An educational specialist visited our ministry several years ago on what I thought was a trip to gather information about informal education overseas. After she sat through a teaching session I was leading, I asked if she had any feedback. Out flew a piece of paper with notes on in, and her suggestions and observations began to roll. There was no apology or hesitation as she voiced areas that needed improvement. Her full engagement took me off guard, but still it struck me as strangely refreshing and energizing. I thought about her feedback for months and made a number of very helpful changes.

Good coaches engage quickly and fully. Their spirit is hopeful and expectant, full of confidence that the player has the capability to change and convinced that change will benefit the player. What makes engagement effective is the absence of judgment, guilt, doubt, or condemnation. The coach engages with openness and optimism that believes the best and looks forward to positive results.

A Coach Needs to Shape

Engagement is most powerful when it's accompanied by specific steps that lead to change. After my brother identified my wayward pole plant, he needed to show me what the proper movement looked like and then coach me through practice to break the old habit and imprint the new one. This involved modeling, directed observation, and then several days of focused practice. By the end, however, the new way of turning seemed natural to me, and I didn't have to think about it. What I received from him was more than just information—I myself had been shaped.

In a spiritual setting we must remember the three most powerful change agents available to us: the Word of God, the Spirit of God and the people of God. We can also take important cues from 2 Timothy 3:16, which lists four key activities: teaching, rebuking, correcting, and training. These same four tools are the essential elements of shaping, though sometimes one has more emphasis than others because of the nature of the problem being corrected.

When the matter is one of lack of knowledge, we respond by teaching. A quick lesson on turning theory was essential for me to understand why my pole plant was so important. For a brief time out there on the slopes, my coach became my teacher because change couldn't happen without additional information.

When the problem is a lack of motivation, rebuke is in order. If I had refused to change, my coach might have sternly pointed out the consequences of ignoring his instructions and urged me to correct my error. Confrontation might have been needed, the kind that takes place in the locker room at half-time when the team is not executing the right plays.

When the problem is a lack of understanding, correction can bring us back on track. Often misconceptions or faulty pictures bind us to bad behavior. A youth leader may be convinced that students must like him in order to have impact on them and thus be unable to lead them in a powerful way. For his leadership skills to change, underlying beliefs must change.

When the problem is a lack of experience, training is needed. Though I understood the new pole plant in my mind, it had still not become part of my behavior. I had to practice the turn over and over, on a less demanding slope where someone else could continue to observe me and give feedback. Training involves practice and repetition to build new habits. Often it takes concentrated effort before the new behavior becomes fluid and natural.

Remember to apply energy to the point that will bring about the most strategic change. Peter Senge expressed it this way: "The bottom line of systems thinking is leverage—seeing where actions and changes in structures can lead to significant, enduring improvements. Often leverage follows the principles of economy of means: where the best results come not from large-scale efforts but from small well-focused actions." He continued with a warning: "Beware the symptomatic solution. Solutions that address only the symptoms of a problem, not fundamental causes, tend to have short-term benefits at best. In the long term, the problem resurfaces and there is increased pressure for symptomatic response. Meanwhile, the capability for fundamental solutions can atrophy."[3]

Remember, too, that most people can focus on only one to three areas of significant improvement at a time. As a coach, you're not looking for perfect performance but the building of long-term habits and the correction of chronic problems. If the issue you've identified really is crucial, even change in a single area can bring significant results to the entire ministry.

A Coach Needs to Support

For a number of years I worked with young people on military bases. Several times one of my officer friends explained to me, "The men don't do what is expected, but what is inspected." We trust those in ministry have a higher intrinsic motivation, but generally regular checkups make it much more likely that a given change will become permanent.

Part of the support a coach provides is returning to an issue at a later date and making necessary corrections or adjustments to continue progress in the area. But change always pulls against the forces of inertia and requires facing the twin giants of doubt and fear. In other words, growth is difficult and takes energy and courage. Support must be provided on the emotional level so that forward progress doesn't grind to a halt.

An essential role of a coach is that of cheerleader. His confidence and resolve is infectious, and the thumbs-up that follows a good play is tremendously energizing to the team. Not long ago after I sent a report to my ministry coach, he fired back a three-line e-mail that included the following line: "You're not just a good leader, Dave; you're a great one."

The burden of bringing about the change he had recommended was weighing heavily on me that day, but all of a sudden it seemed light. I sat up straighter, felt new courage in my soul, and plowed into the responsibilities of my day with new energy. All because of a three-line e-mail. His support and encouragement mean the world to me.

We see this kind of spirit all through Paul's writing. As he communicated to his team from prison on the sidelines, he expressed confidence in God's work in his companions' lives, deep love and belief in them, and specific praise for work well done. He also supported them in prayer, taking their situations to the Lord every time they came to mind.

Whenever I leave a coaching session, I try to pin down some kind of follow-up or support. Sometimes we arrange a "checkup" by phone or reserve a follow-up meeting. Sometimes the people I'm coaching have a specific assignment due by a particular time. When I see them the next time, I ask about specific progress in the areas we discussed and sometimes bring additional thoughts or resources to the table that I've gathered since our last meeting. I will often jot notes and give them a copy so we can return to issues we discussed and review them.

Every new habit or fresh area of growth is fragile at the beginning, like a small sapling that's just taken root or a broken bone just reset. It needs extra support to stay in place until the roots take hold and the new pattern strengthens to the place where it can continue on its own. As time passes, the need for support decreases to the point where new growth retains its shape, even without outside influence.

A good coach doesn't function alone. Rather, he builds a coaching team and even helps players learn to coach one another. First, we need to coach in teamwork with God's Word and his Spirit. Second we need to become master coaches ourselves, skillful at seeing, engaging, shaping, and supporting. But also we need to equip others around us to do the same. Strong leaders create environments in which younger leaders grow and flourish and are often then sent out to reproduce in other settings. The deliberate creation of a "coaching culture" that encourages feedback does this.

The end we strive for, of course, is God's glory. When leaders become more effective disciples and bear much fruit, his name is lifted up and exalted.

Notes

1. For a discussion of these principles in business, see Peter M. Senge, *The Fifth Discipline: The Art and Practice of the Learning Organization* (New York: Doubleday/Currency, 1990).

2. Christian A. Schwarz, *Natural Church Development: A Guide to Eight Essential Qualities of Healthy Churches* (Carol Stream, Ill.: ChurchSmart Resources, 1996).

3. Senge, *The Fifth Discipline*, 101.

21.

Caring for Finances

GENE POPPINO

THE B-WORD IS A DIRTY WORD to most youth workers. Say *budget* and you'll here a chorus of groans, followed by a litany of whining and grumbling. What is it about money and ministry budgets that inspires such emotion? Why do many youth workers prefer a root canal over developing their annual budget?

There are at least three reasons the average youth leader hates the budgeting process.

The first is ignorance. We don't understand it. Our personal budget never demanded a great deal of skill (because we never had any money of our own), so it isn't a focus of our attention. When it comes to the youth ministry budget, many simply don't know enough to confidently put it together.

The second reason is lack of experience. Typically, a church budget needs to be planned up to eighteen months in advance. The average youth worker thinks about eighteen hours in advance. Even many experienced youth workers plan only four to twelve weeks out. Forecasting ministry needs more than a year in advance requires a plan that's often not yet developed. We don't know what we're going to do, so how can we know what it will cost? Also, a characteristic of many good youth workers is spontaneity. A budgeting process that forces them to forecast expenditures next year violates their spontaneous nature.

The third reason is the subtle perception that it's not really *ministry*. We work with kids. Teaching, discipling, counseling—those are the significant parts of ministry. Budgets are a bother.

What Did Jesus Think about Money?

Jesus talked about money more than any other single subject—more than about sin, salvation, evangelism, or love. Do our attitudes reflect his priorities?

When Jesus told the parable of the talents (Matt. 25:14–30), the big issue was not *how much* money each man received but how he handled what he was given. Handling financial resources in a wise manner was a test of deeper character, and that character was rewarded with greater wealth commensurate with competence.

In Mark 6, Jesus instructed his disciples about resources when he sent them out to preach. Calling the Twelve to him, he sent them out two by two and gave them authority over evil spirits. These were his instructions: "take nothing for the road except a walking stick: no bread, no traveling bag, no money in their belts. They were to wear sandals, but not put on an extra shirt. Then He said to them, 'Whenever you enter a house, stay there until you leave that place. If any place does not welcome you and people refuse to listen to you, when you leave there, shake the dust off your feet as a testimony against them.' So they went out and preached that people should repent. And they were driving out many demons, anointing many sick people with oil, and healing" (Mark 6:8–13).

Clearly, they were operating on a sandal-strap budget, and that was just as Jesus intended. Having no money was not a hindrance to effective ministry. The point is plain, *Jesus*-ministries are not about money or a lack of it but about using to best advantage whatever resources the Lord gives us.

The apostle Paul talked about financial responsibility as evidence of his love and sincerity of calling (1 Thess. 2:3–6, 9; Acts 20:33–35; 1 Cor. 9:3–14). How he handled both his personal and ministry finances were evidence of his character and credibility. His financial integrity was above those who ministered for personal profit (2 Cor. 2:17). How money and resources were handled was reaffirmed as a test of faithfulness, just as the Lord had demonstrated in his life and teaching.

Too many youth workers learn the hard way that their attention to finances is inadequate. Bob was a visionary youth leader. His charisma and passion for Christ combined with a buoyant optimism thrust him to positions of real influence early in his ministry. People trusted him and credited him with experience and vision beyond his years. His visionary stance and charismatic leadership style made him the point man for a large community outreach event—a combined effort of eight or nine churches. The venue was booked, a big-name band and speaker secured, and publicity went out.

On the big night the crowd that trickled in barely paid enough to cover half the expenses. Bob had no backup funding, no plan B, only embarrassment and a shortfall of thousands of dollars. Beyond that, Bob's credibility was gone. It took more than a year for all the bills to get paid, and longer before he was trusted with significant leadership again. Even years later, those on the periphery of the event sometimes question Bob's competence. They didn't know the details, but they remembered Bob blew it.

In most churches there are two unforgivable sins: sexual misconduct and financial irresponsibility. Failure in either area is an automatic ejection. With so much resting on such issues, it's imperative our Bible colleges and seminaries train young ministers to budget and manage finances. It doesn't matter whether we work in a church with great financial resources or a church with financial limitations. Good stewardship begins with a heart that properly understands and values money as a tool given by God and then develops the skills to use it wisely.

A Budget the Board Will Love

You're kidding, right? Who really loves budgets? But I'm serious. Men and women who work in the business world love numbers because they know numbers represent significant results. In ministry, business-minded people see beyond the dollars and cents to good stewardship. A good youth ministry budget can inspire confidence and a greater commitment to the ministry.

But how does someone without experience or giftedness in fiscal planning get it done?

Get Help

If you're not trained in handling money, find an accountant or financial guru who will help and coach you through the process. I came to my present church seventeen years ago from a smaller, shrinking congregation that budgeted $250 per year for youth ministry. I spent the annual budget just taking kids to Dairy Queen. I stepped into a congregation five times larger with a budget nearly sixty times greater. I was ecstatic over the financial resources finally available to me.

Then came the kicker—I had to plan how that money would be used. I guess I thought it would be like a personal checkbook, and I could just use the money as needs arose. But, no, I had to have a plan for the whole year. When it came time to propose a budget for the following year, I still didn't have a clue where to begin. My help came from an elder on my youth committee. He was a detail type who loved numbers. As an engineer for Boeing, he knew how to break down expenses and analyze costs. He also knew the needs of our youth ministry. John saved me that first year and for the next couple of years of ministry. He did our student ministries budget while I looked over his shoulder and answered questions about goals and programming. Eventually, I understood the process and needed less and less help. After five or six years, I was doing it on my own.

Don't pretend to know more than you do. Acknowledge inexperience or lack of skill and find someone to help.

Examine Past Budgeting

Has there been a youth ministry budget? How was it established? What factors caused it to go up or down? Who created budgets, the board or the pastor?

A big question that will reveal a great deal is, does the church have what Stephen Covey called an "abundance mentality" or a "scarcity mentality"? An abundance mentality is the attitude that there is plenty out there for everyone. Covey explained it like this: "Most people are deeply scripted in what I call the Scarcity Mentality. They see life as having only so much, as though there were only one pie out there. And if someone were to get a big piece of the pie, it would mean less for everybody else."[1] In a church with a habit of scarcity thinking, there will be a not-so-subtle competition for finances. It will feel like one group will lose if another group gets a bigger budget.

Some churches budget with faith, others only with a spreadsheet and a bottom line. How does it work at your church? My first three churches had no previous youth pastors and no history of youth budgets. At my current church, my predecessor, Roger, successfully led the youth ministry for seven years. He established a healthy youth budget and a healthy pattern of increases based on numerical growth and strategic ministry goals. I benefited from Roger's history of good management and trust.

Often, youth workers are called to pioneer the vision for youth ministry support. They may experience firsthand the adage "Pioneers get the arrows." In established ministries someone has already taken those shots, and you'll inherit healthy attitudes about financing youth ministry.

Submit a *Vision* before a Budget

Most significant decisions in life are vision-driven. This is especially true when it comes to money. People support what they believe in, and few churches will create a budget without believing it's a worthwhile investment. To establish a vision for financial support, it's essential to have clearly stated goals, a plan for results-oriented programming, and specifics for how the money will be used. Where there is no vision the budget will fail. The numbers in your budget must be clearly tied to the vision for what you expect to accomplish with that money.

My first full-time position was in a 250-member church in Vancouver, Washington. The church was one of the oldest churches in the state and had some of the oldest people too! It was in a rural area just beginning to see urban sprawl. Farmlands were becoming housing projects, and demographics of the area were rapidly changing. The new public high school was built in a field next to the church and opened its doors the year I arrived to begin a youth ministry. Though students surrounded us, our youth group had only six active high schoolers and they had almost no impact on their campuses. Four of them attended the high school next door.

As I was praying about how our church could impact the students next door, I would sit and watch hundreds of kids walk past the church to a local market during their lunch hour. They had time, they had an open campus, and they obviously walked past the church. Why not invite them over for lunch? And it began with that simple idea.

I went to our congregation and said, "We've got thousands of unsaved students next door. They wouldn't dream of coming to church for no reason, so let's give them a reason. Let's do lunch for them. Invite them all over during their two lunch hours. We'll get a band, put on a teaser concert while they're eating, and invite them back to church in the evening." Remember, I was spinning this vision to people in their sixties, seventies and even eighties. These were farmers who still hadn't quite adjusted to a high school in the middle of what used to be pasture, and now they were being asked to reach out to kids. God bless them, they said yes even though they were only vaguely aware of what it might cost.

It took weeks of preparation to arrange the food. Most surprising were the negotiations with the school, which didn't mind kids walking down the street to smoke, shoplift from the little store, and pick an occasional fight. But let them go to *church?* Well now, that was a *big* decision! Finally, the day arrived. Volunteers lined up to make sandwiches, put out cookies and chips, and provide food to twelve hundred students in two thirty-minute shifts. What an undertaking for a team of people who had finished raising their own kids fifty years earlier!

The students came. Hesitant at first but finally streaming over in droves after word got out that there was all-you-can-eat free food next door. Hundreds showed up for that first lunch. Those dear church people were way beyond their comfort zone. Not only were hundreds of unchurched high school kids all over the church property, but there was loud Christian rock music playing with drums! Our servers turned off their hearing aids so the band was less loud. They smiled at kids and made sandwiches for all they were worth.

That night the kids came back. Some got saved. Soon our youth group began to grow and eventually thirty students received Christ that first year. Here's the point: When it came time to plan for the next year, our dear church folks remembered how God used that event to save kids, and they were *motivated* to make sure our church calendar and *budget* were ready to do it again. They had a *vision* for what could be accomplished, and they wanted to provide the resources to see it happen. They became vision-driven, not survival-focused.

A budget is merely a tool for accomplishing vision. When we tell stories of life change and how church resources played a part and as people dream of impacting lives, the reason for the budget comes into focus. People see it and get on board with it because it becomes their vision too.

Do Research to Understand the Big Picture

Being able to answer the following questions will demonstrate both knowledge and competence:

1. What are youth budgets in comparable-sized churches?
2. How does your proposed budget break out *per student* for the year? How does that cost compare with ratios in either children's or adult education expenses?
3. Be able to explain why youth ministry costs what it does. An example might be the use of prizes or awards. Prizes for young children at the end of a week of VBS might be a pencil with Scripture verses or a small key chain with a cute animal character on it. Awarding that type of prize to teens would be insulting. For teens, CDs, T-shirts, or concert tickets score big. Teen prizes simply cost more than children's. A youth budget will reflect that.
4. If the youth group is increasing in size numerically, is the budget keeping pace? If the youth group grows 20 percent but the youth budget increases only 5 percent, then there is a decrease in the support the church provides per student.
5. Are there start-up costs or catch-up costs to consider? Is this a new ministry? If it is, there are start-up costs for sports equipment, curriculum, prizes, and other resources. If the ministry has recently been through a down season or a long time between youth pastors, resources may be out of date or depleted. Be able to identify essential ministry tools for the work to start well.

Talk about Options for Ministry Funding

Ideally, every youth ministry would be so valued and appreciated that the church would be anxious to establish a healthy budget to see the work done well. But there are many reasons a church may not be able to fully fund the ministry. When you share your vision for what you expect God to do in the ministry, be able to discuss alternative financing, such as:

Student Fees: According to the Center for Parent/Youth Understanding, a 1998 study revealed that the average U.S. teen has discretionary income of ninety-eight dollars per week.[2] Because teens have few bills or indebtedness, they easily spend it on things they want—like cosmetics, entertainment, and cars. An important direction in funding youth ministry must consider that it's not necessary for a church to subsidize every ministry event. In many cases, it's reasonable for students to pay the full cost of activities, camps, and retreats. Church budgets can provide the important resource base for a variety of ministries without having to spend huge sums of money for every youth event.

What about students who can't pay the cost? Isn't there a danger of providing ministry only to those who can afford it? Many churches address this important issue through some type of scholarship program. One youth pastor specifically invited parents whose children were grown to provide camp scholarships. Because they were no longer paying for all the school and church activities of a middle or high school student, would they "adopt" a student and sponsor that young person for camp each year? Many people responded with great empathy, and those who understood the high cost of a student's attendance at events provided scholarships.

Of course, nearly every group will charge for camps and retreats. The issue to consider is where to draw the line. What events should incur a user fee, and what ministry activities should be covered or subsidized by the church budget? Obviously, user fees have limits and not all ministry expenses should be covered this way.

Fund-Raisers: A long tradition in many churches is fund-raising for various programs or ministries. Car washes, bake sales, candy sales, slave auctions, and other sales are as much a part of the annual program as Bible study. One advantage of fund-raisers is that many churches have successfully used them to raise significant sums of money for ministry. Youth speaker Duffy Robbins probably pointed out the down side best when he told a church board, "If I had wanted to get into retail work, I would have applied for a job at K-Mart."[3] If fund-raising becomes a major emphasis of the work, the real ministry of making disciples will suffer.

Low-Cost and No-Cost Activities: Many things in youth ministry can be done for little cost. Many games require only simple equipment like Frisbees or footballs. Not every Bible study and youth group meeting needs purchased refreshments. If refreshments are crucial to the success of a gathering, students can be assigned to bring them, spreading out the cost so that no one pays too much. No-cost events like hikes, biking, game nights, and talent shows all can be done with a little creativity and planning and provide important ministry accessible for every student.

The disadvantage to doing only low-cost and no-cost activities is there are limitations on how much you can do for free. Those limitations, especially when doing outreach events, may diminish the appeal of the event for a typical unchurched student.

Accept Compromise Graciously

If you don't get everything you think you need, work for incremental change and begin preparing your budget for next year. Even a small change in a budget is a move in the right direction. Adopt a broad view of the process and renew your efforts to communicate clearly your ministry vision and financial needs.

One youth pastor was asked during particularly tense budget negotiations if the youth could make do with no increase in their allotment for a year. Although it would mean certain resources would be delayed, he agreed, seeing the pressure several other departments were facing. He replied, "I see the more desperate needs in other departments, and I'm committed to the success of our church, not only the youth. I think the money is needed more in other areas this year. Youth will tighten our belts and make it work with less."

A year later, his willingness to sacrifice for the team was remembered, and several other staff were quick to point out it was time the youth department received an increase. His budget was increased significantly that year, but, more importantly, the whole team began to look out for the needs of one another's departments. Because he refused to approach the budget with a scarcity mentality and didn't fight for his share, greater progress was made in successive years.

Express Appreciation for Your Elder's Vision and Work

Most church boards are made up of godly men who face the daunting task of overseeing the church ministry while holding down jobs and caring for families. They often struggle to balance the needs of all departments while coming up with a fair distribution of limited money. Theirs is no easy task. Too many youth leaders, disappointed over not receiving the budget they requested, pout like children who didn't get the cookies they wanted. They act as if not receiving their full budget request was a personal rejection and subtly communicate that to the board. Instead, remember to say thanks.

Budget Basics

What items should be included in a budget? Every church budget is different, but certain things are basic. Below is a sample high school ministry budget from a church with a Sunday morning attendance of around 2,500 and a high school ministry of more than 250 students. Included here is their *Charter of Accounts*:

Sample Charter of Accounts

Curriculum/Ministry Resources	*$2,340*
Area Bible Studies	*$500*
HS Winter Conference	*$1,200*
HS Winter Camp	*$2,420*
HS Summer Camp	*$0 (entirely funded by user fees)*
Events	*$1,200*
Miscellaneous Expenses	*$800*
Lay Leadership Training	*$2,000*
Youth Missions/Evangelism	*$1,000*
Printing—Sent Out	*$1,500*
Supplies	*$700*
Operational Equipment	*$1,250*
Equipment Maintenance/Repair	*$300*
Personal Ministry Expenses	*$1,900*
Seminars and Classes	*$300*
Professional Enrichment	*$1,200*

The above budget is a snapshot of ministry finances in a certain location, of a certain size, in a certain economic bracket. A smaller church or a church with less history of youth ministry will obviously start at an entirely different level of funding. In the above example, the categories can be instructive, but they aren't intended to be examples of how much money should be allocated in every area. Churches creating a budget for the first time may have only four or five lines to express the needs and vision of the ministry. In a very simple or concise budget, *curriculum, activities, supplies, camps and retreats,* and *reimbursed ministry expenses* could easily capture all necessary expenditures. Each budget must fit the needs of the ministry, the church culture, and the level of detail requested by the board.

Avoid Asking Forgiveness—Do It Right the First Time!

I scream inside every time I hear a smug youth worker say, "It's easier to ask forgiveness than permission." The thin veil of humor fails to adequately cover the irresponsibility, immaturity, and disregard for authority so often represented in this worn-out statement. No matter your spiritual successes, no matter how big your ministry, you'll get fired for serious financial misman-agement. Forgiveness will not be enough for your reputation to remain intact.

For godly stewardship, healthy management, and a high level of financial integrity, the following steps are essential.

Keep Good Records

Whether it's recording reimbursable business mileage for your car or turning in receipts for ministry expenses, you must have a consistent system for keeping records.

Recruit Gifted People to Manage Details

Most youth pastors love camps and retreats, but when that line of students forms at registration, they're not at their best taking money, checking registration forms, and noting who has paid. Get someone who's detail-oriented to keep the paper trail.

Be Honest

A common aspect of working with students is that a lot of cash can flow through our hands. We're always collecting money for an event, activity, or materials. Sometimes the distinction between "my" money and "group" money is blurred. If you rationalize, "I'm on my way to the youth retreat, and this is something I need at the retreat, and they don't pay me enough anyway. . . ." and you "borrow" group money for personal expenses, you set yourself up for spiritual catastrophe. One youth leader began to compromise in how he handled petty cash and ended up getting fired for stocking his personal snack drawer from the youth group refreshment fund.

Pay Attention to Big-Ticket Events

Camps, retreats, and large events with a big cash flow or budget must be carefully planned and managed. Take a typical youth camp, for example. Plus or minus 10 percent on the number of students attending a week of camp is a substantial attendance margin. If your camping ministry is a fifteen-thousand-dollar event, 10 percent translates to a loss (or gain) of fifteen hundred dollars. Is that margin planned into your budget? To manage larger sums responsibly, several essential steps need to be taken.

Create Margins: Create margins or have contingency funds for unexpected but inevitable costs. One year, we were doing our regular water ski camp with seventy-five high school students sleeping in tents when Idaho had its greatest rainfall in one hundred years. There wasn't a dry sleeping bag in camp the next morning. Or the morning after that. Daily trips to the local laundromat to dry sleeping bags were an unplanned but very necessary expense.

Know Your Break-Even Point: What is the minimum number of students needed to pay the basic expenses for this event? Is it reasonable for that number to sign up, or are you taking a big step of faith? Though you need to live and minister by faith, it must be wedded with wisdom and common sense. Plan a budget that will allow your necessary expenses to be covered by the minimum number of expected attendees.

It's a Tool—Use It Well

Some people love technology. They have the latest computers, PDAs, cell phones, laptops, satellite radios, even global positioning satellite maps in their cars. Some people are into only gadgets, but others really use all of those electronic communication and information tools. They talk about their increased efficiency, convenience, and profitability.

I'm not one of them. I was dragged kicking and screaming into the computer age. I was one of the last people on the face of the earth to get a cell phone. (I know this because as soon as I got one, everyone else called me on it!) The irony of my computer-challenged life is that my wife, Anne, is an information systems assistant. She not only knows how to use the tools, she speaks the language. Under her gracious but persistent training, my hate, dread, and skepticism about the world of electronic tools have softened over the years. Don't get me wrong. Microsoft will not be calling anytime soon for me to join the company. But I'm no longer computer-illiterate. I rarely crash it anymore, and my need for tech assistance has dropped off significantly. I even grudgingly admit there are times I feel lost without e-mail, my cell phone, or computer. They are now tools I need to get the job done.

Attitudes about church finances can easily mirror the same fear, dread, and disdain I had for technology. Whether it comes from lack of experience or a previous bad experience, a leader must conquer any attitude that causes him or her to resist budgets and careful financial management. Money is a God-given tool, and our job is to use it as God intended. Good management of finances is part of good stewardship.

Once upon a time there was a ministry that faced exponential growth and extremely limited resources. Some of the leaders could think only that the scarcity of resources meant the ministry would have to disband. There just wasn't enough to go around. One leader saw it differently from the rest. He stepped forward, did a quick inventory of the limited supplies, and then invited everyone to a church dinner. With only a couple of loaves, a few fish, and some serving baskets, thousands had both physical and spiritual needs met.

As we balance all of the complicated issues around money in the twenty-first century, we need the reminder that Jesus owns it all, creates it all, and supplies it all. It's the same today as it was in the first century. What he asks us to do is to remember our ministries are never about money but about depending on him. We're not about saving as much money as we can or doing everything as cheaply as possible. Remember, he praised Mary for her generous anointing even though others grumbled at the expense (John 12). On the other hand, he reminded the disciples they didn't need a lot when he sent them out. "'Take nothing for the road,' He told them, 'no walking stick, no traveling bag, no bread, no money; and don't take an extra shirt'" (Luke 9:3). Ministry happens with and without money. It's not the issue. His call to us is to serve with passion for and confidence in our Lord, regardless of this Earth's resources. Then as now, it's all about Jesus.

Notes

1. Stephen Covey, *The Seven Habits of Highly Effective People* (New York: Simon & Schuster, 1990), 219.

2. www.cpyu.org, bulletin published December 1998.

3. Duffy Robbins, *Youth Ministry Nuts and Bolts: Mastering the Ministry behind the Scenes* (Grand Rapids, Mich.: Zondervan, 1990), 187.

22.
Working with Parents

DAVID JONGEWARD

WHEN I STEPPED IN THE DOOR, the phone was ringing. I hurried to answer it, thinking it could be a family member trying to reach us, knowing we'd been out of the state for a two-week vacation. The voice was female, but strong, determined, and abrupt. "Lori has just run away from home, and it's all *your* fault." I was a youth pastor, and this was a parent of one of the girls in my high school youth group. She was obviously frustrated and concerned, but why was she blaming me? She went on. "We put Lori in *your* youth group, so *you* could teach her and disciple her, and now she ran away. What are *you* going to do about it?"

What was *I* going to do about it? Was it *my* fault this happened? How could it be? I was only the youth pastor. Why was this *my* responsibility? I found myself feeling defensive. I knew enough about crisis to know that it was better to just listen and try to encourage than to let my defensiveness dictate the conversation. But her accusation haunted—and hurt me.

The next few days meant helping to pick up the pieces of a family squabble, calming down an angry, and frustrated young teenager, and encouraging the parents to hang in there. But something far deeper and more significant happened—something that would change the way I did youth ministry.

Questioning the Role of Parents

God used that phone call to make me reconsider my role and the parents' role in youth ministry. These questions struck at the very core of my view of youth ministry and, ultimately, changed my whole philosophy. I began to think about a number of related issues:

- What exactly is my God-given role and responsibility as youth pastor? What should be the responsibility of anyone doing youth ministry?

Am I responsible for the spiritual growth and development of these young people?

- What is my authority? What authority and right do I have to minister to these young people?
- What is the role and responsibility of parents? If parents are ultimately responsible for their kids' spiritual growth and development, then how does my role harmonize?
- How do I see parents in youth ministry? Are parents a hindrance or a help? A problem and a pain or a pleasure to work with? Do I view parents as partners in ministry or as problems in ministry? Should I work with parents in youth ministry or work without them?
- Ultimately, are parents just a necessary distraction to effective youth ministry, those we just have to put up with? Or are they a necessary dimension of effective youth ministry without whom we can't do ministry?

In searching for a biblical basis for youth ministry, I looked up "youth pastor" and "youth ministry" in *Young's Analytical Concordance.* Neither was there. But the Bible sure has a lot to say about the family, the home, and the role of parents. Passages such as Ephesians 6:4 indicate that fathers (parents) have the responsibility to "bring them up in the training and instruction of the Lord." Deuteronomy 6 (and other chapters) and Proverbs 22:6 describe the teaching and training process, with a strong implication that this is the parents' rightful role. God reminded me that parents and family have the divine authority and, therefore, should have priority in youth ministry, not the youth pastor or youth staff. Ultimate authority and responsibility does belong to the parents. Then why are the parents mostly left out of church youth ministry?

Paradigm Shift

I determined before God to rethink my whole philosophy of youth ministry, to reevaluate all my youth programs and activities in light of the authority and priority of the home, family, and parents. I even needed to think of ways to educate and motivate parents about their God-given role and responsibilities. My whole strategy and way of doing youth ministry needed a paradigm shift.

I concluded that all youth ministry should be subject to the sanctity of this parental chain of command. Any authority or basis for ministry to youth is a privilege that is granted or requested by the parents of those youth. Whether parents actively give us the right or passively allow us to minister to their teens, the ultimate authority resides with them. Just because many parents fail to take this authority and responsibility seriously doesn't mean youth workers should ignore this God-given principle and bypass the parent. Ultimately, the youth worker is there to support, supplement, and cooperate with the parents in training their youth. This is God's design. Youth ministry is really a *team ministry working with parents*, not a competitive ministry in which youth workers fight with parents for the time and attention of young people.

Parent-Sensitive Youth Ministry

If this paradigm shift is to take place in our youth ministries, we must look at several practical considerations and implications:

Parents and Planning the Youth Program

When we plan programs, meetings, activities, and retreats, we must consider and respect parental authority. We youth workers can become so overzealous with planning all of these wonderful events that we forget to consult or communicate with parents. We charge off in our own direction, according to our own agenda, and wonder why parents resist us or don't eagerly support our programs. If your ministry team works with parents, planning will take on a whole new perspective.

What do parents think in general about the youth program? What do parents think about the quality and quantity of programs? Are all youth meetings, events, and activities necessary, and are they accomplishing something significant and intentional? Some youth ministries are guilty of overbooking events, regardless of family commitments and schedules. Teens are very busy these days, juggling many responsibilities—school, sports, jobs, church, and family. Certainly we should ask teens for their input concerning the planning and scheduling of youth events, but we also need to ask parents.

I developed a parental survey shortly after my view toward parents shifted. I asked for their suggestions about our programs and ideas of how to better support the family structure and assist them. I also wanted to better understand their expectations of our youth ministry and be more sensitive to their feelings and ideas. I then invited them to a meeting to discuss their opinions and brainstorm creative ideas.

As a result, we made several significant program changes. For example, every week offered a Wednesday night youth group *and* a Sunday night youth fellowship after the evening church service. The parents felt this was too much. For parents, Sunday evening was a good time to be home with family and to socialize with other church families. So we cancelled Sunday's program. At the parents' suggestion, we organized a monthly fellowship for parents and their teens. Junior high teens and their parents met after church at Pizza Hut, and the senior high teens and their parents met at Pizza World. After eating together, parents talked together about issues they faced as parents, while their teens enjoyed the video games. There was no pressure or expectation to attend, but those who did loved it. This took little time and effort to plan. It affirmed the parents' agenda and also gave my wife and I a wonderful time to interact with them.

Sensitive Topics and Issues

Are there any topics or issues that you want to teach in your youth group that should first be approved or cleared by the parents? I found some parents are very conservative and very sensitive about certain topics. I needed to be cautious and respect their feelings. Even if we disagree, we must fairly and accurately represent the views and values of believing parents when we teach.

One year, our youth staff decided to show a sensitive video about abortion. Although the picture was not graphic, it was visual enough to be quite traumatic and emotionally disturbing and clearly portrayed the horror and pain of abortion. We knew some parents might disapprove, so we wrote a letter to inform them of our plan and invited them to view the video at a parent meeting. That was our best-attended parent meeting ever.

Throughout my years of youth ministry experience, I learned (sometimes the hard way) that when in doubt about any possibly sensitive topic, video, or experience, consult parents first. Don't just proceed. It's far better to get approval first than it is to have to deal with frustrated, angry parents the next day in your office. You show your commitment to them and your respect for their authority and feelings by doing this. You also earn their respect and trust.

By the way, there are simple ways you can secure parental input about your youth ministry programming. Establish a standing parent committee. Place parent representatives on your youth committee. Include parents on your staff. These simple moves will keep you sensitive to their priorities.

Parents and Program Conflict

What happens when parents and youth programs conflict? Maybe parents don't want their teens to attend certain events. What's your response? Do you really believe that parents have the final authority to decide the level of their kids' involvement? Wise counsel would be to do whatever you can to support parents and their choices for their teens even if it means they may not attend your youth group. But I think there are ways you can communicate with the teen and the parent to resolve the situation.

Shane was a boy who started coming to our youth group because of his interest in one of the cute girls. Not long after, he met Jesus Christ and invited him into his life. He suddenly became very involved in all aspects of our youth ministry. But soon his non-Christian parents became frustrated with his absence from home and forbade him from coming to youth group.

Shane asked me, "Do I obey my parents, or do I obey God and come to church and youth group?" I encouraged him to respect his parents' wishes and stay home but quickly added that his attitude might make a huge difference. If he obeyed with a poor attitude, he would compromise his testimony. If he responded respectfully, it would honor the Lord and might even affect their attitude toward church. I thought he should demonstrate a special love for his parents by volunteering to help around the house, communicate love and appreciation to them often, and generally show them the love of the Lord through his words and deeds.

Several weeks later, Shane came bounding into my office with an exciting story. His parents asked him, "Do they teach you to love and obey your parents at that church and youth group you go to? If they teach you to do that, then you can go all you want!" Shane not only returned to church and youth group with his parent's blessing, but soon he was bringing his parents. In a matter of time, his parents became Christians, spurred by Shane's loving obedience. Not every story turns out this well, but God can work out the conflict if we honor parental authority and follow the proper line of respect that he has authorized through the home and family.

Parents and Teen Problems

In a crisis or counseling situations with a young person, be sure to represent fairly and accurately the authority and position of the parents. I've seen too many youth workers take kids in and discuss serious issues in their lives without involving the parents or respecting their God-given authority. Keep in mind these points when you're involved directly with a young person in a crisis, problem, or parental conflict.

- After you listen to a teen's problem, try to think how the parent would respond. Never counsel or do something that would violate the parent's authority or values in that teen's situation.
- Always tell teens that God has given them the parents he wants them to have, and that disobedience of or rebellion against parents is not godly. Encourage them to obey, honor, respect, and love their parents, and to be honest with them.
- Encourage the teen to think or view the situation from the parent's viewpoint. You may role play with the teen to help him think through

possible responses or thoughts that their parents would have in that situation.

- Show strong commitment to the parents (and their God-given authority) as you counsel and discuss solutions with the teen. Never encourage or allow a teen to lie, cheat, disobey, or disrespect their parents.
- Be willing to communicate to the parents the nature and details of the problem or crisis. Parents have a right to know what's happening with their teen. If you think you want to protect the parent from knowing certain information, you may be usurping their parental authority by not telling them.

Sometimes a student will come to talk to you about a topic that will get them into deep trouble with their parents. What do you do when they preface their comments by asking, "Do you promise not to tell?" The answer is always a gentle no. Tell teens you love them and want to hear what they have to tell you, but they will have to trust your judgment and believe you will do the appropriate thing with the information they tell you.

You want them to trust you with personal information, but knowing this information may put you in an awkward situation regarding confidentiality. Never promise to keep things a secret. Some information really needs to be shared with their parents (and other authorities). It's best if they talk to their parents. They may need your help and encouragement to do so. They may feel more comfortable if you volunteer to go with them when they talk to a parent.

Proactive Communication with Parents

A change in thinking about parents means thinking proactively about ways to communicate, cooperate, and work with them. We can't passively wait for parents to come to us with their input, ideas, and feedback. If we do, most of the feedback is likely to be critical or negative, and then we tend to react defensively rather than respond positively. But if we take the initiative to communicate openly with parents, we involve them in the ministry. Then most problems with parents will diminish considerably, and the effectiveness of our ministry will increase. Several key things should be communicated:

Communicate Purpose

Parents need to know your philosophy of ministry—why you're doing what you're doing. You must know why you exist, where you're going, and what you're trying to do, and then be able to communicate that to others. Every youth staff member, parent, and kid should know the overall vision, direction, and goals of the youth ministry and program.

Develop an overall mission or purpose statement, as well as a purpose statement for each of the main ongoing youth programs (for example, Sunday school, youth group, discipleship group, socials). Then for each special event (retreat, camp, etc.), design a specific purpose statement along with the goals for that event. When you communicate this kind of information to parents, it helps them understand what you're trying to accomplish and gives them a greater sense of confidence in you. They'll pray for you more effectively and will be more motivated to help you. Without vision, even parents perish.

Communicate Program

Once you know your purpose, then your program grows out of that purpose. Parents have a right to know and need to know details about the youth ministry program. They need to know the actual schedule of program events, times, places, support staff who will be supervising and responsible, and the transportation needs and the costs. Obviously, this requires planning and organization, followed by proper and effective communication. Youth workers are notorious for not planning ahead and winging it. Nothing frustrates a concerned parent more than the one in charge not knowing these kinds of details.

It's a good idea to plan the basics of your program (themes, topics, times, and places) at least one year in advance. Every three months, plan more specifically. For every month, add the final details. Then communicate this program to the parents, giving them a schedule of the main topics and events. If there is a retreat that will cost one hundred dollars, parents need to know how to plan their finances at least several months ahead. As a parent of four kids myself, my wife and I just can't afford to be spontaneous and flexible (with our time and our money) at the whim and last-second plan of every youth event.

Communicate People

By sending their kids to your youth program, parents are passing their parental rights and authority on to others to assist them in their job of parenting. They have the right to know who's working with their adolescent children. And we should help them know the youth program staff. Establish criteria and guidelines to ensure youth workers are mature and qualified. Parents need to have the confidence that their teen is being treated carefully, respectfully, lovingly, and safely by all youth workers. Proactive communication between youth staff and parents is crucial.

Communicate the Positives

Parents need and want to know the positive characteristics and qualities you see in their youth. They don't often know the way their adolescent child is growing and serving. They want your affirmation, confirmation, and support about their teens' character development. Brag about kids in front of their parents. Tell parents what you enjoy and like about their son or daughter. Compliment parents about their young people. Within the context of positive statements, it's easier to discuss problems, concerns, and areas of growth.

Communicate Problems

No one likes to hear about problems, and yet parents must be in the know and involved whenever difficulties surface. Parents should be among the first to know the details of problems (quite often they're the last to know). Trust needs to be built with parents so when problem issues arise, immediate and appropriate communication will result. I have seen many youth workers wait until they're ready to kick the kid out of the youth group before they consult the parent. If youth ministry is a team ministry, then parents and youth workers should confer all the time about kids, especially in areas of concern or problems.

How to Communicate with Parents

Communication can happen formally and informally, intentionally and spontaneously. There are several ways that youth workers can communicate with and to parents:

Mail

Communication by mail (especially e-mail) can be simple, fast, and effective. With today's computer technology, there's no excuse not to communicate regularly with parents (unless they don't have e-mail). Mail can be in the form of regular newsletters or calendars of upcoming events. These can offer timely reminders, informational items, or inspirational and motivational messages. They can be directed to a whole group or individual. Parents never complain about too much communication.

Phone

At times a personal phone call or visit is necessary. Mail isn't appropriate for certain kinds of dialogue and discussion. There is something about a phone call or face-to-face interaction that is more individual, personal, and may be more appropriate for some kinds of communication. Talking through a personal or sensitive problem or concern should be done privately and personally—certainly not publicly or over e-mail.

Meetings

Meetings, meetings, meetings. Ours is a very busy society, and no one likes another meeting. But a meeting can be a very meaningful and significant way to communicate with parents. You should have a parent meeting at least once a year, for no other reason than to introduce your youth staff and the year's program. But a lot more can be done through meetings:

- *Information:* Parents need to know basic information about the youth ministry, its purpose, programs, the people (staff), any positive items, and any problems or concerns. A group meeting may be the best format to communicate some of these items.
- *Inspiration:* Parents need our encouragement, affirmation, appreciation, and emotional support and motivation in their role as parents. In a meeting this can have great impact. A brief devotional challenge or inspirational thought goes a long way.
- *Instruction:* Sometimes parents need basic information about upcoming youth or church-wide events. A group meeting provides an opportunity for parents to clarify misunderstandings and gives you an opportunity to further explain or justify decisions, directions, and details.
- *Input and feedback:* Solicit parental input, feedback, and evaluation. Sometimes a group meeting is the best time and way to get a consensus or overall evaluation about something. As people share their feelings in a group setting, parents get a sense of what others feel and think, which may spur further suggestions or creative ideas. This may be intimidating, but you can receive good input that may save you lots of time or energy later, or may even help you save face.

Mingling

Face-to-face interaction is always best. Be proactive at finding ways to mingle, mix with, and meet parents of your youth. When you're at any church gathering or social event, set goals to meet, get to know, and hang out with parents. Learn how to "work the room" and start conversations. Take advantage of every opportunity when parents are present to interact with them.

When everyone comes to church on Sunday morning, how about standing at the front door and greeting them when they come in? When people mingle after the church service, do you stick around and mingle as well, or do you leave? On the night of the youth group meeting, stand at the curb and greet parents when they drop their kids off. Be as visible as possible with parents, whenever you get the chance.

Involving Parents in Ministry

Invite parents to be part of planning all aspects of youth ministry. Having a parent youth committee or parent representatives on your youth planning committee can do this. You may ask for volunteers or you may carefully select parents to represent junior high, senior high, and college age ministry. I've had very good response from handpicking parents I think would contribute and then inviting them to join us in planning the youth program. Most don't volunteer because they're not asked.

Other than only helping in the planning, why not involve parents in the actual youth ministry? As with much of ministry development, it's wise to start slowly and at lower levels of commitment and involvement first (like driving or cooking) before moving them up to teaching or leading a small group. Maintaining good, open, and honest communication all along the way is crucial to the effectiveness of involving parents in ministry. Also, make sure you listen to a teen's feelings before you invite his or her parents to be involved.

I already touched on this idea briefly, but I can't emphasize it enough. Youth workers are generally fearful of allowing parents to give input and feedback about what we are doing. If we don't invite their feedback (proactively and positively), we will get it sooner or later (critically and negatively). So ask for their feedback regularly and invite their responses beforehand. Evaluation can be formal or informal, deliberate or spontaneous, but it needs to be intentional and regular.

Also, parents pray like none other. Ask parents to intercede for the ministry. Prayer may be their most important contribution. Here, information is key. Give parents a weekly list of prayer requests to help them pray effectively.

Resources for Parents

It's crucial to provide parents with resources that will assist, support, encourage, inspire, and motivate them in their role and responsibilities as parents. The youth pastor and youth ministry can be a tremendous support in the initiation, organization, promotion, and facilitation of a variety of such resources. What kinds of resources can the youth ministry provide?

1. Seminars, discussion groups, or conferences can instruct, train, and encourage parents on a variety of topics and issues.
2. Support groups address various situations (single parents or divorced parents) or various topics like drugs, alcohol, teen pregnancy, or sex abuse.

3. Printed and media resources—magazines, books, tapes, videos—can stimulate parental development.

A philosophy of youth ministry that acknowledges the primary authority and responsibility of parents and the family creates the active communication with and direct involvement of parents in the ministry. Youth workers shouldn't view parents as a distraction to effective youth ministry. Rather parents should be treated as a necessary dimension of effective youth ministry. We can't do without them.

23.
Working on a Team
GENE POPPINO

IT WAS THE BEST OF TIMES, it was the worst of times, it was the age of wisdom, it was the age of foolishness . . . it was the spring of hope, it was the winter of despair . . .

It was our weekly staff meeting.

The opening lines of Charles Dickens's *A Tale of Two Cities* capture the sometimes wonderful, sometimes dreadful interaction of our pastoral team. We'd like to see things eye to eye. But as often as not, we leave meetings wanting to poke someone in the eye. Team dynamics are rewarding, stimulating, frustrating, or draining, depending on the day. The team experiences the full spectrum of emotions inherent in working with others. A good staff team will intentionally cultivate the joys and boldly face the challenges. As Jesus told his staff, "By this all people will know that you are My disciples, if you have love for one another" (John 13:35).

And You Were Expecting . . . ?

I'd only been at my new church a few months when my senior pastor introduced me at the state-wide denominational meeting as the "best youth pastor on the West Coast." Everyone knew it was hyperbole, especially me, but the affection he expressed in that introduction touched me deeply. His confidence was comforting and inspiring. I became a better man after that day because my pastor believed in me and I felt safe even while taking risks. That day was so significant not only because it affirmed and encouraged my soul, but because that degree of public acknowledgment occurred only once in twenty-seven years of full-time ministry. Most in youth work want to hear their senior pastor's encouragement and affirmation. But many rarely do.

More commonly, we hear youth pastors complain that their senior pastors don't trust them and instead seem to resist their best ideas.

What is it about the relationship between the senior pastor and other staff pastors that creates discontent? Why is tension more common than unity on many church teams? How should we work so that the seeds of discord are never sown in our interpersonal relationships? It begins with our expectations.

Visit the dairy farm and you'll see cows, you'll see cows giving milk, and you'll see the digestive by-products cows produce. Proverbs 14:4, one of my favorite passages of Scripture, says, "Where there are no oxen, the feeding-trough is empty, [or "clean," as it's sometimes translated] but an abundant harvest [comes] through the strength of an ox." I paraphrase it, "Where there are cows, there will be cow poop." What else would you expect? If you're going to raise cows, expect to spend shovel-time in the barn. It's part of the job. What's true on the farm is true in relationships as well.

Many times we *expect* one thing when reality is something very different. If we anticipate no problems in youth ministry and no parents complaining about what we do and expect everyone to like us and understand and appreciate what we do, we'll be disappointed. Our unrecognized expectations can be the source of acute disappointment and disillusionment. Consider your expectations for working with the pastor or others on staff.

- Do you expect the senior pastor to cheer you on?
- Do you expect others to take the initiative in their relationships with you? Do you think they will meet with you regularly, ask you about your personal life, or take an interest in your ministry?
- Do you expect to be respected and considered a professional in your role?
- Do you expect a spirit of team and cooperation among the staff?
- Do you expect a perfect pastor?
- Do you expect the pastoral team to understand what you're trying to do in youth ministry and how difficult it is to shape the next generation of Christ-followers?
- Do you expect the senior pastor to disciple you or be your close friend?
- Do you expect a strong sense of team, with each looking out for the others?
- Do you expect to start new programs or set new directions in ministry, or will you be expected to carry the previous youth pastor's work in the direction he established?

When you think about your expectations for ministry and staff relationships, often you'll find you've set the bar pretty high. High expectations aren't necessarily sinful or unbiblical; they may simply be unrealistic. Their idealism may not take into account the fallen nature of our world or the reality of inter-personal dynamics. Good self-management requires dealing appropriately with expectations. You can't check your expectations at the door. They don't go away easily. But you can identify them, understand how they affect you, and take steps to deal with them.

Team Is Taught in Scripture

Team ministry is clearly demonstrated in Scripture. Take a look at Jesus and the disciples, Moses and Aaron, Paul and Barnabas, Peter and John, Paul and Timothy, and a long list of others. These teams accomplished ministry while they experienced tensions, disagreements, conflicts, and even betrayals.

According to God's Word, teams *choose* to live with certain practices embedded in their relationships.

> Therefore, God's chosen ones, holy and loved, put on heartfelt com-passion, kindness, humility, gentleness, and patience, accepting one another and forgiving one another if anyone has a complaint against another. Just as the Lord has forgiven you, so also you must forgive. Above all, put on love—the perfect bond of unity. (Col 3:12–14)

> Obey your leaders and submit to them, for they keep watch over your souls as those who will give an account, so that they can do this with joy and not with grief, for that would be unprofitable for you. (Heb 13:17)

> First of all, then, I urge that petitions, prayers, intercessions, and thanksgivings be made for everyone, for kings and all those who are in authority. (1 Tim 2:1–2a)

Kindness, compassion, gentleness, patience, forgiveness, submission, prayer, and thanksgiving make staff relationships work. Without this spiritual glue, a staff team is unlikely to stick together under the daily pressures of spir-itual warfare. Teams take work and the first work is deep inside each of us.

Team Begins with a Good Fit

Have you ever tried on a very expensive pair of shoes and found they hurt your feet? Good quality does not always mean good fit. Staff teams are like that. Faithful, godly leaders may not work well together. Building a good team requires us to look beyond the quality of individuals, their competency, or character—though we often blame those things for conflict—and con-sider fit.

Personality

People are outgoing, others quiet and shy. People are secure and bold, others filled with insecurity. Some are intuitive, others dense. There is no right personality, but not all personalities work well together. When you're considering joining a staff team, look at personality and consider these variables:

- Goal setter or problem solver?
- Personality type?
- Birth order—oldest, youngest, or middle child? Which are you?
- Sense of humor or serious thoughtfulness?
- Relational or professional approach? Is the ministry primarily relational or corporate?
- Flexibility and spontaneity or careful planning and strategizing?
- Directive or participatory leadership style?
- High trust or high accountability/control?
- Are decisions made in a team setting, or do individuals use their professional expertise to get the job done?

At first glance, these might not all seem to be about personality. But they predict a great deal about how people will interact and where conflicts might arise.

Perspective

When looking at fit, consider the senior pastor's perspective on ministry. What is his ministry philosophy? (Can he clearly articulate it?) What books, education, or speakers have shaped his passion? Is he a shepherd of people or a rancher overseeing staff who shepherd people?

While being considered for a youth pastor position, I was being interviewed by the senior pastor when the conversation shifted to books. We were both enthusiastic about a particular book we'd read recently on ministry philosophy. That conversation revealed our shared passion and vision for ministry which lasted throughout our years of serving together.

Values

Fit involves shared values. What are the team's values—balanced living, adequate time off, recreation? Or are the team members workaholics? Is there a high priority on family? Do their families see the authenticity of their faith? How is success measured—by numbers or by increasing spiritual depth? What's valued—growth or maintaining the status quo, ministering to those already attending church or reaching out to the community?

While being interviewed for his first full-time position, a youth worker asked the senior pastor how many hours a week he would be expected to work. The pastor replied, "Sixty to seventy hours is an average week. That's what I do." Thinking the pastor was kidding, the youth worker laughed. The pastor, surprised and a little offended, asked what was so funny. It's not surprising he had to resign a few years later for health reasons. He claimed to value balance, but his lifestyle proved otherwise. For a good fit, look at values.

Self-Knowledge

As you consider fit, know yourself—understand your strengths and weaknesses. Do you need a strong sense of camaraderie, or do you work well on your own? How much independence do you need? Do you want to address the overall direction of the church, or are you content managing your own area? Are you fearful, unsure, insecure? Has a previous ministry left you in need of recovery and nurture? What about your life stage? Can your particular needs (single, newly married, married with children) be met in this environment?

The Right Interview

How do you decide whether it's a fit or not? A lot of staff conflicts would be avoided if the right questions revealing fit were asked in the interview process. But lots of youth workers are so glad to be considered, they interview simply hoping to impress and win a job. They fail to make the interview mutually revealing. They win the job and only later discover the fit was a poor one.

A good fit doesn't mean a *perfect* fit. In every relationship there will be differences in personality or style. But the interview should reveal shared ideas and beliefs. Like a marriage in which two people with diverse backgrounds and habits choose to overlook some differences for the sake of love, a good ministry fit recognizes and appreciates differences between team members. However, if those differences are radical, adjusting will require too much energy and compromise for one or both teammates. In that case it's better to find another position where the sense of team is greater.

It's Not What You Know, but How You Say It

Fit is important to building a great team. Communication keeps it together. Like instrumentalists in an orchestra who need to hear one another to play in tune, a team needs to hear one another to stay together. Good communication is more than meetings, e-mails, or memos. It's how you speak as much as what you say. It's incarnational, personal, and intentional. When God wanted to communicate, he sent a prophet, he wrote a book, he sent Jesus. And when Jesus expressed the Word, he didn't do it only one way. He said it, showed it, shouted it, whispered it, and read it from Scripture. Communication on Jesus' team varied according to circumstances and need. To keep a staff team on the same page today, you have to know how to share information.

Know When It Needs to Be Written

I laugh every time I remember the predictions that computers would bring us to a paperless society. A quick survey of my office will tell you that paper is in no danger of becoming obsolete. Mail, memos, proposals, lessons, notes to self, and advertisements pile up and can bury us in an avalanche of print. Learn when you need to write and how to write well.

Churches too commonly hire youth workers without providing a job description. Expectations and goals are only assumed, but they should be spelled out in writing. Without the clarity, boundaries, and expectations of a written job description, a ministry job is like strolling through a minefield—something's going to explode.

Write your mission statement. The team can't grasp and support your vision unless you've communicated it clearly. Spell out your top five ministry priorities along with key result areas.

A great way to aid staff communication is to put them on the youth group mailing list. Written information about activities, events, costs, dates, and times keeps the team invested in your ministry. It's easier to support what you know.

Know When Efficiency Works against You

There's a big difference between efficient and effective communication. Efficient is the fastest, shortest, most concise. Effective is sensitive to what requires time, discussion, and personal connection. I've trained youth workers outside of North America and have found that several African countries value relationships highly. They're not concerned much with efficiency. They have an elaborate system of greetings whenever someone arrives or departs. Meeting each level of village and church leader, having a cup of tea with them, giving formal greetings from our churches, our country, our family, and anyone else we know conflicts with my North American culture. I had to be in the country two days early just to meet and officially greet the hierarchy. *Efficient* would be to fly in, go straight to the seminar location, teach, and fly home. But effective communication would have been zero. Without meeting me, my hosts wouldn't have been able to connect with what I taught.

Soil needs to be tilled before planting. Often, relational soil needs tilling. If you simply send a memo, write a proposal, or e-mail the team, don't assume you've been heard. Like planting seeds in hard soil, your plan might get a slow start. You sometimes need to till relational soil—at the hall printer, in the church kitchen, at a ball game, or in an African village—before you can best be heard.

Know When to Tell Stories

Staff teams may communicate via reports. Annual reports, attendance reports, budget reports, reports containing statistics and financial details, reports that may seem tedious are each appropriate. Sometime, instead of giving a report, tell a story. Our ministries are about life change. God's radical work in people's lives inspires. It takes work, but telling a great story builds momentum for ministry. Learn to keep the team invested in the vision by telling stories of life change.

Jean Milliken recently joined our church staff after serving as the national director of women for Sonlife Ministries. She immediately changed the structure of our women's ministry. What caught our attention were her stories about women whose lives had been changed. She talks little about programs or structure; she simply tells about how a woman in a Bible study responded to Christ or how another became so committed to seeing the city change during a prayer walk that she started a new ministry. Nearly every week Jean shares another exciting story about life change. After hearing a story from Jean, petty administrative details pale and our vision is renewed.

Know When to Invite Feedback

Most of us cringe when we think about performance evaluations. But if your church doesn't have a regular review process between the senior pastor and associates, I recommend you take the initiative and speak with your senior pastor. Ask, "How am I doing? Where can I grow in ministry or in life? What do you see are my greatest strengths? My greatest weaknesses?" By inviting his review of your ministry and your personal life, you get honest feedback that allows you to develop in areas that might otherwise create problems. Most supervisors dread the evaluation process too. Your invitation may provide a much-needed opening.

Know Your Pastor's Dreams

Communicate support for your senior pastor. It's natural to be particularly passionate about your own ministry—for your own work to consume your thinking and energy. But on a staff, we're partners with one another. We're committed to one another's success. Choose to join your senior pastor's team by understanding his dreams, his vision, and his personal goals. It can be lonely at the top. Pressure on the pastor as the chief shepherd and "go-to" guy can drain him. When you share his vision and goals, you partner with him as a leader and friend.

Know When to Connect Personally

A frequent complaint shared by many youth pastors is the lack of personal relationship with their senior pastors. Pastors rarely initiate the relationship. Sometimes, the age difference is a barrier. Often the senior pastor never gets around to developing relationships in spite of good intentions, and at times he simply has different relational needs. It doesn't mean you're doomed to a superficial relationship. Take the initiative. Send a birthday card. Invite him out for coffee or a meal. Find a sport you both enjoy. Send a note affirming a great sermon. Pastors preach their hearts out and sometimes the only feedback they get is "good sermon" from someone shaking their hand at the back door. You understand his goals, his vision, his dreams—you can affirm how well his sermon communicated the passion of his soul.

Each of us has an emotional "bank account" with those around us. If our input into their lives is positive, affirming, and consistent, we make deposits into the account. If our interactions are negative, critical, or emotionally charged, we make withdrawals. To weather the inevitable harsh times, we need a positive balance in the bank. Keep a positive balance by having fun together, sharing empathy or encouragement, and by working together toward common goals.

Know When to Deal with Conflict

Conflict is inevitable. Sometimes it's subtle, sometimes intense. Like fire, conflict is not necessarily bad, but left untended it can become a brush fire sweeping through a staff team. A youth pastor friend of mine serving in a local church disagreed with his senior pastor on several issues. Their untended disagreement smoldered in every staff meeting, turning into increasingly hotter disagreement. Escalating tension continued until the senior pastor became so heated that in anger he swept everything off his desk, picked up his phone, and threw it against the wall. That was a wildfire. Knowing both parties involved, I still marvel that it got that far. Both were mature men who loved the Lord. Yet neither had addressed the embers of their conflict until the conflagration engulfed them.

Don't let conflict smolder. The earlier and more quickly we deal with disappointment, disagreement, or perceived injury, the better. Being able to speak honestly about feelings without blaming or deflecting responsibility is a first step. Learning to speak graciously is another. Speaking the truth in love isn't always easy, but it's right.

Qualities of a Team Player

The quality of a team is directly related to the quality of its individuals. We choose how we work together. We also choose the kind of people we are inside. God has put the body together so it works well as each of us exercises our unique gifts and abilities (1 Cor. 12; Rom. 12; and Eph. 4). What personal characteristics can we develop to contribute best to a church staff?

Cooperation

A good team player is equally concerned about the success of every ministry in a church. Team players set goals and programming in context with other ministries and cooperate in the use of physical and financial resources.

I spoke at a youth worker seminar in Spokane, Washington, and heard the sad story of the conflict between a church's high school ministry and its Awana program. The leaders of each program were so at odds with one another about facility use that they found ways not only to bad-mouth the other program but also to actually sabotage it. The youth ministry was accused of pulling up the Awana circle lines, and the Awana group was accused of putting padlocks on all the equipment closets so the youth ministry couldn't use the game materials. The senior pastor in that church had the unenviable task of sorting out the conflict between two groups that had only personal interests at heart. Unfortunately, the children and youth suffered.

Criticism, a Quiz of Character

A good team player can hear constructive criticism without defensiveness. Vance Havner said in ministry you need the mind of a scholar, the heart of a child, and the hide of a rhinoceros. Rhino hide has its limits though. Proverbs 27:17 says, "Iron sharpens iron, and one man sharpens another." We need to hear the hard things. None of us has immaculate perception. Each of us benefits from the observations of our peers, even if they make us uncomfortable. God's plan for us is not primarily about building a better ministry but about building a better minister. Godly peers are often the tools. As we hear and respond to the criticism of others and allow the truth of their words to correct our hearts, we sharpen both our ministry skills and our character.

A team player also refuses to listen to criticism about other staff. Be disciplined to cut off a speaker at the first sign of inappropriate criticism and explain, "I'm not the person who needs to hear this. You need to speak directly to that pastor. I'll tell him you have a concern and will be making an appointment within the week to speak to him personally." If each pastor on staff maintains that response to criticism, you'll find many more people will lose their critical spirit, or they'll take the appropriate path to speak to the person involved.

Earn the Right to Be Heard

Don't expect respect, earn it. The average youth worker is fresh out of school, under thirty years old, and new to a church. In the minds of most people, that spells *rookie*. We need to come to the team with a passion to listen and ask questions. We need to earn the right to speak before expecting to contribute to overall church direction.

Volunteer outside Your Area

You can demonstrate your heart for team play by occasionally volunteering to help other departments. Whether you volunteer in the nursery, help a custodian clean up after an event, or take on leadership of a church wide project, your contribution demonstrates your desire to see the success of the team, not just your own ministry.

Search My Heart, Lord

Where two or three youth pastors gather, someone will tell he's being picked on! To hear some talk, you would think they work in the worst church in the world. Looking deeper reveals some of the wounds are self-inflicted. You can shoot yourself in the foot with the following:

Attitude

It could be described as a "youthy attitude." After spending so much time and energy relating to students, we pick up their attitudes. You know the one—tinged with disrespect for authority, an antiestablishment bias, a sense of rebellion, a suspicion of authority, and sometimes an edginess that can only be described as "Yeah, so what." I'm not talking about an attitude laced with sin. But youth culture tends to express itself with language and mannerisms adults don't understand. Youth workers who spend their whole lives with youth learn to speak the language of youth. Unfortunately, when we carry that language into the boardroom, we discover the rest of the team doesn't understand.

Unchallenged Immaturity

Youth workers are generally older than the students with whom they work. Students rarely challenge the immaturity of an adult youth worker. We can be oblivious until someone like our senior pastor brings up our behavior. No one else seems to be bothered so we think the problem is his not ours.

Communication Style

Youth workers typically communicate with an edgy style. We develop a shock-and-awe way of expressing things. Bluntness works with youth, but it shocks adults.

One of the clearest examples of this was when Christian author and speaker Tony Campolo, in a well-publicized speech, talked about world hunger. Campolo spoke about the incredible needs of people around the world and how our apathetic Christian culture "didn't give a s——" for the needs of others. Campolo then went on to say more people were concerned that he used a vulgarism than that people were dying of starvation. That clever turn of a phrase, the edgy style, appealed to youth workers. Those who lacked Campolo's credibility and stature in the Christian community tried to use his language and ended up getting in real trouble. Many were bewildered that a famous international speaker got away with using a word that got them fired.

Weak Detail Orientation

Your greatest strength can be your greatest weakness. Youth workers often have high relational skills and make decisions intuitively. These strengths may have the appearance of winging it to the rest of the team. Spontaneity can be effective, even appealing to youth. But a staff team can view it as irresponsible or immature. Take the time-challenged pastor who brings the church van filled with kids back several hours late and can't figure out why parents are upset. The rest of the team will see the youth pastor's bad management of money as poor leadership.

Insecurity

Personal insecurity is common in most of us. It's an especially difficult quality if you're beginning a new ministry and aren't yet confident in your strengths and giftedness. Personal insecurity may cause you to communicate defensively. The team may see you as stubborn or resistant.

Selfishness

Personal selfishness, while obvious to others, can be hard to see. It shows up when you want the world (or the team) to support your vision, but you're not willing to support others'. If everything is about you and your ministry, look out.

You might think the world should adjust. Whether it's personality quirks, hair and clothing styles, or body piercings, expecting the world to look beneath the surface and see the real you communicates selfishness. Demanding it doesn't work.

The Medicinal Herbs of Grace

The law of the harvest says we reap what we sow. Great team relationships come when we sow grace—five graces actually: Prayer, love, forgiveness, understanding, and gratitude cure our sinful selfishness, our petty differences, and our critical spirits. Sow them generously and reap the results.

Prayer

How much do you pray? A lack of prayer often reveals feelings of self-sufficiency and pride. Those who truly understand their dependence on God regularly and passionately call on him. How often do you pray for your staff team? How often do you ask God to bless them and their ministries? Do you pray specifically for their fruitfulness? How do you pray when there's conflict? It's hard to be bitter when you pray regularly for someone. The grace of prayer helps us to see through the Father's eyes.

Love

Love is action, not emotion. When we love as the Bible teaches, we take initiative and reach out. We do good to others whether we feel they deserve it or not. We take an interest in them. We show compassion and kindness. We do the actions of love whether the strong emotions of love are there or not. Extending the grace of love to the team grows our hearts and increases our capacity to love even more.

Forgiveness

Romans 5:8 says, "But God proves His own love for us in that while we were still sinners Christ died for us!" God extended forgiveness to us before we could even ask. How much more should we extend forgiveness to those around us! We all fail. Hurts are inevitable. Healing begins with forgiveness. Sow the grace of forgiveness even if it's not requested.

Understanding

We often mistrust what we don't understand. It's important that you work to understand others on staff. Understanding includes looking at traits mentioned earlier—personality, birth order, level of security, and so forth.

Understanding leads to compassion and support that allow us to extend grace when behavior might lead to suspicion about character or motives.

Gratitude

Finally, consider the importance of gratitude. I was at a youth ministry conference at Multnomah Bible College during a particularly difficult time with my church board and senior pastor. While there, a friend graciously listened to me complain for a time, then asked me, "Have you thanked God for your circumstances?" The question caught me off guard, and at first I resented it. I wanted to say, "Haven't you been listening? What do I have to be thankful for? They're blind, unkind, and unfair." Using the gentle nudging of my friend and Scripture—"Give thanks in all circumstances for this is God's will for you in Christ Jesus"—God changed my heart. It changed how I thought about those around me and how I prayed for them. I began to thank God for them and for all he was doing in their lives, and in doing so I began to remember the good in them. My gratitude moved from being an act of the will to a heart of growing appreciation. Only a few circumstances ever changed in those relationships, but God got my heart to the right place as I began to pray sincerely, thanking him for my brothers in ministry.

Ultimately, I believe God puts us on teams to sharpen our lives and develop our character. Embrace this process. Fleeing from difficult relationships at the first sign of trouble is a mark of immaturity. God is more concerned about developing a good *minister* than a good *ministry*. Often he chisels and sands us, using our pastoral team.

Therefore, God's chosen ones, holy and loved, put on heartfelt compassion, kindness, humility, gentleness, and patience, accepting one another and forgiving one another if anyone has a complaint against another. Just as the Lord has forgiven you, so also you must [forgive]. Above all, [put on] love—the perfect bond of unity. And let the peace of the Messiah, to which you were also called in one body, control your hearts. Be thankful. Let the message about the Messiah dwell richly among you, teaching and admonishing one another in all wisdom, and singing psalms, hymns, and spiritual songs, with gratitude in your hearts to God. And whatever you do, in word or in deed, do everything in the name of the Lord Jesus, giving thanks to God the Father through Him. (Col. 3:12–17)

Part 4

Staying Solid in Ministry

24.
Leading as a Servant

DAVID SCHROEDER

THAT IS WHAT we live for, David."

I followed his gaze across the living room to the opposite wall and a painting titled *The Reunion*. The artist captured a look of sheer joy on the face of Jesus as he embraced and welcomed one of his children into heaven. Turning back to my friend, I gripped his feeble hand and said, "I agree wholeheartedly."

Diagnosed with Lou Gehrig's disease years ago, my friend will experience that moment with Jesus very soon. His time on earth is quickly drawing to a close. When Jim soon looks into his Savior's face, he will hear these words: "Well done, good and faithful *servant!*" (Matt. 25:21a NIV, emphasis added).

I wonder why, when it's all been said and done, Jesus will use that word to identify us? Why not son or daughter or leader or warrior or anything besides *that* word? Servant. Honestly, I don't like the implications of *servant*, and if you don't either, then read on. Perhaps one of the most difficult concepts in the Word to fully embrace, the idea of being a servant is not only countercultural; it's counteridentity. Yet this very identity is emphasized throughout Scripture for us to live.

This chapter is not about skill, knowledge, strategy, or philosophy. It is about you, youth minister. It is about your heart, attitudes, and core identity. The skill of youth ministry you will learn over time, honing your strategy with wisdom acquired through experience. The heart of youth ministry is *you*, and you either are a servant or you're not. While skill is primarily learned, a servant is mostly molded. While skill develops growing confidence, service exposes emerging humility. While skill is quite important to youth ministry, the heart of a servant is *essential* to it.

Yes, you may be personally successful and not have a successful ministry, but you can't succeed in ministry in the long run without personal vibrancy.

Your character is not only the foundation your ministry will be built upon, it's also the garden of life from which the fruit of ministry will continually grow. In other words, the expression of your gifts and skills in ministry must always be fueled by the increasing depth of your character. If not, one day your tank will run dry, and your skills will not sustain you. Some have imploded for this very reason.

I love youth and I admire youth workers. Theirs is a crucial calling. Of the many youth ministers I know, the ones I believe to be the most fruitful in their ministries are those who combine a developing skill set with a growing servant-leader identity and attitude. These are truly inseparable for the man or woman who dreams of a lifetime of impact and influence.

Now I'm thinking you're thinking, *I've heard this all before.* Indeed, you likely have, but I ask you these questions: Are you really living it? When you think of words that describe you, does "servant" readily come to mind? Would others identify you this way? Does your heart resonate with the concept, or do you have some level of aversion to the whole idea?

To answer these questions well, we need to speak the same language on the subject.

The Posture of a Servant

Scripture is saturated with the concept of servanthood. A few examples: The descriptions of the Incarnation in Philippians 2 reveal that the very identity of Christ is tightly tied to the "nature of a servant" (v. 7 NIV). One of Jesus' primary teachings to the disciples was on service (John 13). One of the apostle Paul's most frequent identifiers of himself was "a servant (bond-slave) of Christ." It is the word we'll be called when receiving Christ's welcoming embrace.

I began this chapter with the story of my dying friend Jim because for me he lived the definition of a servant. A chaplain in the U.S. Army, he was my "boss" in Darmstadt, Germany. My wife and I served at the time in the Cadence youth ministry division called Malachi Ministries. While Cadence International ministers to the entire American military community, Malachi staff specializes in reaching the teenage dependents of military personnel.

During most of our five years in Darmstadt, Chaplain Jim Bishop was the senior Protestant chaplain. My friend, pastor, shepherd, and mentor, he was a delight to partner with in reaching the military community for Christ.

While I may have worked for him, he *served* me. His attitude continually and consistently reflected Christ's. "What can I do for you, David?" was the question he asked me most. I remember the day he discovered I couldn't receive AFN (Armed Forces Network) television at our German apartment.

Knowing I enjoyed sports, he began to tape football and basketball games for me to view later. He looked for ways to support, encourage, and lift me up. This is the posture of a servant: It is to "in humility consider others as more important than yourselves" (Phil. 2:3b).

At the heart of a servant is humility—obvious, I know, yet so very elusive. A servant recognizes needs in others and moves toward them in humble service. An accurate assessment of our own humanity enables us to faithfully put others' needs before our own. That sentence means: We are unworthy yet loved. We are sinful yet forgiven. We are needy yet filled. Because of God's love for us, we are free to humbly yet powerfully serve others.

The greatest barrier to a humble, servant posture is simply pride—an improper view of identity that blinds us to the needs of others and hinders our movement toward them. "Do nothing out of selfish ambition or *vain conceit*," Philippians 2:3a commands us (NIV, emphasis added). The problem with pride is its incredible ability to hide from the person suffering with it. While others around smell its insidious odor, the one afflicted travels on, merrily ignorant to its presence and negative impact. Pride destroys. Like cancer slowly spreading through the body, pride strangles the spirit of a person with its malignant death. We must take it seriously or suffer the awful consequences: stunted growth, defensiveness, bitterness, strained and broken relationships, and a chronic emptiness.

The core message of pride is the subtle demand that others should be more like us. We don't state this directly, but our attitudes and actions expose us. We think we're right most of the time. We reek with arrogance. Continually evaluating and criticizing others based on our grid of values and thoughts, we give little consideration to the possibility our values and perspectives might be tainted by sin, pain, and negative experiences.

Hardening of the categories ensues. Defensiveness permeates. Spiritual malaise is inevitable. Pride has done its deadly work, squeezing the life from us.

Youth worker, is your life saturated by humility or strangled by pride? You can't fake humility. Lowering your gaze and kicking at the dirt when given a compliment doesn't mean humility presides. Rather, a heart confidently centered on the cross gratefully enjoys and embraces affirmation as a gift from a gracious God. A servant's humility is core to his or her identity, and it permeates everything.

The cure for pride is first exposure, then brokenness and repentance, and finally humble service. We desperately need the Holy Spirit faithfully using God's Word and God's people to gently illumine and expose the true state of our hearts. It's in these moments we discover our true mettle. Either we go the easy route and rationalize the truth away, or we courageously traverse the high road of faith and embrace the exposed reality. Determinedly facing one's own deep and stubborn sin of arrogance is the posture of a servant. This posture, not of groveling but rather of gratefulness for grace, releases the servant to passionately and powerfully love others.

The Power of a Servant

Another man, another feeble and frail hand to hold—this time, my father's, as his cancer-ravaged body breathed its last breath and his spirit departed for heaven. Only one year ago, the memory remains poignant and meaningful. I miss Dad deeply. My dear friend, he and I shared a beautiful relationship. Because John Schroeder embraced the posture of a servant, he also experienced the power of a servant: impact!

A simple and kind man, my father made it his life's priority to serve others. In his last ten years of life, he professionally served others in his job as a grocery clerk. Unable to retire, he joyfully accepted this employment as a gift from God and as a place to minister. Arriving at work early every day to pray with other employees earned him the nickname "Chaplain." He led employees and customers to Christ. He radiated the joy of Jesus. He touched lives for eternity—the *power* of a servant.

We live in a culture largely devoid of grateful-hearted servants. Power means gaining the edge on those around you. Climbing to the top, no matter who's stepped on, is the ultimate goal. Service is often no more than a slick way to manipulate others to buy your product and make you succeed. True servants are difficult to find.

That's why people like my father stand out—humble servants who truly and genuinely love others. And this is *true* power. As I see it, the most powerful person in the room at any given moment is *not* the person with position or prestige, but rather it's the person most determined to love and bless the others present. The person with the mind of Christ who sees the true state of others' hearts, whose own heart stirs with compassion, and whose energy moves lovingly toward the others. This is the power of a servant!

Not only do we battle our inward propensity toward arrogance and self-ishness (Phil. 2:3a); we also battle the outward influence of our culture. A culture that parades arrogance, control, and positional power as if these are expected and accepted. The only remedy for such destructive influences is to passionately pursue the servant heart of Jesus—allowing him to transform us into his image and then experiencing the influence he produces through us, his servants.

The Product of a Servant

I remember his words well. They're embedded on my heart. As an extremely insecure junior higher, I knew of little evidence to support his conclusion. Yet he spoke with such confidence and love I couldn't dismiss his words. I can't remember his name, but as the missionary speaker for our camp, he enjoyed our respect and admiration. When he asked me for some time together, I couldn't imagine what he had in mind. Well, he wanted to say these words to me: "David, I've been watching you all week, and I believe that someday you will be a great leader."

Over the years as I've struggled to grow as a servant-leader, the words of that missionary keep working their way into my heart. They've been like an anchor and a guide continually centering me on my calling, despite my nagging insecurities and doubts. He spoke vision to me. He saw what I did not. He *served me* with his belief, and I am indebted to him for it.

Servants have molded my values, perspectives, and attitudes. People like my dad and mom, Chaplain Bishop, the unknown missionary, and so many others have all produced in me a deep desire to serve others, as they served me. All living things reproduce after their kind, as do people. Youth worker, I'm confident you want to make a difference, to produce disciples of Christ who, in turn, also make a difference. You are built for it, and, as I've said, yours is a high and noble calling.

Yes, teach and train your disciples. But remember, their character will be molded by what you model. What you model will be determined by who you are. You will not produce servant-hearted disciples unless service is at the core of your essence as a person. Only truth taught congruent with truth lived will transfer to your disciples. No other route to transformational impact exists.

And we must transfer a servant's heart. Our world, churches, and families desperately need servant-hearted leaders who faithfully and powerfully lead and love other people. Servants will beget servants. So I must ask again, "Are you on the road of servanthood?" Yes, a difficult and perilous journey it can be, but so much is at stake. Stay on the path, my friend. Embrace humility as a close and valued friend. Become a servant.

Serve Christ, Your Commander

A danger exists in this discussion. One could easily conclude that a servant is some sort of a doormat, weakly responding to others of greater strength and status. Not true! It takes incredible strength to set aside your rights and desires in order to bless another. It takes great security to refrain from promoting yourself over others. It takes amazing character and courage to live the life of a servant.

Leadership and service are not as incompatible as they may seem. In fact, I believe they're inseparable. A leader should be defined by service. Not all servants are leaders, but all leaders must be servants! He or she may be casting great vision, empowering leaders, organizing strategies and methodologies, mobilizing resources, and shaping core values, but he or she must be doing these things with a servant's heart and attitude. If this fundamental ingredient is missing, a leader's product and power will be incomplete and often impotent.

Focusing on serving Christ rather than pleasing people is essential to staying on course. I've struggled throughout much of my life with the desire to have people happy with me. Who wouldn't want this? Unfortunately, it can be a heavy ball and chain to your leadership. Too great a focus on others' opinions contributes to a shotgun approach to ministry with no real direction and purpose. Criticism easily derails the vision and discourages the leader. Momentum can suffer and chaos can reign.

Serving Christ means developing teams of people who will give consistent and important input. But it does not mean acquiescing to the loudest and strongest opinion to keep the peace. A servant must be willing to at times offend others, leave some behind, and walk the lonely path of leadership. A quick look at the lives of Jesus and the apostle Paul will undoubtedly substantiate these truths. We must first serve Christ, then others.

Serve Your Church

All youth pastors must carry within their hearts a great and high regard for the local church. Effectiveness depends upon it. The church is, after all, God's idea and strategy for reaching the nations. Yet I'm amazed how many youth workers hold some level of disdain for the church. Or better said, disdain for *their* local church. Due to negative experiences within this context, it's both easy and dangerous to develop a critical spirit. One thing is certain concerning a negative spirit: It will leak out of your every pore and greatly undermine your credibility and ministry.

We must embrace the church with all its flaws, idiosyncrasies, pitfalls, and, yes, sinners! A servant recognizes he or she is a part of a beautiful yet fallen and broken community of believers. A servant responds to this flawed community with patient graciousness. A servant releases fellow sinners to grow in an atmosphere of love and grace. A servant appropriately reveals his or her own struggles and difficulties to the community, giving others permission to be human as well. A servant revels in the church.

Youth pastors move too often. Certainly, legitimate reasons exist for this reality: a great mismatch of gifting, passions, theology, or philosophy of ministry; a complete lack of support and trust from the parents, church, or pastoral staff; or a pressure-and-performance-oriented senior pastor whose leadership style may be abusive.

However, I believe most youth workers move on either because of unrealistic expectations about the church, or because they never fully embrace serving that community of believers.

We must wholeheartedly give ourselves to God's people and fully integrate ourselves into the life of the church. It's been said that people will either get on your nerves or get in your heart. This is true of the local church as well. Although not on our church's pastoral staff, as a layperson I've sought to love this body of believers: I teach a Sunday school class; I disciple men; I manage the men's softball team; I've volunteered with the toddlers; I've participated in work days; and I've spoken at retreats. My wife has been equally involved. We can't do it all, and we certainly need clear priorities to guide us, give us boundaries, and allow us to freely say no to numerous needs and opportunities. However, we can't retreat to our specialized department and neglect integrating ourselves and our youth into the fabric of our church. Serving the greater body will keep us sane and, hopefully, keep us staying put for a good long while.

Serve Your Community

One day you will find yourself settling into your ministry in a local church or parachurch context, if you're not there already. You will employ a strategy that balances winning, building, and equipping. You will impact the kingdom of God through your labor. I pray you will also work to instill in your students' hearts a passion for serving and reaching your community and the world. Vital to the church's vibrancy is its outward focus and vision. Youth ministry and youth workers should lead the charge!

Besides the strategies employed by your youth ministry to reach and serve your community, you personally must also be living and modeling a heart for the lost. Encouraging your students to share Christ with their friends will be all the more potent if you're sharing him with your friends. Only sharing Jesus with unbelieving students is not enough. You must share with your peers, and this means you continually need non-Christian friends.

Your neighborhood is full of them. Reach them! In our neighborhood here in Colorado, we intentionally connected with and shared Christ with our neighbors. I worked with neighbors, played sports with them, took them to coffee, and invited them to our home numerous times and to our church as well. We integrated ourselves into their lives, even bailing one of them out of jail! When we were sharing the gospel with one neighbor friend, he said, "I've wondered what is different about your family, and I've almost come to your door to ask you."

Personally, I found it easier to travel across an ocean as a missionary to tell military people about Christ than I did traveling across the street to share with my neighbor. You'll be much more sensitized to how difficult it is for your students to share the gospel with their friends if you're struggling along with them. They'll respect you more and listen more carefully if you model friendship evangelism for them. Live what you teach and preach. Serve your community.

A Servant's Family

"Joyce, I determine to not use fatigue, stress, or busyness as excuses and justification for relating in a selfish way toward you." I spoke these words to my wife only a few years ago after realizing how often I used the "big three" justifications to excuse myself from sacrificially loving her. Because I am one or more of these things most of the time, it hasn't been easy to live this commitment. I'm determined, however. A servant's heart should be most powerfully evident with his or her family.

Youth worker, should God grant you a spouse and children, I implore you to commit yourself to sacrificially serving them above all. Don't consistently give them your leftovers. Serve them up savory meals of focus, energy, creativity, attention, laughter, memories, and, above all, large doses of love and compassion. Make going home to them the highlight of their day, and of yours as well. Focus each evening (or morning, if you have an evening meeting) on connecting with each of them. Enjoy them to the full and lavish love upon them.

For the last ten years, I have been apart from my family on the average of two to three months a year. Traveling is a part of leadership. To help compensate for these times, the nine or ten months a year I'm home, well, I am *really* home. I leave my work at work. I come home at a consistent hour each day. I focus on my family each evening and do what it takes to wholeheartedly serve them. It's a joy! My wife and four kids are my best friends, and I absolutely love serving them. A good way to serve them is to integrate them as much as possible into your ministry. Our children visited youth group regularly and attended many retreats. They prayed with us for students' souls.

Make your ministry a friend of the family. Serve them with all your heart.

A Servant's Friends

Not too long ago, a friend of mine and I made a "friendship covenant" with each other. We wrote out our commitment to each other and each other's families. With our wives as witnesses, we spoke these covenants to each other. We promised to encourage each other, support each other, stand with each other, and, most of all, stick with each other through thick and thin. We made this covenant because we wanted to express our commitment to each other in a tangible way.

Speaking to you men in particular, I want to warn you of keeping others at an emotional distance. You need godly brothers in your life who know you intimately and thoroughly, who walk with you through life, who confront you when needed, and who stand shoulder to shoulder with you through the dark and difficult days. You were built for community, and community was built for you. Reach both directions across generational lines and develop a variety of friendships with men of many personalities and perspectives. My friends are not only in Colorado; they are in a variety of states and countries. Although I see these friends only on occasion, we're bonded brothers still, growing old together. Pursue friendships relentlessly. You will be richer, more secure, and stronger for it.

A Servant's Foes

I'm not your typical thick-skinned, task-oriented, driven leader. In fact, I'm quite the opposite. I'm sensitive, relational, and emotional. Criticism often hurts. Sometimes it immobilizes me. In my years of leadership, I've periodically struggled with great discouragement, often triggered by someone's negative or critical comments concerning my leadership. This is a part of life and leadership.

We must expect opposition. Anyone determined to make a difference with his or her life will encounter those committed to undermining it. Some critics will simply be goodhearted people who do not realize your need for encouragement and who just expect you to take a good dose of input. Other critics will be more purposeful in their attempts to derail you, discourage you, or even destroy you. Either way, you must learn to expect criticism and learn to deal with it.

I use these three words as a guide through criticism: face, embrace, and erase. *Face* your critics and their criticism head-on. Avoiding it invariably makes it worse. Go after it and lovingly, yet firmly, face it. *Embrace* what's true, even if it be a very small percentage of the "truth" presented. Defensiveness may be the instinctive reaction, but it's also the destructive one. A reactionary attitude mostly escalates the problem and isolates the people. On the other hand, a gentle and genuine openness to truth is surprisingly disarming, even if the input giver doesn't have your best interest in mind. Finally, over time and a sifting process, you can *erase* the untrue and unhelpful criticism from your mind. Move on. Don't let it waste your time and energy because the next round may be just around the corner.

In conclusion, I want to bring you back to the words of my friend, Jim. That *is* what we live for—the moment we see our Savior and he applauds and affirms us as *servants*. Live with the end in mind, for we do not know the day or the hour when it will be upon us. Become a servant. Be a servant. *Well done!*

25.
Spiritual Health of a Youth Minister

JUDY GLANZ

I AM THE VINE; you are the branches. The one who remains in Me and I in him produces much fruit; because you can do nothing without Me" (John 15:5). The truth is, apart from Jesus we can accomplish nothing for the kingdom of God.

Priority of Relationship Must Be with God in Christ

Knowing God Makes You Bold

Daniel 11:32b says, "the people who know their God will be strong and take action." Knowledge of God here is a description of the closest and most intimate relationship possible with the living God. Knowing God and his truth gives you confidence. For example, in Matthew 28:20, Jesus promised to be with us always. We forget this vital truth. I challenge you to practice this by choosing an object to remind you of his presence (after you've memorized the verse). Choose a piece of jewelry or a doorway. Each time you see or touch that ring or bracelet or walk through a doorway, let it be a trigger to remind you of God's presence.

Another way to remember is to practice what I call "inviting Jesus to the party." We do this through silent "arrow" prayer in the midst of an activity or conversation. This can be part of your praying without ceasing. Pray like this, "Jesus, I invite you to this conversation (classroom, party, date, talk, Bible study, relationship)." The truth is, if you're a believer, God is with you always. Acknowledging that truth in prayer is powerful for your walk with him, for your witness and testimony, and for your next words to others or in prayer.

I've heard it said that if you love God and love students, you will make a great youth worker volunteer. But if you desire to serve students and youth ministry for any length of time, it will take more to go the distance. Nothing short of perseverance in the faith, godly character, and a surrendered life transformed continually by the Word of God and the Spirit of God will be needed.

Persevering Faith

First, faith is a gift from God (Eph. 2:8–9). Be thankful for the gift freely given to you. Faith is a shield about us, the apostle Paul said, that's part of our spiritual armor. Practice daily the habit of clothing yourself with the armor God has provided for spiritual battle. Many great books have been written to help us better understand our armor.

Faith grows and is exercised when we choose to believe and live by God's promises. We all stand on our favorite verses. Two of my favorites are 2 Corinthians 3:5–6, "Not that we are adequate in ourselves to consider anything as coming from ourselves, but our adequacy is from God, who also made us adequate as servants of a new covenant, not of the letter, but of the Spirit; for the letter kills, but the Spirit gives life" (NASB). Time and again, God allows me to face a task or ministry or relationship for which I feel totally inadequate. As I pour out my timidity and fear to God in prayer, his Spirit whispers these verses to me. When I choose to believe them, my faith grows as God meets me at my point of need.

Godly Character

Jesus is our standard for character, and he is also the way to acquire it. Remember John 15:5 quoted at the beginning of the chapter? Apart from Jesus, we can do nothing. Godly character is determined and tested in the daily pressures of life. Jesus said to the disciples, "You will have suffering in this world. Be courageous! I have conquered the world" (John 16:33b). He meant to encourage his followers. Stop looking for perfection and a trouble-free life. That's not reality according to Jesus. And he created life so he should know. Romans 5:3–4 says we are to rejoice in our sufferings! Why? "Because we know that affliction produces endurance, endurance produces proven character, and proven character produces hope." There is tribulation and suffering in following Jesus. Face it. Jesus said it would be true. You will have tribulation. Add to that the constant challenge to our spiritual life of the flesh, the world and the devil. How will you cope with the pressures of walking with God in an ungodly troubled world? Rejoice! Praise God in the midst of the trouble. In Luke 22:32, Jesus told Simon Peter that he prayed Peter's faith wouldn't fail. Our only hope to be like Jesus is to do as he did and turn to the Father in prayer and praise.

If you walk with the Lord Jesus, you will have a ministry in the lives of others. If you live in obedience to the truth you possess, you will minister to others. And you will face many of the challenges the Lord Jesus faced as he walked the earth and poured out his life for those who followed him. Do you remember how Jesus grew so tired that even a furious storm could not wake him on a ship? Do you remember how he grew hungry during a fast? Do you remember how alone and agonized he felt in the Garden of Gethsemane? Yet he held fast. Jesus modeled for us a dependent relationship with the Father through prayer. Regularly, he sought direction, courage, wisdom, and strength through prayer.

A Surrendered Life

In Romans 12:1–2, Paul urged believers to give themselves completely to God. That is worship, he said. We live in a culture bombarded with ungodly stimuli that derail us from a mind set on Christ (Col. 3:1–3). But spiritually healthy people surrender to God. They surrender to his will *despite* their circumstances. They surrender themselves *because* of their circumstances. How often should you surrender? At least daily for me and then every time I discover by the whisperings of the Spirit that I've taken control of my life again. Surrender is an issue of will. Who's in charge? Am I in charge of my life or is my Maker? I've discovered that I can be just like Jonah and fight God's will for my life, end up in a storm, get thrown overboard, and discover a big fish. Still, I'll be on my way to Nineveh eventually. It's better to develop a habit of surrender to God at the beginning of the day.

In the Romans 12 passage Paul specifically said to surrender "your bodies as a living sacrifice, holy." Your prayer may go something like this: "Lord, I give you my eyes. I will look at no worthless thing and I will not look upon a virgin. I give you my ears to hear no evil (gossip, including my own complaints, some news reports). I give you my arms to carry out your work, to give hugs of encouragement to strengthen believers and others you direct me to. I give you my legs to walk where you would have me walk. Protect me today from walking into places I don't belong." This is only a beginning of surrendering yourself to God. He will lead you and show you the unsurrendered parts of your life.

A Habit of Prayer

If you don't pray, stay home. Can God work in our ministries and bless us if we don't pray? Absolutely! I'm counting on it. But he commands us to pray.

Jesus modeled a surrendered life of prayer, and he wants us to participate in what he's doing by praying his will back to him. When we pray his known will—his Word—our faith and our ministries will grow as he answers those prayers. Let me explain. What are you praying for yourself these days? Do you pray, "God, help me on this test," or "Give me spiritual eyes to see where you're working today"? Do you pray, "Lord, get me a date with that cute person," or "Lord, give me this high school campus or this city for Christ"? All these prayers are valid. But the fruit of your ministry will be in proportion to your investment in prayer for yourself and your ministry simply because you're talking to the Lord of the harvest and that's what's on his heart.

Listen to one example of how Paul prayed for the churches: "[I pray] that the God of our Lord Jesus Christ, the glorious Father, would give you a spirit of wisdom and revelation in the knowledge of Him. [I pray] that the eyes of your heart may be enlightened so you may know what is the hope of His calling, what are the glorious riches of His inheritance among the saints, and what is the immeasurable greatness of His power to us who believe" (Eph. 1:17–19). I challenge you to research Paul's prayers and to begin to pray for yourself and your ministry as he prayed.

Know Your Calling

Another result of the priority of your relationship with God is to know and be reminded of your calling to youth ministry. Some people have trouble with the terminology *calling*. We're all called to be a minister, they say. Granted, but let's trace God's leading that brought you to your commitment to youth ministry in particular. Let's start with now and work backward. If you're a youth leader, youth pastor, or director, you're God's choice for that position. Even if others are more qualified. Even if others are more gifted. Even if others want your job. How do I know this? Because God places people in positions of leadership and they stay there by his grace. God demonstrates this principle through the stories of Moses, King Saul and King David, and the prophet Jeremiah, to name a few examples.

Self-doubt will rob you of emotional and spiritual energy to do the work God wants you to accomplish. Therefore, I suggest that you take the time periodically to trace the steps that brought you to your current position so you can see and remember God's hand in the process. What Scriptures did God use to help you gain your convictions? Can you see God's handwriting in the process of bringing together Scripture, opportunities, circumstances, and key relationships? Don't let the enemy whisper, "It's a coincidence" or "You got lucky." Let the issue be settled. You were led to this position by the sovereign hand of the living, personal God. You're it. You're the leader. By God's providence and grace you're the leader, so get on with leading and serving God's people. The strength and grace that got you to the position will not abandon you in it.

Today, you may not have a clear calling to youth ministry yet or you may have received it at twelve years of age and it's not yet fully realized. While you're waiting and God's working, Psalm 37 has clear directions for you. Delight yourself in God, the psalmist said. Study his word, worship him, and pray without ceasing. Stay faithful to the truth revealed to you already. Keep laying your dreams and your vision for ministry before the Lord in prayer. Do you have a desire for ministry and no clear plan? Lay that out to God as well. Proverbs 3:5–6 reminds us to "Trust in the LORD with all your heart, and do not rely on your own understanding; think about Him in all your ways, and He will guide you on the right paths." Then keep track of what God is saying to you and doing in your life. This is your story of God's leading in your life and your calling.

Whether you're a veteran youth worker or a newcomer, I encourage you to revisit this process of reviewing God's leading in your life throughout your lifetime. You may not question your calling (God's leading) now, but you may in the future or you may face a decision to go another direction in ministry. I call these times "agonizing reappraisals." All of us at some time or another find ourselves at a crossroad that demands a decision. I'm so thankful that I have the truth of God's faithfulness and leading in my life written down in old journals, which I periodically drag out for review. This process of (1) tracing the steps of God's leading through Scripture and convictions, (2) taking your desires back to God in prayer for confirmation and refinement, and (3) keeping track (journaling) of what God is doing or has done through circumstances and opportunities will serve you well in ministry, in life, and in relationships.

Relationship with God Affects Other Relationships

When John the beloved talked about what we have seen and heard concerning the Word of life in 1 John 1:1–4, he spoke of Jesus. The disciples were with Jesus. They heard Jesus, saw Jesus, touched Jesus. Their life in Christ was being with Jesus. How are we *with* Jesus? We are with Jesus when we spend time in the Word, prayer, and practice (acknowledge of) his continual presence with us. Who is responsible for developing your relationship with Jesus Christ? It's not your pastor, your mentor, or your discipler. It's you!

Since ministry is highly relational, the personal spiritual health of a youth minister is most clearly seen within the context of relationships. How does your relationship with God or your lack of relationship affect others? Let me give you an illustration. You may have to put the book down to pull this off. Let our relationship with Jesus in verses 1 and 2 of John 1 be represented by one arm extended vertically straight up in the air with your hand reaching out as if to grasp the heavens. That's you and me reaching out to God by a choice of our will to abide in him daily and to abide in him moment by moment through the Word and prayer. Verse 3 says, "what we have seen and heard we also declare to you, so that you may have fellowship along with us." Let that represent relationships between Christians by extending your other hand horizontally like a handshake. That is the picture of the body of Christ relating to one another. Staying in connection with God and intentionally reaching out (proclaiming) and loving others.

Now, let's work with this a bit. What if two Christians approach each other with both of their hands raised to God in communion with him but fail to reach out to each other? No connection takes place between the two regarding their life in Christ because both have connected to God but failed to reach out to each other. What if two Christians face each other with hands reaching out to each other and neither raised up to God? The Christian has no message, no spiritual power, only leftover manna. Here the flesh powers ministry and relationship. It is clear that your relationship with God in Christ affects your relationships. This passage and illustration also point out that we must each intentionally reach out to others in the power of Jesus.

The result? Complete joy. Look at what John claimed in verse 4: "We are writing these things so that our joy may be complete." This is joy: Christians abiding in their relationship with the Father by reaching up and with one another by reaching out. This is also a picture of the Great Commandment: loving God and loving others. We need both to keep our spiritual well from running dry. Remember, you can't give what you don't possess. In Exodus 16 the children of Israel were promised manna for food from heaven. Every morning they were to pick up that day's supply, except on the Sabbath. The food of one day wasn't adequate for another. It would rot. We must eat from the Bread of Life daily and have a fresh supply from Jesus to feed on and give away.

The Great Commandment in Youth Ministry

What do you think and feel when you look out at the youth group you serve? If you think or feel anything but love, you must go to the cross with those thoughts and feelings. Say to the Lord in prayer, "Lord Jesus, give me *your* heart and *your* love for these people." There will always be people who are difficult to love. Whether it's a volunteer staff person, an annoying student, or a parent—there will always be people who are a challenge to love. That's natural. We're looking for the supernatural love that comes from God for his people in youth ministry. We're all loved equally and unconditionally by the King. How do we do the same? Pray. Students can tell when you don't love them, so I've discovered that you'd better pray if you doubt that love exists. Get in your "closet" alone with God and exchange what you have for what God has to give you.

We are powerless to love unconditionally and to accept others apart from Christ. Remember John 15:5b? "Without Me," it reads, "you can do nothing." First Timothy 4:12a is a familiar passage for the young: "No one should despise your youth." This verse has been an encouragement to me in the past as a new believer and as a young minister. But after thirteen years of youth ministry, I found myself on the other side of this verse. Now I was older and no longer young. I found myself despising the music, the clothing, and the actions of the youth culture I was committed to serve. I looked out on the youth group as a whole and felt annoyed. Only the transforming love of God could change my heart and attitude toward his precious lambs. Instead of looking at a sea of faces, God allowed me to see individuals for whom Christ died. I still don't like their music or their clothes very much. But I love them in Jesus, truly because he loves me and daily refills my heart with love for his people.

Developing Spirituality in Ministry Relationships

Typically, a youth leader relates with the senior pastor, the church staff, the board (deacons/elders), volunteers, students, and parents. As a youth counselor and parachurch minister, you'll be in relationship with those in leadership, coworkers in the ministry, and those you're trying to reach. Youth ministry is relationally *intense!* How will you relate to all of these people? Let's look to 1 Timothy 5:1–2. Four relationships are mentioned in the text. Paul clearly referred to these relationships as family members because the body of Christ is family.

Relating to Fathers

Paul admonished Timothy (and all of those who minister) to relate to older men as fathers. We are not to rebuke them harshly but to exhort them as our own fathers. I don't know about you, but that intimidates me right off! When was the last time I exhorted an elder or parent? Wow! I'd say intimidation and avoidance more typifies this crucial relationship.

A relationship of exhortation presupposes that the relationship exists, that this relationship is valued, and that there is reciprocity between the older and the younger member. This is not a one-way relationship. When was the last time you even had a conversation with your senior pastor or supervisor in ministry? The Phillips translation says, "Don't reprimand a senior member of your church, appeal to him as a father" (v. 1a). We're talking about a relationship of respect and honor.

The skill of working with authority figures and submitting to their authority must be learned and applied. This is extremely important for youth ministry. First, because our Lord Jesus modeled respect in his relationship with the Father, we, too, should follow his example. Second, the apostle Paul commanded submission to authority. Third, youth ministry needs an example of how to honor one another from leadership on down. Be advised. This is countercultural behavior. That means few people will be modeling this around you. You must, however.

Some of us are at a disadvantage here. We come from homes lacking appropriate male leadership or homes with nonexistent father figures. Luke 6:40 tells us we can't give away what we don't have. So I suggest you find one. Ask God to guide you to a spiritual father in the faith and intentionally invest time with that person for the purpose of understanding, valuing, and modeling a submissive attitude toward leadership.

The number-one reason youth pastors leave their ministry positions is the relationship with the senior pastor. When the youth minister leaves a position, it's devastating to students and staff volunteers. The enemy of our souls and of the church is working hard to destroy leadership relationships. This relationship is important. Whether you're a youth pastor, leader, or volunteer, evaluate your relationship with your authority figure. If it's not what it could be, should be, or you desire it to be, remember that love initiates. Take the initiative to invest in this vital relationship.

Relating to Brothers

The next relationship is with younger men or brothers. Paul said simply, "Treat the younger men as brothers" (v. 1b NIV). I grew up with four brothers. Two were older and two were younger. We had the typical fights and disagreements, mostly about who got to be boss when Mom and Dad weren't home and who got the car on the weekend. One of my most precious memories about my brothers, both younger and older, comes from my high school years. Although I wasn't the average American princess, my brothers treated me with respect and kindness. Because of their good treatment I decided when I was fifteen that my dates would have to treat me at least as well as my brothers did if they expected to continue the relationship. Consequently, I treated my brothers well too. We took care of one another. That's what brothers and sisters do. We worked, played, ate, and grew up together.

What a great picture for the family of God doing ministry together! As brothers and sisters in Christ, laboring alongside one another for the kingdom, we are to grow up into him, who is the head, until we all attain to the maturity of Christ. We're not alone in this adventure, and we're not at odds with our brothers in the ministry. We're on the same side and in the same family.

As a staff team, do you take care of one another? Do you share meals, sports, hobbies, as well as personal burdens and the concerns of ministering to students? Do you take the time to give and receive thoughtful gifts, cards, and encouragement to one another? I remember one year receiving a huge surprise coming home from work. Some of the staff guys had delivered and neatly stacked a cord of wood alongside the carport, for my fireplace. I felt cared for by my brothers in Christ.

In John, we're told to love one another and pray for one another (chap. 13). Paul encouraged us to bear one another's burdens and encourage one another (Gal. 6). But our natural tendencies are worldly when it comes to brothers. We compete with them; we argue with them over who's right or wrong, stronger or weaker, a better communicator, better athlete, and on and on. But remember, Paul said in 1 Corinthians 12:24–25 God is the one who brought us together "so that there would be no division in the body, but that the members would have the same concern for each other."

I challenge you to begin to practice the "one another" passages with your staff team, particularly if you're at odds with a brother in Christ. I believe there was a clear reason Jesus told us to pray for our enemies. Your brother in Christ may not be your enemy. He may just drive you crazy. But if you commit to praying for him, begin to bear his burdens, and encourage him by the power of the Holy Spirit, your heart will be changed.

Relating to Mothers

Paul told us to treat the older women as mothers. Mothers command respect as participants with God in giving life, serving, nurturing, and mentoring. Mothers are important to the Lord Jesus. In John 19:27, Jesus spoke to John from the cross, "Here is your mother." From that day on John took Mary, the mother of Jesus, into his household and cared for her. There was no hesitancy to meet Mary's need for a home. We know that John had his own biological mother, but he stepped up and took care of Jesus' mother as well, at the Lord's bidding. Older women, mothers, are important to youth ministry.

When I first started youth ministry, I respected the mothers of the students. I wanted them to know who I was, and I wanted to support their goals for their adolescent children. However, it wasn't until much later that I began to welcome and value older women on the youth staff team. One year, God brought to us a fifty-year-old woman. She had already raised two daughters and wanted to lead a Bible study and invest in the lives of some young girls. I was skeptical. Could she still relate to adolescent girls? Would the girls respond to her leading? In God's wisdom and timing he also brought to the youth group that year two fifteen-year-old girls who were being raised by their fathers. This was a match made in heaven! She was exactly what those girls needed by way of a godly role model, discipler, and a voice of maternal wisdom.

Relating to Sisters

The last group Paul addressed is younger women. We are to relate to them as "sisters, with absolute purity" (v. 2b NIV). How do you relate to younger women (staff or students) or colleagues in your ministry? God judges the thoughts and intentions of the heart. I've found Philippians 4:8 helpful. We are to relate to young women with purity, in kindness, with gentleness and integrity. Integrity means that we don't use people for our own purposes. You'll find little help from our hedonistic culture, which models and teaches young women to use their bodies to get what they want while encouraging young men to take what they want from girls.

But ministry relationships are much more subtle. We would not intentionally use others for our personal or ministry gain. And yet, because of naïveté or lack of understanding we can damage relationships and short-circuit ministry opportunities. For example, if a young man doesn't understand the way God has wired women to respond romantically, he may unwittingly invite the affections of a young girl. Girls are wired to respond to men through words that imply "I'm noticing you," through discussing dreams for the future, and through touch. Girls are also likely to respond to men who show strong spiritual leadership.

The unwise staff volunteer who leads a Bible study may simply think he's being friendly with a young woman, giving her a hug, telling her she looks nice today, noticing her hair, perfume, and smile. Then, as the leader of the study, he may call on the girl, affirm her answers, and invest time talking about God with her. Perhaps he may even spend time praying with her and for her relationship with the Lord. While there's nothing inherently wrong with these actions, the combination of them together may invite sin into the relationship.

The weight and potential of all of these relationships can be overwhelming. Were it not for the fact that God is at work making us adequate for the task (2 Cor. 3:5–6, NASB), we would either buckle under the strain or withdraw from ministry altogether. And perhaps we'd withdraw from society from the sheer overload or do great damage to others. God promises that his grace will make us sufficient for the task (2 Cor. 12:9). And that includes in youth ministry relationships.

Attending to the Important

Our only hope to go the distance in youth ministry is a close union with the living Christ.

The world has a lot to offer students to keep them interested, entertained, and feel important. Few of our church youth budgets can match the techno magic and *wow* factor of worldly media enterprises that lure young people. But as youth workers we have so much more to offer students than entertainment and the latest media show. We have Jesus. We have relationships to offer them. John 17:3 says, "This is eternal life: that they may know You."

If we stay close to him daily, moment by moment, and walk with him, we'll have his strength, power, wisdom, love, direction, peace, joy and all that he promises those who love him. Without a vital love relationship with the eternal that overflows to others, we youth workers don't have much else to offer students that can compete with what's available to them outside the church. It wouldn't satisfy them or us anyway. Only Jesus will truly satisfy the longings of human hearts. "Let us strive to know the LORD. His appearance is as sure as the dawn. He will come to us like the rain, like the spring showers that water the land" (Hos. 6:3).

26.
Staying Fresh for the Long Haul

GENE POPPINO

HE WAS ONLY THIRTY-ONE years old when his world began to crumble. Five years into full-time youth ministry, he wondered if he could face another day. Every small task was overwhelming. Planning the next Bible study or youth event seemed an insurmountable challenge. He dreaded working on even the smallest task. The youth group was going well and numerical growth had come quickly and held steady over the years of his ministry. No trauma had occurred to account for the depression and despair that left him smothered and oppressed. Only five years into ministry, burnout scorched not only his energy but, at times, his very soul. How soon would he become a statistic— one of those who didn't last in youth ministry?

For years we've heard the statistic that the average youth worker stays between nine and eighteen months in a church. Short-term ministry is said to be the cause of much bad youth work, poor morale in youth groups, and distrust between youth workers and youth. I don't believe the statistic is accurate for most churches, and I think that more and more youth workers are in it for the long haul. Without a doubt, however, there are very few *old* youth workers. A youth worker in his forties is a pretty unique individual, and the number of active youth pastors older than fifty is even more rare. Why is that? Why do people working with teens burn out early? Why are there so few "lifers"?

In professional sports, athletes reach their physical peak in their late twenties or early thirties and few are still playing after age forty. In youth work it's tragic that those with more life experience and greater spiritual wisdom somehow feel less effective with youth as they age. Unlike athletic strength that diminishes with age, spiritual depth and maturity increases with greater life experience.

Longevity in youth ministry is not only possible but also needed. Just as an athlete stays in shape through a regimen of exercise and diet, a youth minister practices disciplines for the long haul.

Get Back in the Boat, Jonah!

When considering great heroes of the Bible, I have to admit I never dream of being Jonah—a disobedient prophet, an unwilling preacher, a whiner when revival came, and prejudiced to boot! Jonah was the poster child for ministry with bad motives. Maybe God tells us the story of Jonah precisely because so many of us are like him. We have our own idea of how we want to serve, who we want to serve, and when we want to serve. If ministry doesn't fit our criteria, like Jonah, we complain and pout.

Have you ever thought about why many youth pastors lose their sense of calling, quit youth work, and move into other ministries? Some are led by the Lord into other ministries and are called to work with teens briefly. We respect those God has used for a short season of youth ministry and celebrate when they're called to the next role. But what of those who started career ministry with passion and enthusiasm and abandoned it prematurely? Some, like Jonah, may end up running away because they started with flawed motives that finally cracked under the real-life pressures of youth work.

Why Did You Choose Youth Ministry?

Jonah's heart wasn't so pure when he jumped on the boat for Tarshish, but God provided a fishing trip to give him time to reconsider his motives. Today, many fail to reflect on why they want to work with youth. Checking motivation before embarking on ministry may save some from having a whale of a time in that first ministry. Four motivation flaws show up often in those choosing youth ministry.

Trying to Regain Lost Experiences

At a youth seminar in Portland, Oregon, a number of years ago, the speaker asked a room full of youth workers, "How many of you were nerds in high school?" Hands shot up all over the room. "How many of you still feel like nerds today?" Most of the hands went up again. Then the kicker: "How many of you are still trying to be cool and you're using your youth group to make yourself feel 'in'?" The somber silence gave mute testimony that the point had struck home. Some people go into youth ministry hoping to finally be accepted after their own disappointing high school experiences. Youth ministry is not the place to regain lost experiences.

Trying to Find Affirmation

Derek's parents divorced when he was young. Every other weekend, Derek visited his dad, but he dreaded even that short time with him. In his dad's eyes, Derek never did anything right. Nothing he did was good enough. Living with his mother during the week, Derek was generally ignored. His basic needs were met, but he never felt loved or wanted—until a friend invited him to his youth group. From the moment he walked in, he knew this place was different. Bob, the youth pastor, showed an interest in Derek and spent time with him. The youth group responded too. By the time Derek graduated from high school, the youth group was more like family than his parents were. That was why he chose to become a youth pastor. He felt loved and affirmed when he was around kids. He eventually got fired for moral failure. As he sought to have emotional needs satisfied by students, he became sexually involved with a high school girl. His hunger for affirmation took him down a deadly path.

Power

Students are younger, typically used to being told what to do by parents and school personnel, and when raised in the church are taught to respect their pastors. A youth pastor who likes to be in control of people will find opportunities in youth ministry. Using the Bible and spiritual authority to coerce students through guilt into doing what he says, he cultivates loyalty to himself and sets himself up as the petty ruler of a kingdom of teenagers. The more subtle power wielders will continue for years without being confronted. God tells them, "'Not by strength or by might, but by My Spirit,' says the LORD of Hosts" (Zech. 4:6), but they don't hear. Thinking they're developing disciples, controlling leaders create legalistic, guilty students who experience little true spiritual transformation or passion for Jesus.

Glory

Steve grew up in the youth ministry at Grace Church. Grace was known for having the biggest and best youth group in the denomination. Eric, Grace's youth pastor, was in demand as a speaker all over the country. Eric often shared glowing success stories from his ministry, and Steve basked in the reflected glory of his youth pastor. He loved the reaction he got whenever someone would find out he was a student-leader at Grace. Sometimes adults would ask him ministry-related questions because of his position in the youth group. It made him feel important. When it came time to go to school, a youth ministry major was an easy choice. After all, because he learned it all from one of the best, he would be good at it too. Several years out of college, struggling in a small ministry that didn't appreciate him, Steve found that ministry wasn't glory. Disillusioned, he eventually quit and joined Microsoft where the hours were as long but the pay way better!

The list of flawed motives is longer. People have chosen to begin a career in youth ministry out of guilt (no one else will do it), boredom (I don't know what I want to do so I'll work with youth), even loyalty to a popular leader (who often moves just after you start working with him). Those who start with flawed motives rarely last long in ministry. They need a stronger foundation.

Not Just Motives

Out-of-balance Lifestyles

There are other reasons people fail to sustain energy and passion for youth ministry beyond flawed motives. Most common is lifestyles that are so out of balance the youth workers ultimately drop from fatigue. Youth work is exciting, energetic, fun. How can you worry about your day off when your work has so much play in it? Between the weekly activities and studies, the late-night discussions, early-morning prayer groups, games and campus events, life with a youth group can be as exciting as a roller-coaster ride.

Early on, when the youth worker is single, or when the married couple have no children of their own, the nonstop schedule is mostly fun and there is little awareness of needing more private time. But like a honeymoon, this stage of life doesn't last. Constant activity works for awhile, but ultimately, overwork will bankrupt both the body and soul of a spiritually committed youth worker. Too many youth workers find themselves looking longingly at greener pastures simply because they can't figure any other way out of the mess they've created with their schedules. As one youth pastor explained when he changed churches, "I just couldn't figure out any other way to get two weeks off!"

A popular but destructive idea that circulates widely is the value of an open-door policy. It says, "A good youth worker will be available to youth whenever they need you." The mantra of availability has been repeated so often that many believe it's biblical. But practicing this model of ministry can be dangerous.

First, kids need Jesus more than they need us. Letting students become dependent on you as a youth leader actually harms their dependence on Jesus. Guard yourself against letting your messiah complex take over and make you think you're indispensable. Second, to be healthy each of us needs private time, rest time, and if married, romantic time. It won't happen if your office and living room are always open to kids who have nothing better to do than drop by and include you in their current crises.

A life without balance is either confused or missing priorities. When we don't know what's most important, everything becomes equally demanding, equally time-consuming. Living by priorities helps us say no to some things in order to focus passion on the most important things. Balanced people think clearly about what's mission critical to youth ministry. They leverage their time for greatest impact and avoid being on-call all of the time.

Passion Shifts

"I used to love lock-ins, but now the thought of staying up all night with a bunch of rowdy kids fills me with dread. I'm just getting too old for youth work." Nonsense! Not wanting to go all night without sleep and taking days to catch up with your normal sleep cycle isn't a sign that you've gotten too old for youth work. You've gotten too old only for lock-ins!

Many youth workers fail to adjust to their changing life stages as they age. When you're nineteen years old, going to college, and helping out with a local youth group, you're in a different life stage than a thirty-year-old, married, father of two. It's great to have the iron constitution of a twenty-year-old, especially when you're single with few responsibilities. We need twenty-year-olds in youth work. But eventually, everyone grows up, begins to need regular sleep, and takes longer and longer to recover from a three-day retreat. Things that used to be fun with youth lose their novelty the sixth time around. The excitement fades, and when it does, a youth worker used to living on adrenaline often interprets it as a loss of passion for the work. It isn't a loss of passion; it's a *shift* of passion. The shift should take you toward increasing maturity and depth in youth work, not out of youth work.

Disciplines for the Long Haul

Growing up on the Oregon coast, I watched the Seaside Marathon from my house each year. Runners of all shapes, sizes, and speeds would come by over a five-hour span. The winner each year would complete the race in less than two and one-half hours. The rest of the field would string out for several more hours. One year, I remember the very last runner to finish the race came in so long after everyone else that the runner's banquet was over before he crossed the finish line. This last runner took more than eight hours to cover the twenty-six-mile distance!

I watched him when he came by my house at the twenty-mile mark, all alone with dusk settling, his pace little more than a shuffle. Grit and determination showed in his single focus of putting one foot in front of the other. No matter that there was a celebratory banquet going on someplace else with food and comfort. No matter the finish-line banner had been taken down already. He knew his goal and he wouldn't be satisfied until he achieved it. And he did, crossing the finish line some three hours after every other racer had showered and eaten dinner. I don't remember the name of that *eighty-year-old runner*, but his perseverance left a lasting impression. He was running a marathon when many of his peers were confined to walkers and wheelchairs. He practiced disciplines to stay healthy for the long haul.

Who are the marathoners in youth ministry? What does it take to be an eighty-year-old who still impacts youth? How do we get in that kind of shape? Perseverance like that requires managing the priorities of our lives in four areas: spiritual, physical, mental, and emotional.

A Well-Tended Fire of Spiritual Passion

First, let's be clear about one thing—burnout is sin. It comes from being so driven in our work we never rest. Our driven-ness is generally accompanied by the attitude, "I've got to do it!"

I remember when a well-known pastor in our area had a severe heart attack. As my pastor prayed for his friend, he prefaced the prayer by telling how this man had worked so hard for the Lord that his tireless efforts had worn out his heart. In other words, he killed himself working for the Lord! Something in me recoiled at the idea that it was noble to overwork and die prematurely. Known for his type-A, driven personality that needed to be part of every decision made in the church and denomination, he was famous for being available to anyone day or night. At his funeral many spoke of how the pastor "was always there when I needed him." When he died, he died well loved and mourned by everyone in his church—except by his own wife and children. Their bitterness was barely contained, and privately his children called him a fraud. He had known how to work for the Lord but not live for the Lord.

Not all will burn out so dramatically, but most will battle the same temptation to pursue ministry over the care of their soul. It might start innocently, likely it will be subtle, but before we notice, we're working more and more and tending our souls less and less. A. W. Tozer challenged Christian workers generations ago to put first things first: "We're here to be worshippers first and workers only second. We take a convert and immediately make a worker out of him. God never meant it to be so. God meant that a convert should learn to be a worshipper, and only after that he can learn to be a worker . . . The work done by a worshipper will have eternity in it."[1]

John Ortberg went further: "Burnout isn't usually the result of trying to give too much. It is the result of trying to give what isn't really in me."[2]

Tending our own spiritual disciplines is the first great practice of those who run with endurance. Do you know what feeds your soul? It must be more than just *doing* devotions. What practices most stimulate your appetite for God? When do you feel closest to the Lord? How often do you experience those times? Are your times in prayer, reflection, and in the Word deepening year by year? Too many believers learned something about "devotions" when they were teens, learning a formula for spiritual feeding that was designed to start them in the habit when they were young. But like training wheels on a child's bicycle, those practices were props to help beginners. As we grow in Christ, we must develop our appetite for more of him and more of his Word. We must continually go deeper spiritually, not only work harder.

Guarding Physical Health

It's too easy to discount our body's need for regular care. "Do you not know that your body is a sanctuary of the Holy Spirit who is in you, whom you have from God? You are not your own, for you were bought at a price; therefore glorify God in your body" (1 Cor. 6:19–20). Physical health may be taken for granted when someone is young, but youth doesn't last. Looking in the mirror as my temple has expanded with age, I have no illusions about staying young. Physical health, though, is not just about staying young and in shape; it's about practicing habits that keep our bodies in condition to serve the Lord. There are some common areas of neglect.

Sleep: Scientists, doctors, and mental health experts agree that the human body performs best with seven to eight hours of sleep each night. I think about that statistic often during all-night lock-ins or while patrolling camp after lights-out. However, it isn't the occasional late-night ministry event that's our biggest problem. Many of us simply exercise poor personal management and stay up too late. Without enough sleep we feel sluggish, anxious, and impatient. Habitually getting too little sleep creates health problems, emotional problems, and mental dullness.

Exercise: In youth ministry we're always on the go so we don't need to exercise, right? Depending on your ministry style, that may be true. Many, however, think that youthful energy is a God-given right and it will always be there. The quiet, persistent aging process creeps up on them, and pretty soon they want to play goalie in every game so they don't have to run up and down the field. Long-haulers know that exercise must be a regular part of their lifestyle.

Weight: I'd rather not have to mention this one. I read somewhere that the average American gains one and a half pounds each year after age thirty. By that statistic, I'm pushing eighty! When I came to my present church, which is significantly bigger than my previous ministry, my senior pastor told me I would have to learn to be a "larger church youth pastor." So I put on thirty pounds. Living large isn't supposed to be a weight thing! You have to admit the youth ministry lifestyle is a tough one. Youth events involve eating, and we're not talking health food. Pizza, chips, ice cream, soda—the diets of typical teens are bad enough for them, but for a youth pastor who lives on that stuff for thirty years, it is positively destructive. Our weight, cholesterol, and blood pressure belong to the Lord. We must develop the disciplines to curb our appetites and eat like adults who plan to live a long time.

Recreation: Playing is an important part of refreshment. Caring for our physical needs involves doing things that are fun and entertaining and that provide a mental break. A friend of mine manages a large equipment company and consistently runs under a great deal of pressure. His recreation is sailing. One day we were out on his catamaran. The wind was up, and it was a perfect day to fly a hull, which means balancing the boat just right to lift one hull off the water. It's an exhilarating experience that requires intense concentration. If you dig the bow of the hull into a wave, the boat stops suddenly and flips over. To top it off, I was on a trapeze wire hanging over the water from the flying hull. It was an adrenaline rush. At that moment John looked up at me and yelled, "Just try to think of one thing you were worried about before coming out here!" He was right; there was room in my mind for nothing except sailing.

Nurturing the Emotional Core

Two demons inhabit the world of youth workers and do more to damage long-term ministry than anything else—*stress* and *loneliness.* Passion for ministry combined with unhealthy attempts to establish our self-worth through work causes many to overwork and lose all margins in their lives. At the same time, focusing on youth can separate a youth worker from adult peers, resulting in the loss of friends and consequent loneliness.

Dealing with stress is like jumping out of an airplane. You can't *sort of* do it. When you go skydiving, you either jump out of the plane or you don't. Controlling stress so it doesn't become distress is our responsibility, and it can't be a halfhearted effort. You can't blame others for your stress, either. We all make our own choices about the pace of life and the margins or boundaries we put in place. We naturally follow the line of least resistance and overcommit, overwork, and end up distressed. Dr. Henry Brandt asked, "Why are

Christians not in the least embarrassed over the absence of peace and rest in their lives?"[3] Commonly, we even get into one-upmanship contests in which we describe our schedules, hours worked, and the great pressure we're under, all the while looking for sympathy or to impress. What we need is a rebuke. God did not design us to live under constant, unrelenting pressure that robs us of the fruit of the Spirit. A youth pastor who fails to manage this area of life will burn out, and burn out isn't a badge of honor but evidence of sin.

The loneliness we experience in the midst of crowds of youth and church people is all the more dangerous because it goes unrecognized. A full schedule of meetings, events, counseling appointments, and travel hides the erosion of relationships. Any adult who pours life and energy into teens will naturally experience an inner drain of emotion and compassion. Without replenishing relationships from adults, including peers, mentors, and friends outside the youth ministry world, lonely youth workers begin to look for something to ease their pain. We've all heard the stories of moral failure as a youth worker develops an attachment to a student and falls into a sexual relationship. Others secretly salve their loneliness with pornography.

Youth workers who go the distance in ministry develop friendships. The relationship that receives first priority is the one with a spouse. Next come friendships with peers. Real friendships take time. You can't expedite intimacy. They need to be scheduled, protected, pursued.

Sharpening the Mental Saw

"If I have to teach 'Marriage, Sex and Dating' one more time to kids who think they invented sex, I'm going to scream! I'm ready to throw them up against a wall and just yell, 'Don't do it!'" My passionate outburst after one Sunday morning lesson occurred during my twentieth year in youth ministry. I used to love helping kids work through their sexuality and find God's plan for dating. But on that day I felt I had said it too many times. I didn't want to say it again.

For thirty years I've been working with kids between the ages of thirteen and eighteen. No matter how old I get, they will always be the same age and need the lessons taught at their teenage maturity level. Less and less mental stimulation occurs while preparing youth Bible studies for the umpteenth time. To continue to grow intellectually, we need to study outside our focus on youth.

We all know the illustration of the woodcutter who worked hard but accomplished less and less because the saw he was using grew dull. Stopping to sharpen the saw took time, but the sharper saw quickly proved an advantage as it cut more with less effort. In our ministries it's not only about putting our shoulders to the wheel and going at it as hard as we can for as long as we can.

We need to take time out for sharpening ourselves. Lifers find ways to regularly sharpen the saw.

Reading: Books that stimulate your thinking about theology, ethics, science, literature, and history keep you thinking beyond the next youth talk or Bible study. Don't read to prepare for a presentation. Read to deepen your own thinking.

Retreating: Take study leaves. In some churches they're built right in the job description or contract. Scheduling time away from the *daily-ness* of ministry for reflection, reading, and prayer will sharpen your mind and heart. Freshness comes into our lives when we break from the routine of work to renew our perspective.

New opportunities: It's easy to get into routines that become so predictable they become ruts. Someone once described a rut as "a grave with the ends kicked out." To last in ministry for a long time, you need new challenges and stretching experiences. You can volunteer to do something entirely outside your job, like coaching a school team or serving at the local soup kitchen. If you're qualified, teaching as an adjunct professor of youth ministry at a local Christian college may give you an outlet for sharing skills and passions that are beyond what you can teach to most high school students. Leadership in local youth worker networks, denominational roles, community positions like the school board or city council, or joining an orchestra to use your talents in music are some other ways to expand your universe.

Mentoring: We never learn so much as when we're teaching others. This can be especially apparent when we mentor or disciple emerging leaders. Their questions will stimulate us to defend our positions, force us to think more deeply, and evaluate our assumptions. Sharing vision and insight with them can fuel our passion and help us reconnect with the reason we started in youth ministry in the first place.

Looking Forward from Here

Ministry for the long haul will be built on good motives, will live life in balance, and will maintain the disciplines to run a long way in the same direction. Allow me to conclude with a very personal reflection.

I began my first paid church youth position in 1974. Driving seventy-five miles each way from the Bible school I was attending, I worked in a church of sixty-five people in a small rural valley. From that first small youth group, I've served in three more churches over the years. My longest tenures were eight years at my last church and seventeen years where I am now.

I am also the thirty-one-year-old whose world crumbled when agonizing depression overwhelmed me. I began the chapter in this book with my personal story of depression and burnout. I didn't quit ministry, but I came close. For me, it was a wake-up call to change my lifestyle. Some of those changes are reflected in this chapter.

At fifty, I don't do things the way I did when I was younger. It takes longer to recover from a weekend retreat or a camp. I don't play football with high school guys anymore—it takes too long to heal. But I'm still a kid at heart (and sometimes in behavior!). Adults misunderstand me at times. My sense of humor can offend our pastoral staffers, but more often it just goes over their heads. My wife occasionally cringes when I start a story at an adult party, knowing full well that I can forget the people I'm with and gross them out with too much information about the flu outbreak at camp.

Kids used to think of me as an older brother. My own sons grew up and went through our group, and I became like a dad to many. Now my sons are grown and married, and I'm older than most of our youth group's parents. Occasionally, some kid will affectionately call me grandpa. I smile, but on the inside, I cringe. I figure I've got about twenty more years of youth ministry in me. What will I remind people of then?

I just graduated a class of seniors who were only a year old when I came to this church. Seventeen years ago I changed some of their diapers, a fact I remind them of when needed. The second generation of youth group kids, children of youth in earlier ministry years, entered high school this year. It's fun to see the second generation of disciples come through.

With all of the changes, with all of the challenges, *I still love youth ministry.* A few years ago, I had my twenty-fifth anniversary in youth ministry at age forty-five. Expecting to keep at it until I'm seventy, I figured that was the halfway point. With grace, a good church, and opportunities that stretch my heart and keep me young, I can see doing this for a long time to come. I don't think I've peaked yet. Hebrews 11 records the list of people in God's Hall of Fame of faithful witnesses. They're shouting to the next generation, "It's worth it! Keep going!" I'm not a Hall of Famer, but speaking on behalf of all of us committed to long-term youth ministry, I say to those coming behind, "It's worth it! Keep going!"

Notes

1. A. W. Tozer, *Worship: The Missing Jewel of Evangelism* (Christian Publications, 1996).

2. John Ortberg, *Leadership Journal* (Spring 2000), 30.

3. Henry Brandt, *When You're Tired of Treating the Symptoms, and You're Ready for a Cure, Give Me a Call* (Wolgemuth and Hyatt), 27.

www.TruthQuestBible.com

Get Deep. Get TruthQuest.